In Search of Manhood

I0025121

ALSO BY DON H. CORRIGAN
AND FROM MCFARLAND

*"I fart in your general direction!": Flatulence
in Popular Culture* (2023)

*American Roadkill: The Animal Victims
of Our Busy Highways* (2021)

*Nuts About Squirrels: The Rodents That
Conquered Popular Culture* (2019)

In Search of Manhood

*American Men's Movements
Past and Present*

Don H. Corrigan

McFarland & Company, Inc., Publishers
Jefferson, North Carolina

LIBRARY OF CONGRESS CATALOGING-IN-PUBLICATION DATA

Names: Corrigan, Don H., 1951– author.
Title: In search of manhood : American men's movements past and present /
   Don H. Corrigan.
Description: Jefferson, North Carolina : McFarland & Company, Inc., Publishers, 2024 |
   Includes bibliographical references and index.
Identifiers: LCCN 2024030473 | ISBN 9781476695600 (paperback : acid free paper) ∞
   ISBN 9781476653600 (ebook)
Subjects: LCSH: Men's movement—United States—History. | Masculinity—
   United States. | Men—United States—Social conditions. | Men—Identity.
Classification: LCC HQ1090.3 .C665 2024 | DDC 305.320973—dc23/eng/20240802
LC record available at https://lccn.loc.gov/2024030473

BRITISH LIBRARY CATALOGUING DATA ARE AVAILABLE

ISBN (print) 978-1-4766-9560-0
ISBN (ebook) 978-1-4766-5360-0

© 2024 Don H. Corrigan. All rights reserved

*No part of this book may be reproduced or transmitted in any form
or by any means, electronic or mechanical, including photocopying
or recording, or by any information storage and retrieval system,
without permission in writing from the publisher.*

Front cover image: © Master1305/Shutterstock

Printed in the United States of America

McFarland & Company, Inc., Publishers
   Box 611, Jefferson, North Carolina 28640
      www.mcfarlandpub.com

This book is dedicated to my uncles Johnnie, Stanley, and Jim, and to my father, Howard, who took me camping and fishing and imparted fine lessons on the journey to manhood. All four served in the military during World War II.

—‹‹‹•›››—

I also salute my father for teaching me, as a boy, "to put up my dukes and fight like a man." That was an appropriate lesson for manliness in the context of his times, but I trust there are better lessons for the future in the quest for manhood.

Table of Contents

Acknowledgments

Many scholars, researchers, journalists, and university colleagues, as well as friends and family, merit acknowledgment for inspiring and contributing to this book. As mentioned in the book's dedication, I feel particularly indebted to my late father and late uncles. My dad was very supportive of my writing career, even as he was extremely skeptical of what I might do with a degree in English composition. My uncles Stanley McCarron, Jim Huling, and Johnnie Corrigan were all avid outdoorsmen, full of laughter and kindness, who enjoyed taking me on fishing trips and camping trips. They were all worthy models of manhood.

This author has been extremely fortunate to have pursued two careers simultaneously: one as a newspaper editor and the other as a college professor. The newspaper position permitted me to explore my interests in writing about gender issues and men's groups. Reader reactions to the resulting articles on fathers' rights groups and male liberationists could be swift and animated. I am grateful to these lively readers and should note that the vitality of their responses was a major factor in why I took on the mission of writing this book.

My newspaper coverage of American men's movements began with my reporting on protests at St. Louis theaters against Hollywood movies. The protesters cited cinema sexism against men. For these stories I interviewed leaders of fathers' rights groups. Subsequent stories on men's movements put me in touch with the National Congress for Men, local Million Man March participants, Promise Keepers participants, and citizen combatants with the 1st Missouri Volunteers and other state militia movement members.

The 1st Missouri Volunteers permitted me to observe their outdoor training exercises. I was able to converse with them about the mostly male militia movements both in Missouri and in the United States. The mythopoetic men of St. Louis provided information on their outdoor activities and on their creative literature and poetry. The militia members in their combat practice fields and the mythopoetic men in their sweat lodges offered a stark contrast on how men have searched for their manhood.

In my career as a college professor of journalism and mass communications, I have experienced the intellectual stimulation of joining and participating in a number of professional organizations. Those organizations range from those of college media advisers to the Associated Collegiate Press, from the Association for Education in Journalism and Mass Communications to Investigative Reporters and Editors.

The organization that I wish to acknowledge for the purposes of this book is the Popular Culture Association, which encourages research and writing on a wide range of topics. I have been a member for more than three decades, and my work has been primarily with the Men's Studies Division, which researches masculine identities and male-and-female gender issues. I am most indebted to professors who have headed this division and encouraged my research, including Dr. Merry Perry of West Chester University of Pennsylvania and Dr. James Alan Temple of St. Mary's College of California. My research with the Men's Studies Division of the Popular Culture Association has been useful in constructing many chapters of this book.

The Popular Culture Association affiliation served as a venue for introduction to MAMSA, the Masculinities and Men's Studies Alliance. As a MAMSA member, I have enjoyed many paper presentations, readings, and discussions by scholars at conferences around the country. Among the research papers that I have enjoyed are Harry Brod on Clint Eastwood and Lorena Bobbitt; Don Deardorff on Promise Keepers and the male resistance; Richard McGowan on Ellen Goodman and male-bashing; Jennifer Moon on *Fight Club*; Robert Nill on white power and skinheads; Jason Payne on male parody in *The Big Lebowski*; and many more.

As an academic, I have witnessed campus demonstrations over the years involving men's rights groups and by women's rights activists. College professors at Webster University in St. Louis, who have provided useful background for articles and for this book, include Kate-Kelly Pease, Ann Geraghty-Rathert, Kate Parsons, Kathy Corley, Karla Armbruster, Gwyneth Williams, and Kit Jenkins. St. Louis writer Suzanne Venker, who authored "The War Against Men," also has provided useful background on the men's movement and a female perspective on men's issues.

Finally, the assistance and patience of my family should be acknowledged here. My wife, Susanne, has always exhibited exemplary forbearance as I take on writing projects. These endeavors always take more time than originally prognosticated. This means fun times are delayed and, in some cases, simply lost to the ether.

My children Brandon and Christa also have provided valuable assistance with this book. They grew up to be successful journalists and communicators, even as I advised them to seek other, more profitable careers (as my father did in my case). The "kids" provided many interesting memories in their days as children. These recollections can be quite useful when contemplating issues of fatherhood and manhood. I admit that I do not miss Brandon's Pinewood Derby competitions. Nor do I miss coming home from work to find that Christa and her girlfriends have cut all the nice hair off their Barbie dolls.

Special kudos should be accorded the editorial staff of the weekly *Webster-Kirkwood Times* in St. Louis, the newspaper with which I have been associated for five decades. My news colleagues, Jaime Mowers and Melissa Wilkinson, were most supportive with stories about their own fathers and male relatives. Melissa updated my AP Style knowledge on the use of personal pronouns in a new era of journalism. Ursula Ruhl and Kevin Murphy have always been extremely helpful in offering their unique skills and advice on graphics and photos for all my books.

More special kudos have to go out to the folks at the crown prince of popular culture books, McFarland, in Jefferson, North Carolina. Managing Editor Layla Milholen always has been receptive to my sometimes-offbeat book ideas, whether they involve red squirrels and Marshall McLuhan, roadkill jewelry and recipes for fresh roadkill possum, or flatulence in mass media and popular culture. Her guidance and suggestions have been most appreciated, whether my books are humorous or in a more serious vein.

Finally, I wish to thank readers of books. There still are some readers of print left, no matter what the young communications professors suggest about an end to ink on paper. The readers who come to book presentations and signings always are appreciated. They come with good questions and much-needed intellectual curiosity in an age of artificial intelligence.

Preface

Masculinity Studies
and the Manhood Quest

"Men are not born, they are made," declared Michael Kimmel and Michael Messner in their 2001 anthology, *Men's Lives*. These two pioneers in men's studies emphasized that from infancy, to boyhood, to manhood, male human beings do not follow a predetermined biological imperative encoded in their physical makeup. Men are socially constructed. Men make themselves, but they rely on social, historical, institutional, and organizational influences in the effort to make themselves masculine—in the search for manhood.

The postscript for this book describes how my own search for gender identification began early in life, when I learned the hard way that it was not acceptable to play house with girls in the neighborhood. Young boys need to battle and brawl in backyards. They need to play Khoury League baseball and elementary school basketball. I took up those challenges, but somehow I could never get away from the girls. As a newspaper reporter later in life, I became one of the first male reporters to find a berth on the women's pages. That was in the late 1970s. These sections no longer exist in today's newspapers.

My early encounters with gender issues led me to cover and write gender-related stories throughout my journalistic career. Those stories blossomed into academic papers for the American Culture Association (ACA) and Popular Culture Association (PCA) as a part of my academic career. The academic papers and presentations led me to join MAMSA, the Masculinities and Men's Studies Alliance. Through this association, I became acquainted with men's studies thinkers such as Kimmel, Messner, Joseph Pleck, Susan Faludi, Herb Goldberg, Robert Okun, Lionel Tiger, Susan Bordo, Warren Farrell, James Doyle, Paul Nathanson, Francis Baumli, Richard Haddad, Ellis Cose, and Harry Brod.

The work of these scholars and authors in the area of men's studies

1

has provided guidance on most of the chapters in this study. The book begins by examining the political and mass media icons that have had an impact on men as they seek answers on how to make themselves masculine. Among our country's past and present political leaders, who should men choose to learn from and to emulate—Dwight Eisenhower or Adlai Stevenson? Richard Nixon or George McGovern? Ronald Reagan or Jimmy Carter? George H.W. Bush or Al Gore? Barack Obama or Donald Trump?

The male icons of Hollywood movies present even more interesting possibilities as models for masculinity. In fact, as men seek answers on how to make themselves masculine, the popular culture icons of cinema are much more powerful influences than our political or military leaders. Among our country's past and present cinema and television icons, from whom should men learn and who should they choose to emulate—John Wayne or Jimmy Stewart? Clint Eastwood or Alan Alda? Charles Bronson or Sidney Poitier? Tom Cruise or Tom Hanks?

This book moves from the celebrity iconography of masculinity to the institutional and organizational influences that men have relied on in the effort to make themselves masculine. The search for manhood led to the rise of a number of all-male enclaves in the half century before 2000. Men joined movements such as Promise Keepers, Million Man March, mythopoetic explorers, and men's liberation and father's rights groups. All of these groups were influenced by the icons of politics and cinema. When it comes to men's liberation and fathers' rights organizations, it's noteworthy that members reacted personally to political figures and to characters on the silver screen.

Some scholars contend that the men's movements before 2000 were a response to the rise of the women's liberation movement and feminism starting in the 1960s. With the beginning of a new century, the influence and attraction of the older men's movements began to wane. New men's groups literally crashed upon the American scene, perhaps in response to the jarring trauma of the 2001 terrorist attacks on New York and Washington, D.C. These groups reflected a new militancy and polarization in American politics.

The third part of this book examines some of these vocal and very visible militant men's groups. New militant men's organizations and militia groups promote an older, more reactionary version of masculinity. The groups include the Proud Boys, Oath Keepers, Patriot Front, Fraternal Order of Alt-Knights, Three Percenters, and others. They take extreme positions against feminists, gays, globalists, immigrants, progressives, and Black Lives Matter. In one sense, these groups constitute a reaction to some of the "softer" and more humane visions of what manhood should be—with some of those conceptualizations emanating from liberal men's groups and university gender studies programs.

The final chapters of this book analyze the contrast between the more thoughtful men's movements before the turn of the century and the more militant and physical movements after 2000. The chapters pose critical questions: What drives men to become battered and bloodied in extreme efforts to make themselves masculine—in their searches for manhood? Did a reactionary masculinity result in men being arrested and jailed for participation in the January 6 Insurrection at the U.S. Capitol in 2021? Does the idea of "toxic masculinity" constitute a conspiracy to demoralize American males, as some conservative politicians insist? Or is toxic masculinity real and leading us into a dark and dystopian future?

This book separates itself from much of the past men's studies scholarship because this study is "boots on the ground." Rather than relying on theories and formulations about masculine identity, the author has been in the trenches with men who've been searching for answers to the manhood quandary. Sometimes this has involved visiting militia camps with armed men in combat exercises; other times it has involved mixing it up with fathers' rights demonstrators who are angry with the feminist movement and trends toward female empowerment.

One question continues to nag the author through his several decades of reading men's scholarship, listening to male politicians fixated on gender issues, and covering alt-right men's groups intent on restoring a patriarchal vision of America. That question is simply this: How do men ever hope to succeed in their many efforts to make themselves masculine—to find the holy grail of manhood—without the counsel of one half of the globe's population? The arduous quest for manhood would seem futile without the participation of women.

Introduction

Masculinity as a Political Platform

Every four years, Americans are told that their presidential election is critical, a watershed event, a crossroads, a defining moment, the most important decision to be made in their lifetimes. For voters who've been around the ballot box a few times, all the election blather is just trite and tiresome—except that in the year 2016, it was all true. Serious problems in America and the world awaited the next chief executive: nuclear weapons proliferation, Chinese and Russian expansionism, America's allies under strain, traumatic climate change impacts, an increase in costly natural disasters, immigration issues, and continuing unrest in America's big cities.

When Donald Trump came down his hotel escalator in New York City in 2016, along with his latest trophy wife, to announce that he would be taking on crime and "tough hombres" as the next president, the political experts were not so impressed. This was a cornball event, staged in a less-than-presidential setting, with adulatory fans who were allegedly paid to clap and be supportive. There was no way this reality TV star, with a shady past and a track record of failed businesses, was going to take the country by storm and win the Republican primary, never mind the critical 2016 general election.

The pundits swore the American public would never entrust the fate of the nation to a reality TV star. These political experts failed to consider that Donald J. Trump was the ultimate popular culture icon. He also was savvy about using the TV medium and adept at positioning himself as a credible political candidate. He was "very rich"—rich enough to be profiled on television's *Lifestyles of the Rich and Famous*. He appeared as a take-charge, decisive boardroom CEO on television's *The Apprentice*. He was a manly kind of man, according to men who knew about such things.

Trump's electoral victory was unexpected and startling. His triumph revealed that minds heavily influenced by popular culture can lose track of what should really matter. A reality TV star with no political experience, a limited attention span, and less intellectual capacity somehow was victorious over a longtime political veteran, a smart woman with White House experience as well as a track record as a U.S. senator from the populous state of New York.

A major theme of this book is that popular culture matters. Pop culture and media iconography can matter. They can matter more than political platforms, white papers on policy issues, or even economic self-interest. The politician who reminds us of our favorite movie cowboy, our favorite TV cop, our favorite celluloid "Daddy Warbucks," our favorite fighter pilot on the silver screen can matter. Such a politician can matter "bigly," to use one of Trump's popular made-up word creations. A manly pop culture politico can matter much more than the serious politician. We've known about this for a while, haven't we?

We've known that popular culture matters, and Donald Trump is hardly the first political candidate to win office on the basis of his pop culture bona fides. Ronald Reagan was the most dramatic example of this phenomenon in the 20th century. A well-known movie star, he was the charismatic host of *Death Valley Days*—the longest-running TV series about manly men in the Old West.[1] Reagan easily made the pivot from TV to being a prime-time politician. He won two terms for the presidency of the United States by substantial margins.

The 2003 election of Arnold Schwarzenegger to the governorship of California was another triumph of pop culture and another dramatic moment in American political history. After "The Arnold" won the top leadership post in Sacramento by more than 1.3 million votes, the pundits asked how a foreign-born body builder and wrestling star out of liberal Hollywood could win the approval of conservative Republicans. How could an actor with a thick accent and with no prior political experience capture the most important leadership post in the most populous state of California? How could he win so many Golden State votes of both Democrats and Republicans?

The answer is simple: Arnold Schwarzenegger was "Conan the Magnificent" in movieland. He was the most masculine and famous barbarian of comic books, television, and cinema. Schwarzenegger also was the "The Terminator," a cyborg with incredible powers in an epic about saving the human race. His election as the real governor of the state of California attracted national and international interest. The news media nicknamed him the "Guvernator." The pop-culture governor immediately went to work to break up and terminate the gridlock among state legislators in the California capitol. How could he do that? To get things moving in the statehouse, Schwarzenegger took aim at recalcitrant Democrats and drew on a catchphrase from his bodybuilding career. The towering, muscular Republican governor trashed Democratic state politicians as "girly men."[2]

The potent slur against male political opponents brings us to another major theme of this book. Republicans—from the centrist Schwarzenegger and other moderates of yesteryear to the extreme right of today's party—have sought political gain by portraying their liberal opposition as "girly men," as weaklings, as gender-confused sissies too weak to lead. In contrast, these conservatives have identified themselves as the keepers of the keys to masculinity, the virtuous and manly deciders, the definers of manhood itself.

The initial chapters of this book examine politics and presidential races through the prism of popular culture from the time of Dwight Eisenhower to 2020. Eisenhower was a manly hero of World War II, a conflict that produced many movies glorifying U.S. military leaders. Richard Nixon was no war hero, but he latched on to the machismo of a cowboy actor named John Wayne to further his political career. Ronald Reagan was a popular culture movie icon in his own right, but he also advanced his political ambitions by adopting the language of Clint Eastwood's "Dirty Harry" character.

Popular culture can be so incredibly important in America. The power of mass media matters. And masculinity in America matters.

This book is roughly divided into four sections.

The initial chapters examine how popular culture and masculine iconography have affected decisions on who leads America. Subsequent chapters examine how questions about masculinity, and a new search for manhood, led to the rise of all-male enclaves. Men organized themselves into movements such as men's liberation and father's rights groups, the Promise Keepers and mythopoetic explorers, and the Million Man March. For the most part, these groups were introspective and professed not to be interested in politics. Many scholars contend the men's movements before 2000 were a response to rise of women's liberation and the feminist movement starting in the 1960s.

With the beginning of a new century, the influence and attraction of the older men's movements faded. New men's groups crashed onto the American scene, partly in response to women's liberation, but also because of the jarring trauma of the 2001 terrorist attacks on New York and Washington, D.C. The new men's groups now seem far less concerned about introspection or laboring over definitions of masculinity. They're far more concerned with reviving traditional masculinity, with projecting male power, and with being a force in American politics.

The third part of this book examines some of these very visible and militant men's groups: the new militant men's groups and militias promote an older, reactionary vision of masculinity—and it's on steroids. These groups include the Oath Keepers, Proud Boys, Fraternal Order of Alt-Knights, Patriot Front, and others. They take radical positions against gays and globalists, immigrants and feminists, liberals and progressives, and Black Lives Matter. They take pride in being battered and bloodied in confrontations with the people whom they hate. They are locked and loaded. Some of them have been arrested and jailed for their participation in the January 6 Insurrection in 2021.

Whether their leaders are jailed or in prison, experts on extremist groups say they are not going away. What's more, many of our politicians have taken up the cause of the extremist men's groups. Our politics are on steroids and conservative politicians have joined the extreme men's groups with their animosity for progressives, liberals, feminists, gays, globalists, immigrants, and Black Lives Matter. Like the men of the militant groups themselves, the extreme politicians are locked and loaded. They campaign with political advertising that shows them aiming high-powered weapons at progressive candidates and reducing liberal policy papers to confetti. Laws restricting open carry on city streets and the regulation of automatic weapons also have been reduced to tatters by the extreme right in Congress and in state legislatures.

The extremist politicians know that being manly and supporting militant men's causes can win Republican primaries and even general elections. The manly candidates act as tough guys ready to subjugate "wimpy" liberals. They declare that they will remove progressive books from schools and municipal libraries. They vow to put an end to any "homosexual agenda," the display of rainbow colors, and drag shows that could corrupt the minds of minors. Republican senator Josh Hawley has written a male manifesto claiming that schools, Hollywood movie makers, and cultural elites are out to make boys ashamed of being male. Hawley hopes to make political hay with his sermonizing on the evils of liberalism and his preaching that male values are under assault.

Alt-right, toxic male rhetoric is dangerous. It's not patriotic to put America and its citizens in danger. As this book was going to press, Donald Trump was again urging Americans to "fight like hell" to get him back into office in 2024. Former Republican governor Mike Huckabee solemnly promised that if prosecutors blocked Trump from "winning or even running in 2024, it is going to be the last American election that will be decided by ballots rather than bullets." After Trump's indictment on unlawful possession of classified documents, U.S. Representative Andy Biggs was outraged by the "judicial persecution" of his hero. The Republican of Arizona tweeted: "We have now reached a war phase. Eye for an eye."[3]

The final chapters of this book show that right-wing conservatives and alt-right men's groups have gone too far with their violent political bombast. The extremist rhetoric and attacks on teachers, gender therapists, healthcare workers, judges, prosecutors, and liberal political leaders must give pause. The willingness of militant men's groups to resort to violence became visible with their actions during the January 6, 2021, Capitol Insurrection. This kind of behavior reveals a toxic male persona at its worst with its turn toward raw force, rudimentary combat, and aimless destructive behavior.

The final chapters of this book show that Americans, especially the younger and more diverse generations, have had enough of an outdated masculinity on steroids. There is a desire for a new iconography of masculinity that no longer champions gun-slinging and militarism. There is a longing for a more mature political environment that focuses on pressing issues such as climate change, world peace, and racial healing—rather than on "dirty books," drag queens, and some kind of transgender threat to the integrity of sports. The destructive culture warriors need to be retired. There is a yearning for a new, transformative, enlightened, and inclusive definition of what constitutes manhood. There is a longing for a kinder and gentler America. This is not inconsistent with manhood.

Section I

MACHISMO ON THE POLITICAL FRONT

1

Pop Culture Masculinity and Political Messaging

Republicans have long been a political party determined to project strong, aggressive masculine values reflecting a kind of Old West ethos, a code for life largely created by Hollywood. President Richard Nixon, an ardent John Wayne fan, insisted he would sock his political enemies "right in the puss." President Ronald Reagan challenged his adversaries, global and domestic, with a dare to "make my day," like the tough-talking Clint Eastwood character of Dirty Harry. President George W. Bush grabbed a megaphone after 9/11 and promised the world that the terrorists who brought down buildings in New York would soon be "hearing from us." President Donald Trump bragged that he didn't care much for "shit-hole countries" and was "gonna bomb the shit" out of ISIS killers in the Middle East.

Movie-set toughness plays well with American audiences. Strong and resolute messages are often politically popular with Americans. Past studies have shown the populace likes its leaders to stand tall, to walk with a straight gait, to gaze directly with absolutely no shifting of the eyes, and to speak boldly and with a no-nonsense tone. It's a dog-eat-dog world out there, and according to voting patterns and political polls, it's best to put alpha dog males in charge.

Alpha dog males will bark, growl, bite, and ignore all discordant voices or expressions of doubt. They will intimidate. Alpha dogs can deter threats and scare off enemies who might mislead the pack. Over the decades, Americans have shown their admiration for alpha dogs at the ballot box, at the box office for movies, and at the cash register for iconic pop culture items ranging from superhero comic books to *Rambo* and *Magnum Force* tank tops. Machismo in politics has been a winner, but the future of iconic manliness may be in doubt.

Alpha Dogs, John Wayne—and Eggheads

For Republicans since World War II, the alpha dogs leading their pack have often had an angry bark—no yapping, no yelping. In recent years, the bark of their candidates has become more irate, more indignant, more irascible, and more ill-tempered. During the relatively placid 1950s, Republican standard-bearer Dwight D. Eisenhower did not have to growl or snarl too much. He had already proven his mettle as an alpha male in the European theater of World War II.

In 1952, Eisenhower easily bested his Democratic opponent, Adlai Stephenson, who was portrayed as the epitome of a pampered, privileged, elitist egghead. In a rematch in 1956, the military general from Kansas trampled the former Illinois governor without much of a contest. The egghead once again had a great fall, and Eisenhower won the popular vote by a whopping 15 points and handily won every state outside the South.

Unfortunately for Vice President Richard M. Nixon, the unquestioned masculinity at the top of the Republican ticket in 1952 and 1956 put him in a very questionable light for his own run for U.S. President in 1960. That light already was quite dim for Nixon after operating in the shadow of America's great warrior for eight years. It did not help that Eisenhower considered booting Nixon from the Republican ticket before the 1956 election took place. Nixon got into trouble when he was called upon to defend his secret $18,000 political fund. He was only saved by his infamous "Checkers Speech," in which he conceded receiving a cocker spaniel that his daughter Trisha loved and "that regardless of what they say, we're gonna' keep it."[1]

In the 1960 election against the Democrats, Nixon faced candidate John F. Kennedy, who beat the Republicans at their own game. He was young man of obvious ability and ambition. His masculine appeal for female voters was beyond any doubt. In candidate debates, Nixon appeared uncomfortable while the handsome JFK came off as totally assured. Nixon looked tired and needed a shave; Kennedy was poised and photogenic. Kennedy argued for a "New Frontier" and a revived American spirit to engage the world. Kennedy also talked tough about a dangerous missile gap that had grown between the U.S. and its Soviet adversaries while a drowsing Eisenhower-Nixon administration was asleep at the wheel. Never mind that the so-called "missile gap" disappeared as an issue once Kennedy was elected.

Nixon and the Republicans rebounded. They learned the lessons from their 1960 defeat. When a "New Nixon" returned to the political scene in 1968 after eight years of Democratic rule, he was ready to rumble. In this election, the liberal Hubert H. Humphrey was the tired man who was unsure of himself. An intellectual and reformer, Humphrey looked weak up against Nixon, but also up against the brutish and uncouth Lyndon B. Johnson for whom he had served as vice president. Humphrey alternately supported and opposed the policies of his boss from Texas. He was indecisive, a waffler. The tough Texan known as LBJ did little to support Vice President Humphrey as he struggled to get his footing in the 1968 election against the "New Nixon." When Nixon won, a chastened Humphrey came to the White House for a meeting with the new president. Nixon noted after the meeting that Humphrey cried over his loss to him, something Nixon proudly said he did not do when meeting Kennedy after his 1960 election defeat. Nixon did not do tears. Republicans don't cry.

Humphrey's presidential run in 1968 was hindered by a backdrop of eight years of turmoil that included the Kennedy assassination, a transfer of power to LBJ, turmoil in the Middle East, plane hijackings, race riots, a failing war in Vietnam, and unruly youth demonstrations for peace in America's streets. Nixon promised to quiet the streets. He beat Humphrey on a "law and order" platform. Nixon inherited many of the problems of the Kennedy-Johnson-Humphrey years, including a very unpopular war in Vietnam. However, the tough "law and order" message worked once again in 1972 when Nixon was challenged by liberal Democrat George McGovern. And McGovern never recovered from saying, during the campaign, that he would go to North Vietnam "on his knees" to seek peace and the release of U.S. prisoners of war.

In 1972, Nixon unleashed his attack dog, vitriolic Vice President Spiro T. Agnew, on candidate McGovern. Agnew's venomous language and alliterative attacks would foreshadow what was to become commonplace in politics in the next century with the arrival of a new millennium in 2000. Pressed on his views on POWs, South Dakota Senator McGovern had said, "Begging is better than bombing. I would go to Hanoi and beg if I thought that would release the boys one day earlier, but begging won't help if we bomb and aid the Thieu Government." Quoting only the "begging is better than bombing" remark, Agnew trashed McGovern as an appeaser, as "the darling of the advocates of American retreat and defeat."[2] Agnew added that his stalwart boss, Nixon, always negotiated with enemies on his feet, never on his knees crawling before the enemy. Republican leaders don't crawl.

Once again, attacking a candidate for being unmanly won the day in the 1972 election. McGovern lost 49 of 50 states and did not even win his home state of South Dakota. However, Nixon and Agnew's sweet election triumph soon turned sour. Their administration became mired in numerous scandals, including the break-in of the Democratic campaign headquarters at the Watergate Hotel in Washington, D.C. Agnew's vitriol went into overdrive as he blamed Democrats and the liberal press for all their problems. Agnew called out "nattering nabobs of negativism" in the press, "effete snobs" in universities, and said demonstrating students belonged in penitentiaries, not colleges. He proclaimed that liberalism "translates into a whimpering isolationism in foreign policy, a mulish obstructionism in domestic policy, and a pusillanimous pussyfooting on the critical issue of law and order."[3]

No amount of scathing vice-presidential verbiage could save the Nixon-Agnew team from the disgrace of impeachment and resignations. Under siege, President Nixon found himself buoyed by the support of an American icon, John Wayne. And Nixon took immense satisfaction that he resisted his adversaries, just like his favorite movie cowboy John Wayne. Nixon vowed to hit his enemies, like those in the press, "right in the puss." As the stakes in the Watergate scandal ramped up, Nixon actually received public support from his personal hero, John Wayne. And why wouldn't Nixon take advice and encouragement from the man known as "The Duke"—the man whom he and much of the country worshipped.

John Wayne represented American manhood to the max. On screen, he wrestled and killed countless Native Americans who were dismissed as mere savages. Wayne played the charismatic manly man in film classics like *Red River, Rio Bravo, Stagecoach, The Searchers* and *The Shootist*. A controversial 1968 Wayne film that especially pleased Nixon was *The Green Berets*, which revealed a sound American war policy in Vietnam being undermined by weak-kneed liberals and a cynical press. Wayne had earned Nixon's admiration with his tough talk in a 1971 *Playboy* interview in which he declared: "I'd like to know why well-educated idiots keep apologizing for lazy and complaining people who think the world owes them a living. I'd like to know why they make excuses for cowards who spit in the faces of the police and then run behind the judicial sob sisters."[4]

Nixon punched back at his political opponents during the Watergate scandal, just like a real John Wayne cinema character. Wayne himself spoke up in defense of Nixon by reminding the public of the president's achievements in foreign policy in China and in working for "peace with honor" in Vietnam. Wayne believed Nixon was being undermined by carping political critics and a liberal press that was out to get him for mistakes made by Nixon's overzealous underlings. Nevertheless, there came a point when Nixon had no choice but to resign. Even his Republican colleagues found his culpability in the Watergate scandal too egregious to ignore. In disgrace, the "New Nixon" regressed back to his old self, hunched over and whining about his mistreatment.

The complete demise of Nixon-Agnew in 1974 gave way to two subsequent presidents who have generally been deemed as weak and ineffectual, perhaps unfairly. The Republican caretaker president, Gerald Ford, was suspect because of his quick pardon of his predecessor, Nixon. Ford also became the only person to serve as president without being elected to either the presidency or the vice presidency. Ford suffered from a perception of bumbling and stumbling. His clumsiness was frequently satirized by actor Chevy Chase on *Saturday Night Live*. Ford was defeated by Democrat Jimmy Carter in 1976, and Carter served in the White House for one term. Carter himself became the poster boy for limp and ineffectual presidents, as Republicans took great joy in hammering him as profoundly inadequate.

Carter suffered because he inherited a weak economy with high inflation that was compounded by the so-called "OPEC Oil Crisis." Carter put on a sweater and talked to the nation about lowering home thermostats and driving slower to conserve energy. He seemed impotent to persuade the oil-producing nations to increase their oil production to ease inflation and energy demands. Carter was even bested by a swamp rabbit that swam toward his fishing boat in an infamous "killer rabbit attack" incident that made TV news. The ultimate insult to Carter came toward the end of his presidential term when Americans were taken hostage at the U.S. Embassy in Iran. They were not freed until a new president defeated him and assumed office in 1981. That president was Republican Ronald Reagan, a past California governor with an image as a rugged man of the West.

The Gipper, Clint Eastwood, a Wimp Factor

Otherwise referred to as "The Gipper," based on his movie role as college football's George Gipp in *Knute Rockne, All American*, Ronald Reagan knew how to act rough, tough, and tumble. Unlike Nixon, Reagan did not have to rely on icon John Wayne for his maleness inspiration, because as an actor, Reagan was a tough customer and star in his own right. In the movies, he was an athlete, a soldier, and a cowboy. He even played a Wild West lawman in a movie called—what else?—*Law and Order*. On television, he was on *Wagon Train, Zane Gray Theatre*, and *Death Valley Days*. However, Reagan's movie career sputtered in his later years, so he moved on to politics. His manly looks, sunny disposition, and thespian skills helped him win a governorship and the U.S. presidency in 1980.

Reagan easily terminated the presidency of Jimmy Carter by a landslide with an impressive total of 489 electoral votes. During his presidency, he appeared tough, indestructible and credited with vanquishing labor unions, terrorist threats, Soviet power, costly welfare policies, and a liberal judiciary. He also fended off a challenge in 1984 from Democrat Walter

Mondale, whom he jokingly blasted as young and inexperienced. Reagan campaigned against Mondale and said he was ineffectual and would simply carry on Carter's failed policies. Mondale chose three-term Congresswoman Geraldine Ferraro to be his running mate in 1984, making her the first woman nominated for president or vice president by a major U.S. political party. She turned out to be a liability. Americans apparently were not ready for a woman on the ticket. The Mondale-Ferraro team was trounced when election returns were tabulated in November.

In his eight-year tenure, Reagan garnered popularity and political strength by drawing on another Hollywood icon who, like John Wayne, played an ornery cowboy. Clint Eastwood was a ruggedly handsome cowboy in the TV series, *Rawhide*, and a sharp-shooting "Spaghetti Western" movie cowboy in *A Fistful of Dollars* in 1964, *For a Few Dollars More* in 1965, and *The Good, the Bad and the Ugly* in 1966. However, Reagan chose to draw on the Eastwood persona of Detective Harry Callahan. The Callahan character hailed from the actor's *Dirty Harry* movies. Reagan most famously quoted Dirty Harry when he used Eastwood's "make my day" line facing off with Democrats over tax policy. In the movie, Dirty

Harry is challenging the bad guy to make a move on him, if the threatening punk feels he might be lucky enough to take down Eastwood's detective character. Reagan enjoyed enlisting Dirty Harry in his fights. Republicans would again call on Clint Eastwood's help to take down Democrats almost two decades later against Barack Obama.

Reagan has often been ranked as one of America's top ten U.S. Presidents. However, his presidency ended in turmoil in 1988 as a result of the Iran-gate scandal. The wrongdoing involved U.S. weapons funneled to a terrorist state. Political pundits were certain his vice president, George H.W. Bush, would be damaged by the scandal and be unable to beat Democrats when Bush picked

Bill Clinton won the U.S. presidency in 1992 defeating George H.W. Bush, who was hobbled by the "wimp factor." Candidates labeled as "wimps" seldom win American elections, even if they sport impressive military credentials (courtesy *Webster-Kirkwood Times*).

up the Reagan mantle in the 1988 election. However, Bush capitalized on his heroic actions as a U.S. Navy pilot in World War II in the 1988 contest against Michael Dukakis, a Democratic Senator from Massachusetts.

In addition, Bush employed the cutthroat campaign skills of Roger Ailes, who would later head Fox News. Ailes created political ads to make Dukakis look like a weakling, a dufus, and a coddler of criminals. Ailes put together the famous revolving-door commercial accusing Dukakis of allowing weekend furloughs for first-degree murderers not eligible for parole. "While out, many committed other crimes like kidnapping and rape," narrated the commentator for the Republican ad.[5]

The beefed-up Republican law-and-order narrative against Dukakis worked for George Herbert Walker Bush, who became America's 41st president. However, "Bush 41" was unable to sustain a rough, masculine or indestructible image for American voters, even after winning the first U.S. war with Iraq as president. Bush looked silly when he told the public about his "thousand points of light" policies to help out disadvantaged Americans. He was mocked as well and when he asked Americans to "read my lips" on his no new taxes policy then reneged on that promise. His weak constitution was confirmed for some voters when he barfed and passed out at an official Japanese dinner. Bush also moaned over a Newsweek magazine cover about him titled, "Fighting the Wimp Factor," which he decried as the "cheapest shot" in his entire political career.

A young, energetic Arkansas governor named Bill Clinton was nominated by Democrats in 1992 to take on the flagging Bush, who was fighting an economic recession as well as his "wimp factor." Clinton defeated Bush and began an eight-year tenure in the White House. He was a popular president, despite his alleged womanizing and rocky relationship with his wife, Hillary. Republicans tried to paint Clinton as hen-pecked by a woman who wanted to wear the pants in politics and the family, and who was estranged from her husband. Republicans thought they hit pay dirt when they uncovered Bill Clinton's affair in the Oval Office with intern Monica Lewinsky. However, Clinton survived an impeachment and a Senate trial that resulted from lying about the affair. He pulled through with even higher popularity numbers at the end of his two terms as president. Ironically, it was Al Gore who may have been damaged the most by a wild ride as William Jefferson Clinton's vice president.

Gore became the nominee of the Democratic Party in 2000. George W. Bush, the son of "Bush 41" won the Republican Party nomination after an especially dirty primary against challenger John McCain, the conservative senator from Arizona. The privileged son of George H.W. Bush had a reputation for trying to avoid combat in Vietnam in contrast to his father, whose plane went down in combat with the Japanese in World War

II. Somehow, John McCain, who had stellar credentials for combat and surviving as a POW in the Vietnam War, was unable to capitalize on his war reputation against the upstart Bush.

War injuries may have made McCain less attractive and less energetic than the younger Bush. George W. Bush also was packaged as a born-again Christian who looked like a cattle rancher as he posed for the cameras cutting brush. He beat McCain in the Republican primary and then sported his "cowboy rancher look" to defeat Vice-president Al Gore in the 2000 election. In point of fact, Gore won the popular vote, but Bush won crucial electoral votes in the less-populated "livestock states." Environmentalist Gore seemed too much like a stiff academician up against the plain-speaking cowboy, even if what Bush actually had to say was not always so bright.

Manliness Goes Haywire in a New Century

Less than one year after the Bush-Cheney team replaced Clinton-Gore in the White House, America suffered its worst terrorist attack on U.S. soil in the country's history. It's pretty tough to maintain a "tough guy" image in the White House when you have just presided over a terrible, deadly, surprise attack on the nation's number one city and the U.S. Pentagon. It did not help that Bush was reading to school kids from a children's book, *My Pet Goat*, when Osama bin Laden's treachery was unleashed, killing more than 3,000 Americans. Nevertheless, Bush attempted to bounce back from September 11, 2001, with a Dirty Harry approach to what was an international crisis. Standing in the rubble of the World Trade Center buildings in New York City, Bush vowed to track down the bad guys who wreaked havoc on America.

Soon U.S. jets were flying all over Afghanistan. Taliban fighters on camels were scrambling for cover. Afghanistan had provided a safe haven for Al Qaeda terrorists and their leader Osama bin Laden. This poor and unstable country would have to pay for harboring the Islamist radicals who planned the terrorist attack on America. The rockets' red glare flashed upon the mountains of the Hindu Kush at the borders of Afghanistan and Pakistan.

Bush-Cheney also took aim at other nation states and branded them as accomplices in terrorism. Soon George W. Bush was giving speeches against an "axis of evil" made up of Iran, North Korea, and Iraq. The fiery speeches were followed by bunker buster bombing of Baghdad, the capital of Iraq, and a fast-paced U.S. invasion of the country. It was called "shock and awe," but the massive military display of 2003 was later followed by long months of battle, bloodshed, and quagmire.

Hyper-masculinity went into high gear as Bush struggled to find a satisfactory outcome to the increasing loss of blood and treasure in the Middle East. There was a victory announcement on an aircraft carrier with Bush dressed up like "Maverick" from the Tom Cruise movie, *Top Gun*. That was followed by more "axis of evil" speeches and assurances that America's enemies were on the defensive and on the run. Bush's vice president, Dick Cheney, gritted his teeth and defended his early assertions that U.S. troops would be greeted "as liberators" in Iraq. Defense Secretary Donald Rumsfeld insisted the Iraq war was going well, although he did concede that "death has a tendency to encourage a depressing view of war."[6]

Bush also defended the war and referred to himself as a strong leader and as "the decider" who understood America' adversaries: "Our enemies are innovative and resourceful, and so are we. They never stop thinking about new ways to harm our country and our people, and neither do we,"[7] Bush declared. Bush's verbal gaffes mounted as did U.S. military casualties. Americans looked on in horror as flag-draped caskets from Iraq continued to arrive at Dover Air Force Base in Delaware. The world looked on in horror as stories of waterboarding terror suspects and photos of abusive treatment of prisoners were leaked from America's conflict in the Middle East. The Bush-Cheney administration stood behind its "enhanced interrogation techniques" and its use of the Guantanamo Base in Cuba to hold prisoners indefinitely.

By 2008, Americans had had enough of tough talk and the abysmal results of the Bush-Cheney foreign policies in the Middle East. The mastermind of the September 11, 2001, terrorism, Al Qaida leader Osama bin Laden, was still at large and on the loose. There was no light at the end of the tunnel in the war in Afghanistan, and it would drag on for another 13 years. Operation Iraqi Freedom did not deliver freedom for Iraqis, but it did deliver the Sunni government of Saddam Hussein to the radical Shiites who found support from their compatriots in Iran. The Bush administration had launched the war against Iraq on the pretext that its leader, Saddam Hussein, had developed nuclear weapons capability. There was no evidence of a nuclear program or a nuclear arsenal once American troops captured the country.

Americans were not just disillusioned with the Iraq War by the time the 2008 election rolled around. On September 29, 2008, the stock market fell almost 800 points, the biggest point drop in history up to that time. A number of factors were behind the market collapse, but the immediate cause was Congress's refusal to pass a bank bailout bill to stabilize the American financial system after a series of historic shocks. America was losing wars abroad and its international standing. At home, economic upheaval was throwing Americans out of work, decimating family fortunes and retirement programs, and causing loan defaults and home foreclosures.

As the Bush-Cheney team eyed retirement, the Republican Party eyed military hero Senator John McCain of Arizona as its best hope for maintaining its hold on the executive branch going into the November 2008 election. American voters did not seem all that impressed by military credentials at this point, despite McCain's record of heroism in the Vietnam War. The two failing wars in the Middle East, both predicated on dubious assumptions, did not help the cause of the Republicans or John McCain. After a contentious and very close presidential primary between Hillary Clinton and Barack Obama, the Democrats chose the Black U.S. Senator from Illinois over the Caucasian woman U.S. Senator from New York. Former First Lady Hillary Clinton was considered a strong possibility to be Obama's running mate after McCain chose Sarah Palin to be on his ticket. However, Obama chose Delaware Senator Joseph Biden for his running mate, so the 2008 election became a contest was between McCain-Palin and Obama-Biden.

Economic dislocation and foreign policy disasters under the previous Republican administration were major factors that favored a Democratic Obama-Biden win in the 2008 election to replace Bush-Cheney. On November 4, 2008, Obama won a decisive victory over McCain, winning the Electoral College and the popular vote on November 4 by sizable margins. Obama's victory included states that had not voted for the Democratic presidential candidate since 1976. The Obama administration declared that its agenda for the nation was to revive the economy, provide affordable and accessible health care to all, strengthen public education, work toward energy independence, tackle climate change, and wind down the Iraq War in a responsible fashion. Although the Obama agenda was moderate, if left of center, he was accused of having secret plans to provide new welfare programs and reparations for the Black segment of the U.S. population.

Obama became the first African American to be elected to the U.S. presidency, a remarkable accomplishment which alarmed many on the right. During his presidency, he was the subject of a number of both subtle and overt racist attacks challenging his leadership and legitimacy as the occupant of the White House. Just a few of those affronts included mock lynching incidents from trees, a rodeo clown in an Obama mask at a state fair, numerous insults about his birthplace and birth certificate, the use of the n-word in reference to the president, willful disrespect from members of Congress. That disrespect included Rep. Joe Wilson, Republican of South Carolina, yelling "you lie!" at Obama as he addressed a joint session of Congress in 2009. Former president Jimmy Carter told *NBC Nightly News* in 2009: "I think an overwhelming portion of the intensely demonstrated animosity toward President Barack Obama is based on the fact that he is a Black man."[8]

As the first Black U.S. President, a certain amount of racial backlash could be expected in a country with a white majority and that from its inception to its deadly Civil War sanctioned legalized slavery of Blacks. Attacks on Obama, which were probably less anticipated, had to do with questioning his gender and his manhood. Conservative pundits described him as all about demeanor and style, but lacking in any real substance. He was sensitive and thoughtful, but indecisive and far too passive. He was arrogant and impressed with himself, but basically a windbag and ineffectual. He was slight and soft and perhaps even was a "girly-man" with no business being leader of a the most powerful nation on earth.

Republicans sought to use these depictions of Obama to great advantage in the 2012 election to gain back the White House. Nothing illustrated this more than when Republican presidential nominee Mitt Romney called upon that favorite icon of so many Republicans to assist in putting Obama in his place—and out of office. In the 2012 election against the incumbent Obama, the Republican National Convention promised a "mystery speaker" for its final hour. That speaker proved to be Clint Eastwood in his popular Dirty Harry mode. Eastwood's so-called "empty chair skit" was well-received within the convention hall, but less so outside its confines.

Eastwood's skit involved speaking to an empty chair which represented President Barack Obama. Eastwood made his famous "make my day" remark to the invisible Obama, and the conservative crowd belted the line out

Barack Obama won the U.S. presidency in 2008 by defeating John McCain, a celebrated war hero. McCain's own party blamed his loss on his not waging a tougher, more combative campaign against Illinois U.S. senator Obama (Library of Congress).

in unison. The convention was clearly pleased that the man who championed strength and righteousness, and a fondness for guns, was clearly behind Mitt Romney and Paul Ryan. Eastwood said he was inspired by lyrics in singer Neil Diamond's hit, "I am ... I said," where "no one heard at all, not even the chair."[9]

In an August 2016 interview with *Esquire* magazine, Eastwood explained that he was, indeed, likening the first Black president to an empty chair: "That's Obama. He doesn't go to work. He doesn't go down to Congress and make a deal. What the hell's he doing sitting in the White House? If I were in that job, I'd get down there and make a deal. Sure, Congress are lazy bastards, but so what? You're the top guy. You're the president of the company. It's your responsibility to make sure everybody does well. It's the same with every company in this country, whether it's a two-man company or a two-hundred-man company.... And that's the pussy generation—nobody wants to work."[10]

Dirty Harry's endorsement of the Romney-Ryan ticket and his denunciation of "the pussy generation" did not seal the deal for voters going to the polls in November 2012 to make their decision. Obama-Biden won the all-important electoral vote and the popular vote by several million. The following year, the Republican establishment did an autopsy on the lost election and said the party had to change its ways. It had to rebrand itself as a kinder, gentler, and more inclusive political organization. Strategists conceded that the party was viewed during the election as callous toward minorities and dominated by stuffy, old white men. Pundits speculated whether the party of machismo was truly going to turn a new leaf and jettison their past totems and fetishes for cowboy hats, fighter helmets, and Dirty Harry's Smith & Wesson.

In all the elections of the post–World War II period, the old white men ruled and the most manly candidates invariably won their contests in the quest for the White House. Then came the 2008 and 2012 elections when voters preferred a Black candidate to be president who was softer, more intellectual, more civil, and diplomatic. So, what happened?

- Had a changed electorate become more diverse and less satisfied with what older white men were selling?
- Had Americans tired of tough talk that always seemed to result in costly, open-ended military adventurism with no attainable goals?
- Had Americans closed the door on the past? Had they forever turned to a new vision of masculinity that was less reliant on brawn and bravado, and more oriented toward mental acuity and mannerly behavior?

Perhaps these questions were all answered in 2016 when a brusque and caustic Republican candidate named Donald J. Trump demolished a slew of primary candidates with bombast and insult. Although Trump did not win the popular vote to become president-elect in November 2016, he did win the crucial electoral vote with help in critical small states in the Mountain West and the Great Plains. He won the presidency. A television celebrity and popular culture icon in his own right, Trump won because he was a master showman projecting all those treasured Republican values that had worked for the Grand Old Party in the past. Traditional manliness did the trick once again. The door had not closed on the past.

The colorful cockalorum with the trademark orange hair and garish red tie did not draw on the graven image of Dirty Harry and his "most powerful handgun in the world" for his 2016 election campaign. Perhaps that's because the Clint Eastwood character worked no magic for Mitt Romney four years before. Also, Eastwood himself was now a libertarian and free thinker who expressed many ideas that run contrary to the Republican credo. Trump chose to reach back instead to that old Republican standby, John Wayne, who was never shy about expressing his own belief in white supremacy or justifying land grabs from Native Americans when ranchers and cowboys settled the West.

When Donald Trump received the endorsement of the family of the late John Wayne for his presidential run in 2016, celebrity candidate Trump was ecstatic. Trump returned the favor, when accepting the family's seal of approval, by praising Wayne's virility and his many manly attributes. Trump roared: "John Wayne represented strength. He represented power. He represented what the people are looking for today, 'cause we have exactly the opposite from John Wayne right now in this country. And he represented real strength and an inner strength that you don't see very often."[11]

What Trump failed to mention in his praise was that "The Duke's" inner and outer strength was illusory—purely celluloid. Nevertheless, many Americans in 2016 longed for a return of the kind of manhood that Wayne represented, especially for their White House. Their national house seemed to be captive and sullied by some alien force. The electoral triumphs of Barack Obama in 2008 and 2012 constituted the worst kind of snub and denigration of the Wayne model of manhood beyond anything possible to imagine. For some, it was easy and comforting in 2016 to imagine a restoration of the tough-talking, frontier-style America which Wayne's films often capitalized upon—now that candidate Donald J. Trump was on the scene.

2

Owning the Libs with
Pee-wee and Mr. Rogers

Cowboy actor John Wayne has been at the top of the heap when it comes to portraying a powerful, red-blooded man with the right values. His fans in politics have marveled at his ability to throw his clenched fists at villains or to use a rifle to vanquish bad guys. Wayne always was a man's kind of wordsmith as well. He didn't use a lot of fancy adjectives and adverbs in his films, and he was to the point. "What you need in these parts is a marshal that's better at smelling than spelling," Wayne advised the town folk in *Dark Command*. He was boasting that he could sniff out a horse thief from a mile away.[1]

When defining manhood, no one could do it better than the brawling cowboy: "I define manhood simply: men should be tough, fair, and courageous, never petty, never looking for a fight, but never backing down from one either." Wayne never backed down and never blinked. For Wayne, relying on courage to prevail over enemies is about being unshakeable and decisive with a pistol: "It isn't always being fast or even accurate that counts," America's premiere cowboy counseled in *The Shootist*. "It's being willing. I found out early that most men, regardless of cause or need, aren't willing. They blink an eye or draw a breath before they pull the trigger. I won't."[2]

Conservatives most enjoyed Wayne's ability to call out a loser or to put down a wimp. Wayne would ask a chicken-hearted innocent just how far he might want his cowboy boot up his ass. His favorite term for weak-kneed fellows, who were not of his caliber, was "pilgrim." Outing someone as a pilgrim was the worst of insults, especially in the Old West period of John Wayne movies. The unwanted salutation was aimed at greenhorns, from the effete East, who made their way out West but who were woefully unprepared to take care of themselves in a new and hostile territory.

Perhaps the most famous instances of Wayne using the "pilgrim" slur occurred when he castigated the Jimmy Stewart character more than two dozen times in *The Man Who Shot Liberty Valance*. Stewart played Ransom Stoddard, a naïve young attorney with little knowledge of guns, who was convinced he could bring justice to the frontier town of Shinborne. Wayne, as the tough realist Tom Doniphon, was compelled to protect Stoddard from himself and from the hardened outlaws in the Liberty Valance gang.

Right-wing conservatives have taken their cues from that tough realist Tom Doniphon, aka John Wayne. They never tire of castigating their liberal "colleagues" in the halls of government, calling them effete coastal elitists who know little to nothing about defending themselves or their country. They generally put labels on their political adversaries that carry a bit more punch than "pilgrim." House Republicans have been known to tag Democrats as "snowflakes" or "commies." Senate Republicans have been known to diss Democrats as "peaceniks" and "agitators." The derisive language is even more heated at the presidential level with GOP standard-bearer Donald Trump labeling Democrats as "wackos," "dopes," "creeps," and "sick puppies."

In contrast to the pugilistic language of Republicans, Democrats have shown a little more restraint and a softer side. The results of speaking softly over the years, rather than wielding a verbal "big stick," have often been disappointing for them at the ballot box. Democrat Jimmy Carter had fireside chats on fighting inflation and his measured words during election campaigns seemed to result in his eventual defeat. Conservative and mainstream media dismissed him as just another liberal wimp delivering mush.

Michael Dukakis was truly a "pilgrim." The Massachusetts Democrat was shamed in a presidential debate when he tried to give a nuanced response about how he would react to a hypothetical rape of his wife. Democrat Al Gore was dismissed by George W. Bush as "Senator Ozone" after expressing concerns about the threat of global warming and climate change. Democrat Hillary Clinton was degraded as a "tramp" and a "bitch," with "small breasts" and "fat thighs" after 2016 presidential debates in which she tried to focus on national policy issues. Manly conservatives are never afraid of engaging in "locker room talk," if it involves a woman to be branded with the "b" word.

Unlike conservatives who have identified with many heavy-duty pop culture icons for their behavioral role models—characters played by the likes of John Wayne, Clayton Moore, Clint Eastwood, Arnold Schwarzenegger, Sylvester Stallone, Mel Gibson, and Tom Cruise—liberals have resisted adopting Hollywood superstars as their exemplars. One explanation for this reluctance by Democrats may be that they constitute a more diverse party, and the hyper-masculine, white prototypes are not palatable for Blacks, Asians, or women. Another explanation could well be that these characters do not reflect core liberal or Democratic values. This is especially true when it comes to liberals' repudiation of the American gun culture, homophobia, capital punishment, or imprisonment practices in the U.S. criminal justice system.

Liberals shun the heroes whom conservatives love, and they have especially steered clear of testosterone-powered pop culture warriors. Liberals' aversion to exploiting pop culture has not stopped Republicans from branding liberals as well-known pop culture celebrities. These "stars" are of dubious distinction. Intellectual liberals are likened to the erudite, bespectacled dog named Mr. Peabody, who appeared on the *Rocky & Bullwinkle and Friends Show*. Soft-spoken liberals with an academic bent are likened to the benign and gentle fellow known as Mr. Rogers on his children's television show. Popular liberals of various sexual proclivities have been likened to such unusual luminaries as Elvis "The Pelvis" Presley, Corporal Max Q. Klinger of the *M.A.S.H.* television series, and Pee-wee Herman of TV's *Pee-wee's Playhouse*.

Mr. Peabody, Four-Eyed Egghead

Some boys in secondary schools have endured the unfortunate side effects of racking up straight A's, of making the honor roll, of being inducted into Honor Society. They've been bullied for each and every one of these attainments. It's not always so cool to be too smart in American schools. In fact, it's often never cool at all. Young males have drawn the wrath of school bullies, and been met with name-calling and fisticuffs. Among the many derogatory names ascribed to the seriously intellectual kids over the years are: "know-it-all," "four eyes," "egghead" "dork," "Joe Scientist," and "Peabody."

The moniker Peabody comes from "Peabody's Improbable History" segments on the *Rocky & Bullwinkle and Friends Show*, which aired on television in the late 1950s and early 1960s. Peabody is shown to be the smartest creature in existence with an Ivy League degree from Harvard University. He just happened to be awarded that degree when he was three years old. A scientist, a Nobel Laureate, and a two-time Olympic medalist, Peabody invents a "Wayback Machine," and by doing different upgrades and tinkering on the time machine, Peabody and his adopted son, Sherman, meet historical figures whom they help out whenever possible. These notables in need of Peabody's help range from Napoleon to Churchill, from Mozart to Marco Polo.

As the world's greatest thinker, Peabody inevitably developed a pompous, egotistical demeanor. There is no subject that he has not studied and mastered. He is a "superhuman" mathematician who can solve complex calculations with relative ease. At the same time, Peabody is an accomplished historian. Peabody speaks all languages fluently. Peabody has mastered every musical instrument known to man and plays flawlessly. In other words, "Peabody" is a great insult to hurl at someone whom you want to define as pretentious, flatulent, vainglorious, pontifical, and an absolute dweeb.

Among the Democratic presidential candidates who have suffered classification as "Peabodies" are Adlai Stevenson, Michael Dukakis, and Al Gore. Using popular culture to relegate these candidates to absolute nerd status has proven an effective way to diminish their stature and credibility in the mind of the average voter. Who wants to elect an egghead? The common man prefers a presidential candidate who's a regular fellow— the kind of guy that he can have a beer while demolishing a plate of red hot chicken wings. The average voter does not want to be lectured to by a Mr. Peabody on difficult foreign policy issues, on bloated defense funding, or on the deleterious effects of carbon dioxide emissions entering the atmosphere.

Adlai Stevenson may have been the easiest Democrat to portray as an egghead with his bald pate, his perfect use of the English language, and the depth of his intellect. Stevenson was the darling of intellectuals, but there are not enough of those in America to double the population of the state of Wyoming. Stevenson attended an Ivy League school like so many presidential aspirants, but he lacked the good common political sense to play down that affiliation. In fact, Princeton University was where Stevenson could claim to have been an officer of Quadrangle, the school's most desirable eating club; managing editor of the *Daily Princetonian*; and a member of the university senior council.[3] He was defeated in both 1952 and 1956 by president by Dwight Eisenhower, who got his education in the European theater of World War II.

Stevenson deserved better treatment, rather than being diminished as a goofy egghead. He was an honest governor of Illinois, where he reformed the state police, improved the state highway system, cracked down on government corruption, and bolstered the state's image. Stevenson elevated Illinois journalism with his writing in the family newspaper, *The Bloomington Pantagraph*, and also gave stirring speeches that appealed to America's better angels, rather than to Republican Joseph McCarthy's minions, who smeared progressive thinkers as disloyal communists.

Historian David Halberstam wrote that "Stevenson was an elegant campaigner who raised the political discourse" and who brought thoughtful idealism to political life making "it seem an open and exciting place for a generation of younger Americans who might otherwise never have thought of working for a political candidate."[4]

Michael Dukakis and Al Gore also were Democratic presidential candidates who were easy to paint as Mr. Peabody types from the popular cartoon show. Dukakis was portrayed as the consummate dork, while Gore was tarred as a know-it-all bore and the "Joe Scientist" of environmental issues. Dukakis came out of the Democratic convention in 1988 with a 17-point lead over George H. W. Bush, but Republican strategists were expert at belittling Dukakis as someone who could overthink his way into a paper bag, a bag from which he could never escape.

Dukakis tried to counter attacks that he was inept and weak on defense by riding around in an Abrams attack tank for a campaign event. Republicans used the tank footage to make him look like Daffy Duck, or perhaps Mr. Peabody, peering out of the top of the armored vehicle. Political commentators later smirked that he was "tanked by a tank" in the 1988 election.

Al Gore, the Democratic nominee for president in 2000, was another victim of the Mr. Peabody syndrome—defeated by a far more pedestrian intellect. He had a superior command of national and international issues after two terms as vice president under President Bill Clinton. Gore knew far more about world affairs and global terrorism threats than his opponent, the pampered faux cowboy and rich kid of George H. W. Bush. He was a far more articulate speaker than Bush and did not mangle the language or create new words as the fraternity boy Bush was wont to do.

In his campaign, Gore warned Americans about environmental damage to the planet. For this, he was labeled as "Senator Ozone." For his lengthy and detailed critiques of the many ill effects of over-reliance on fossil fuel energy, he was branded as "Al Bore." He was nerdy. An opinion piece in *The Charlotte Observer* noted that candidate Gore had proven "compassionate, dedicated, effective, strong, well-educated, a good family man with strong moral values, who is willing to take risks, who understands and deals with issues," but when presented with such qualifications, "we throw away our long list of criteria and worry about whether he is charming enough. Are we choosing a dinner companion or the leader of the free world?"[5]

Klinger, Peacenik Pansy

Perhaps it's no coincidence that the anti-war television comedy series known as *M*A*S*H* debuted during the 1972 election contest of Democrat George McGovern and Republican Richard M. Nixon. The dark TV comedy

Republicans likened anti-war presidential candidate George McGovern and his youthful supporters to Corporal Klinger, the wacky, cross-dressing enlisted man in the TV series *M*A*S*H* (1972–1983). McGovern lost to Richard M. Nixon in the 1972 election. From left: Harry Morgan as Colonel Sherman T. Potter, Loretta Swit as Major Margaret J. "Hot Lips" Houlihan, and Jamie Farr as Corporal Maxwell Q. Klinger (CBS / Photofest).

was based on the 1970 anti-war movie of the same name, which was inspired by a 1968 novel. The movie was praised as bold, frank, timely, subversive, and fearless. At the same time it was derided as blasphemous, heartless, disloyal, sacrilegious, and demoralizing, especially for American troops fighting in Vietnam at the time. The military needed moral support and bolstering, not blasphemy. The TV series received very similar mixed reviews at the beginning, but as America's war in Southeast Asia became more and more unpopular, the television comedy became more popular—and outrageous.

By far the most outrageous character to develop out of the TV series was that of Corporal Klinger. Klinger, played by Jamie Farr, was a comical, cross-dressing enlisted man trying to find his way out of a war very much like Vietnam—the Korean War. Maxwell Q. Klinger hoped that wearing a dress, as well as a fruit-plate hat on his head, would lead to his discharge. Gays and cross-dressers were not especially welcome in the military. They were considered as cowardly, chicken-hearted, perverse, unreliable—and mentally ill. At the time, the American Psychiatric Association considered homosexuality to be a mental illness.[6] Klinger hoped that his wacky stunts would get him a Section Eight discharge from the service because of mental illness.

Although Klinger's TV character arrived too late for use as a political icon in the 1972 contest between McGovern and Nixon, his specter permeated the election. There was something a little perverse, disloyal and wacky about candidate McGovern and his young anti-war followers. Many of his youthful supporters would do anything to stay out of the military and so were accused of giving "aid and comfort to the enemy." They were attacked as cowardly, chicken-hearted, and unreliable. The whole bunch could have been right out of left-leaning television's *M*A*S*H* show, whose liberal cast supported subversive, traitorous, left-wing causes. At least, that was the view of the conservative right.

The Republican game plan to attack McGovern was devastating, simple, and direct: He was the candidate of draft dodgers, war resisters, hallucinogenic drugs, pornography, sexual revolution, and all manner of wackiness. This line of attack was repeated over and over again in subsequent elections. It worked against McGovern, who lost in a landslide against Nixon. It worked three decades later against Democrat John Kerry in his 2004 race against George W. Bush, who was running for a second term in the presidency. The irony of these right-wing tactics is that they were so at odds with the truth. Both McGovern and Kerry had served their country honorably in the U.S. military and at considerable risk.

Democrat McGovern may have had supporters who looked like hippies, and he may have grown his sideburns too long, but he was far from being a radical subversive. He opposed the Vietnam War as a useless waste of blood and treasure and was outspoken about it. However, he was not the crazy, anti-war, peace-at-any-price candidate. He was not Corporal Klinger. In World War II, McGovern volunteered for the U.S. Army Air Force. He flew 35 missions as a B-24 Liberator pilot over German-occupied territory in Europe. Among the medals McGovern received was a Distinguished Flying Cross for making a dangerous emergency landing of his damaged plane and saving his crew.[7] By contrast, candidate Nixon served stateside for much of his World War II service, yet McGovern was smeared as a chicken and appeaser in their 1972 election contest.

Democrat John Kerry suffered political attacks very similar to McGovern in his 2004 contest against incumbent Republican George W. Bush. In his younger years, Kerry echoed McGovern in calling the Vietnam War a useless waste of life and national wealth, and he was outspoken about it. However, he was not a crazy, anti-war, peace-at-any-price candidate. He was not Corporal Klinger.

In fact, Kerry served in Vietnam as an officer in charge of a Swift boat in 1969. Kerry received several combat medals during his tour in Southeast Asia, including the Silver Star, Bronze Star, and three Purple Hearts.[8] In contrast, candidate Bush dodged service in Vietnam and wrote in his biography that he was not interested in "serving as an infantryman wading across a paddy-field." Bush secured a safe assignment in the Texas Air National Guard, and there was controversy over why he lost his flight status in the Guard and whether he fulfilled all the provisions of his military service contract.[9]

The smears against Kerry and his service were encapsulated in a series of television campaign ads attacking him, advertising which inspired a pejorative term *swiftboating* to describe an unfair or untrue political attack. A group called Swift Boat Veterans for Truth (SBVT) spread the message that Kerry was unfit to serve as president based upon his alleged disgraceful service in Vietnam and his misconduct during the war. SBVT members had close ties to the Bush Campaign. Their efforts did irreparable harm to Kerry's reputation and his campaign. He lost the 2004 contest to Bush in a close election. The claims of the group were discredited. Vietnam veterans who served alongside Kerry, or under his command, tried to rebut all the criticism.[10] They expressed admiration for Kerry's service and his presidential aspirations.

Mister Rogers, Neighborhood Snowflake

Fred McFeely Rogers, better known as Mister Rogers, died in 2003 after a career as an American television host, author, producer, and Presbyterian minister. He was the creator and host of the preschool television series known as *Mister Rogers' Neighborhood*, which ran from 1968 to 2001. He was widely praised for teaching young children about tolerance, sharing, caring, good manners, and self-worth. He provided the young audience watching his public television show with wise and sympathetic counsel for dealing with the death of a pet, sibling rivalry, the first day of school or a family move to a new location. He is credited with helping millions of parents with the responsibility of raising their children.

Mister Rogers won numerous awards for his children's television show and also was the subject of the favorably reviewed movie *A Beautiful Day in the Neighborhood* (2019) in which he was played by actor Tom Hanks. Mister Rogers was the recipient of impressive honorary degrees from 40 colleges and universities. He won Grammy Awards, a Peabody Award, an Emmy for Lifetime Achievement, and a Presidential Medal of Honor.[11] Still, not everybody was wowed by his character and show during his lifetime, nor by the Mister Rogers' legacy after he passed.

Conservatives complained that despite all the good things about Mister Rogers, he was the archetype of "metrosexual wimpiness." Andrew Klavan, the right-wing host of *The Daily Wire,* declared that Mr. Rogers certainly was not the best model for young boys. "Men, real men, are tough" because life is dangerous, Klavan declared. "A nation full of lovable Mister Rogers [types] is a nation suitable for 4-year-olds and 3-year-olds who are controlled by soft-spoken, sweet-talking, all-powerful government authorities [but] … if you really want to have a wonderful day in the neighborhood, call John Wayne and tell him to bring his guns."[12]

One of the habits of Mr. Rogers, which drove conservatives up the wall, was his gentle manner and casual dress of sneakers and a sweater. That casual look was one of the traits of U.S. President Jimmy Carter, who also drove conservatives up the wall and whom they likened to Mr. Rogers. A manly president would not dress in a loose sweater and go on TV to gently lecture the American populace to slow down their cars to conserve energy. Democrat Carter, who served in the Oval Office for one term after winning the 1976 election against Gerald Ford, was constantly beat up for being a wimp for all of his four years. His vocal critics maintained that America did not need a soft-spoken, carbon copy of Mr. Rogers in the White House. America needed a cowboy—even if it was a TV cowboy— when the 1980 election arrived.

"I think [Mr. Rogers'] message of kindness and love and depiction of a quieter, more humble masculinity helped make Jimmy Carter's presidency possible in 1976," observed David Zurawik in *The Baltimore Sun.* "But Carter was one term, and the culture rejected and even mocked his values as it pivoted to Ronald Reagan and his more bellicose vision of 'Star Wars' technology and confrontation with the Soviet Union in 1980."[13]

Elvis, Legendary Hound Dog

Elvis Aaron Presley, who died before his 45th birthday in 1977, has become a legend as the American heartthrob dubbed the "King of Rock and Roll." Elvis Presley is classified as one of the most significant cultural icons of the 20th century. His energized renditions of songs, his sexually provocative performance style, and his potent mix of racial influences across color lines transformed him into a colossal musical success accompanied by plenty of controversy.

However, there was a dark side to Elvis. Republicans tried to transfer the dark side of the man from Graceland in Memphis, Tennessee, to the Arkansas Democrat, presidential candidate William Jefferson Clinton, in their efforts to defeat him in both the 1992 and 1996 elections.

The dark side of Elvis has been detailed in several biographies including Albert Goldman's *Elvis*. The king had serious flaws. Elvis was an arrested adolescent with insatiable appetites for twisted sex and for unhealthy food championed in the American South. But he was a top-of-the-charts musical genius.

Saxophone-playing Bill Clinton, for all his Southern charm and easy-going manner, was accused of many of the same transgressions as Elvis Presley. He was a smooth-talking genius, but Americans were plenty familiar with his insatiable lusts for food, the ladies, and celebrityhood. Like Elvis, he was known for prevarication and drug use, although Clinton maintained he never inhaled with his use of marijuana.[14]

Perhaps the main reason that likening Clinton to Elvis did not work as a campaign strategy is because Elvis Presley wasn't perceived as soft, weak or feminine—at least, at that point in American history. A young man as vital and animated as Presley (or Clinton) could not be a wimp. A movie star like Elvis, who had scantily-clad women on his arms while belting out songs like "Viva Las Vegas," was the envy of a good number of men, not their nemesis. There's a scene in one film where Elvis Presley and Ann-Margret marry. While they didn't actually wed, Elvis Presley and Ann-Margret did begin an affair on the set of the movie, *Viva Las Vegas*. The king had many, many princesses, much to the chagrin of his queen, Priscilla Presley. Stuff happens when you're a vital, manly celebrity.

Pee-wee Herman: Controlled by the Incubus

Pee-wee Herman is a cheerful, flamboyant, fictional character, a TV persona developed by Paul Reubens with a famous Los Angeles improvisational comedy group. Pee-wee Herman's children's television shows of the 1980s, including *Pee-wee's Playhouse*, was the recipient of numerous Emmy Awards. A child-like character inhabiting a very weird universe, Pee-wee attracted celebrities to the show, including Oprah Winfrey, Cher, Whoopi Goldberg, Grace Jones, Little Richard and more.

Pee-wee Herman appeared on *Late Night with David Letterman*, and Letterman was moved to comment: "What makes me laugh … is that [the character] has an external structure of a bratty little precocious kid, but you know it's being controlled by the incubus—the manifestation of evil itself."[15]

The incubus may have inspired Paul Reubens to go to an adult theater in Florida in 1991 to view pornography. He was arrested by police along with several other men for indecent exposure for alleged lewd behavior. The incident caused him to put his character of Pee-wee Herman on the shelf for several years and he had to cease his famous comebacks to personal insults: "I know you are, but what am I?" The arrest haunted him, but did not stop him from eventually going on *MTV's Video Music Awards* and asking, "Heard any good jokes lately?" When the audience responded, he came back with his signature line: "Ha! Ha! That's so funny I forgot to laugh!"[16]

Reubens did not forget his signature television character and came back to TV with his Pee-wee Herman shtick in 1999. Conservative moralists were outraged that "this pervert" could return to the airwaves for more TV time. However, they enjoyed likening many Democrats to the effeminate man-child known as Pee-wee Herman. In their view, the pale-skinned trickster with his giddy expressions and airy prancing personified those Democrats focused on gender identity issues. Democrats who were inclined to pass gay marriage laws, normalizing what conservatives saw as transgressive behavior, were put in the crosshairs.

Rank-and-file Republicans also enjoyed comparing a Democratic candidate for president in 2008 to the slight and skinny Pee-wee Herman. In their view, Barack Obama was a very similar "girly-boy type" who was not to be taken seriously. Republicans may have had a better time using the rather strange celebrity of Pee-wee Herman against Barack Obama than they did using the tarnished star of Elvis Presley against Bill Clinton. However, the party's more restrained standard bearers weren't having it. Perhaps they figured Americans had more serious matters on their minds than pop culture comparisons after the brutal economic crash of 2008. Perhaps they were too respectful and dignified to stoop to trashing America's first Black presidential candidate as some kindred soul or alter ego of Pee-wee Herman.

Neither John McCain in 2008, nor Mitt Romney in 2012, seemed willing to engage in gender slurs and the lowest gutter politics against

Obama. In fact, McCain went out of his way to defend his opponent when a McCain supporter at a campaign event called Obama an untrustworthy Arab. McCain retorted that Obama was a decent family man with whom he simply had policy issue differences. That elicited boos from McCain's amped-up audience. Both McCain and Romney were accused by the conservative right of playing political footsie and not engaging in any real mudslinging aimed at the Democrats. Republicans on the right were convinced that tough guy talk and innuendo can be effective in elections, while the more restrained approaches of soft Democrats, and the likes of McCain and Romney, turned out to be a major loser.

Elections have consequences. Popular culture has consequences in elections. In many of the election contests since World War II, Republicans have often succeeded by comparing Democratic candidates to iconic pop figures that are not always so flattering—that are definitely not manly in the traditional sense. Americans may have enjoyed watching TV characters like the egghead Mr. Peabody on a cartoon, the zany and mischievous Corporal Klinger in a comedy series, the warm and gentle Mr. Rogers on a children's show. However, they have not wanted to entrust the fate of the nation to someone charged with personifying the unmanly virtues of offbeat celebrities.

Republicans have not just triumphed by besmirching their opponents as dead ringers for someone like Mr. Rogers or Corporal Klinger. They've also succeeded by likening themselves to "real men," the kind of celebrities who display a surfeit of testosterone. Republican leaders did not seem so eager to employ such tactics in the eight years of the Obama administration, but their frustrated political base, and a fair number of independent American voters, were more than ready for someone to come out swinging in 2016 at the end of the Obama presidency. They also were ready to anoint a presidential candidate who was not afraid to call a woman ugly, who was not afraid to call a male opponent low-energy or poorly endowed, who was not afraid to engage in a little locker room talk about grabbing women's privates. Was there such a candidate out there?

3

Outrage, Populism, and Making Men Great Again!

In the aftermath of two election losses in 2008 and 2012—to a youngish, but puny, upstart community organizer from run-down south Chicago—the Republican Party found itself in crisis mode. The second inauguration of Barack Obama in 2012 resulted in a whole of lot of head-scratching and finger-pointing for frustrated Republicans. Hard questions were being asked about the "success of the soft guy."

How could this poor excuse for a man, whom they sarcastically described as America's "first woman president," assume the highest office in the land for the second time? How could someone with an un–American name like Barack Hussein Obama defeat a war hero with such an Old West name like John McCain? How could a candidate with derogatory nicknames like "Nobama," "Obummer," and "Odumbo"—courtesy of the right-wing media—end up crushing an upstanding Christian blueblood with the all–American moniker "Mitt" Romney?

Moderate Republicans argued that perhaps the Grand Old Party of John Wayne needed a makeover. After the drubbing of Romney, they pointed out that the GOP had lost the popular vote in five of the previous six presidential elections. The Republican National Committee released the most comprehensive post-election review ever made after an electoral loss. The 100-page autopsy stressed that the party's tent was growing ever smaller and that it was time for a new politics of inclusion. The time had come for outreach to African American, Asian, Hispanic, and gay voters. The party needed to reach out especially to the many women who were alienated by Republican policies of the past and a platform that appeared to be anti-women.

In the 2012 election, women who comprised 54 percent of the electorate went 55 percent for Obama. U.S. Rep. Ileana Ros-Lehtinen, R–Florida, said the party had to stop giving people the impression that opposing abortion is its top women's issue or that it has no use for financially-struggling single moms. Only eight out of 219 Republicans voted in favor of the 2009 Lilly Ledbetter Fair Pay Act, which would guarantee equal pay for women in the same positions as men.[1] The Romney election autopsy also noted the party's problems reaching Hispanics. The nation's fastest growing demographic group was not happy over GOP attacks on immigration. Republicans overwhelmingly voted against the 2010 DREAM Act, even though two-thirds of the nation's voters said illegal immigrants should be offered a chance to apply for legal status.

Despite the damning election autopsy calling for major changes and an overhaul of Republican Party positions, the right wing of the party said the main problem in 2012 was not policy but a milquetoast candidate who did not fight hard enough against the leftist loonies of the Obama-Biden administration. Romney did not champion the party platform against abortion, gay rights, immigration reform, and government regulations that favor minorities. The 2012 loss also was because Mitt Romney was not a mainline Christian. His Mormon religion did not sit well with Evangelicals in the party.

Despite the GOP 2012 election autopsy advising more openness and diversity for the party's future, the Republican base chose to slam the door on reaching out to marginalized constituencies. Instead, it turned to a candidate for 2016 who made an issue over whether the Black president was actually a U.S. citizen or even possessed a valid birth certificate. The base turned to a candidate who came down an escalator at the Trump Hotel and launched his campaign with harsh and divisive words about Mexican "rapists and murderers." Aliens, he said, were entering America in a great deluge as a result of lax immigration policies by Democrats.

The new Trump wing of the party shredded the damning report on the 2012 election. Trump Republicans brushed aside suggestions that they were losing young voters focused on issues about diversity, inclusion, equity, and climate change. Florida Republican strategist Sally Bradshaw, who served as a co-chair on the autopsy report, warned right-wing Republicans that young voters were increasingly "rolling their eyes" at what the GOP represents "and many minorities think Republicans don't like them or don't want them in our country. When someone rolls their eyes at us, they aren't likely to open their ears to us."[2]

Young people had much more to roll their eyes about when Donald Trump became the presidential nominee in 2016, picking up the party mantle from 2012 nominee Mitt Romney. Trump was accused of sexual misconduct by more than two dozen women; he declared the issue of climate change to be a Chinese hoax; he resolved to build a wall to keep out illegal immigrants on the southern border, and he promised that Mexico would pay for it. Instead of backing away from the misogynism of past

Republican idols like John Wayne and Charlton Heston, Trump embraced toxic masculinity and put it on steroids. He used misogynist tactics against the incumbent president, whom the party's right wing dismissed as the "first woman president." Then he used the same tactics against the Democratic Party's actual female nominee for 2016, Hillary Clinton.

In the early days of the 2016 presidential contest, Trump campaigned as much against Barack Obama as he did against Hillary Clinton. He joined the right-wing chorus that for years had been demeaning Obama as womanly and feminine—as if those qualities are somehow inferior and anathema. Matthew Continetti, a cheerleader for the emerging Trump candidacy as well as editor at the Washington Free Beacon, charged that a strong cabal of feminist women surrounded Obama and raised him "after his deadbeat dad fled to Kenya."

The influence of overbearing females and feminists supposedly made Obama bend over backwards on "women's issues, women's concerns, and women's priorities," according to Continetti on a website funded

Conservatives criticized children's TV character Mr. Rogers as a wimpy snowflake. They targeted Democrat Jimmy Carter as the same sort of softy in his unsuccessful presidential race against Ronald Reagan in 1980. From left: Mr. McFeely, Betty Aberlin and host Fred Rogers from *Mr. Rogers' Neighborhood* (1968–1976, 1979–2001) (PBS / Photofest).

by billionaire hedge fund manager Paul Singer. The Free Beacon editor trashed "Obummer" for unapologetically displaying every conceivable naïve trope of womanhood, so "he has as much of a claim as the next girl to be the first woman president. Do not 'other' him. Love him. Celebrate him.... And Hillary: Take note. We already have a woman in the White House."[3]

Conservative political journalism in American aided and abetted Trump in his own assertions that Obama was weak and womanly. *Washington Post* columnist Kathleen Parker joined the pack, attacking the authenticity of Obama's masculinity and questioned his gender identification. Parker confirmed her most conservative readers' suspicions that "Obama's weakness, cowardice, duplicity, thin-skinned scolding and oily forked-tongued-ness is fundamentally womanish." She suggested that his disposition was not that of a male maverick but of a meek woman who wants to talk things out with enemies, foreign and domestic. She dismissed Obama as "a chatterbox who makes Alan Alda look like Genghis Kahn."[4]

Not to be outdone, extreme masculinists on right-wing conspiracy blogs and radio talk shows declared that Barack Obama was gay; his wife Michelle Obama was a cover for his homosexuality; and they both had major gender authenticity issues. Jerome Corsi, one of the "swiftboaters" out to sink the presidential aspirations of Democratic Senator John Kerry back in the 2004 campaign, claimed that as a state senator in Illinois, Obama was a frequent participant in the gay bar and bathhouse scene in Chicago. His lovers were shocked when Obama had the audacity to decide to run for president, according to Corsi.[5] But then their shock turned to high anxiety and fear about telling the truth regarding Obama's lifestyle for fear of retaliation.

Not content to denigrate Barack Obama as a flighty and dangerous homosexual, pundits in the right-wing blogosphere also took aim at Michelle Obama. They told their millions of followers that the Obama couple personified a growing gender dysfunction among the nation's deranged liberals and misguided American youth. The strident voice of *Infowars*, Alex Jones, also took his turn at trashing Michelle Obama. Jones, who smeared the parents of the murdered children of the Sandy Hook massacre as whining fraudsters, went on a wild tear in 2014 questioning whether Michelle Obama was really a woman and whether Barack Obama was really a man.

Jones presented his arguments that Michelle Obama was a transsexual after what he told listeners was his extensive study of the physical attributes of Black women. He said it was time for the Obamas to own up: "These people are the authors of such tyranny that they shouldn't whine and complain when the public doesn't believe anything they are saying—especially every time I look at 'Michelle' or 'Michael' Obama, the First Lady, or First Tranny—something doesn't look right.... She doesn't look like any Black woman I've ever known."[6]

Jones contended that most Black women could support two heads on their shoulders, but Michelle Obama could support three, because her shoulders were so expansive, so broad. Candidate Trump was a total fan of the Jones' brand of craziness, and he was rewarded with appearances on Jones' show. Trump never questioned Jones' authority on Black women or that child victims of mass gun violence were just a liberal fantasy.

During the 2016 campaign, Trump linked via Twitter to *Infowars* articles as credible sources for his own claim that "thousands and thousands" of Muslims in the United States celebrated the 9/11 New York City attack on America. He also linked to Jones' assertions that climate change is bad science and a total hoax to benefit Chinese communists. A few days before one of Trump's August 2016 rallies, Jones posted a video claiming Hillary Clinton had mental health issues, which Trump then recycled in his campaign speeches. Many conspiracy theorists, like Jones, spread deceits about the Obamas and Clintons during the 2016 contest. Among the most outrageous was the delusional "Pizzagate" pedophile conspiracy theory disseminated on many alt-right websites.

Pizzagate claims included stories that a number of pizza restaurants were connected to several high-ranking Democratic Party officials, including Clinton, and were acting as locations for human trafficking and the operation of child sex rings. One of the eating establishments, allegedly involved with the sex rings using minors, was the Comet Ping Pong Pizzeria in Washington, D.C. Harassment of pizza parlors followed the outlandish charges. The Comet Ping Pong Pizzeria endured threatening phone calls, and one armed man entered the Washington, D.C., restaurant intent on causing physical harm to "pervert" employees. The Pizzagate disinformation campaign became part of the far right's wide-ranging QAnon conspiracy fantasies, which began cascading in late 2016.[7]

Candidate Trump did not distance himself from the crank conspiracy theories such as those spread by Alex Jones' *Infowars*. He fired up his conservative base in 2016 with attacks on both Hillary Clinton and Barack Obama. The Democratic Party deserved to be punished for foisting the first Black president on America, and it deserved to be punished again for trying to foist the first woman president on the country. America needed to be great again, with a return to manly leadership.

Obama was an untrustworthy, liberal, elitist, womanish Democrat, conservatives alleged. And Hillary Clinton was even worse. Hillary Clinton was an untrustworthy, liberal, elitist Democrat, who actually was a woman. The Trump strategy worked, but just barely. Trump won the 2016 electoral college vote. He lost the popular vote tally by almost three million ballots. Election observers noted after November 2016 that the GOP had now lost the popular vote in six of the last seven presidential elections.

Without a popular vote mandate in 2016, many political observers suggested that Trump would need to work with Democrats in order to govern effectively as president. Pundits optimistically predicted that Trump would turn down the volume and grow into the office; that he would drop the unfounded claims and his abominable campaign rhetoric; that he would become the moderate that he always had been as a visible, if vocal, lifetime resident of New York City. Other, less sanguine commentators, said it was likely that Trump would become America's first "Chaos President." The "chaos" prediction for the four years of the Trump presidency proved correct.

Over his four-year term, Trump garnered front-page coverage across America for cozying up to Russia's autocrats; turning his back on U.S. allies; claiming love letter exchanges with a North Korean dictator; building an ineffective wall that did not stop immigrants; blaming wildfires for a failure to rake forests; doctoring hurricane forecast maps; suggesting nukes be used to stop hurricanes; appointing close relatives to highly paid posts; firing cabinet officials on a regular basis; and continuing a sophomoric habit of assigning names to political leaders who disagreed with him, particularly women. His failed political rival Hillary Clinton was "Crooked Hillary"; House Speaker Nancy Pelosi was "Crazy Nancy"; Senator Elizabeth Warren was "Pocahontas"; his transportation secretary Elaine Chao became "China-loving Co Co Chow"; and her husband, Senator Mitch McConnell, became "Old Crow."

The "Chaos President" hit rock bottom with the arrival of the Covid-19 pandemic in late 2019. Trump at first tried to deny its severity, then claimed it would one day disappear as fast as it came. He told people not to wear masks and discouraged testing, because that only increased viral infection statistics. He touted bleach and an equine medicine, ivermectin, as possible pandemic cures. When he caught the virus himself, Trump was confined to Walter Reed Hospital for several days where he received superior treatment, with no use of bleach or ivermectin. After recovery, he demanded to wear a Superman logo upon his ostentatious release from the hospital. His plan was to stand up before the news cameras and open his button-down shirt to reveal a "Man of Steel" logo and to showcase his manly triumph over Covid-19.

In the 2020 presidential contest between Trump and Democrat Joseph Biden, the president's handling of the Covid-19 pandemic became a major liability, despite his own superman recovery. By the end of November

2020, almost 15 million people had contracted the virus and more than a quarter-million Americans had died.[8] America accounted for 20 percent of global fatalities. The pandemic caused severe economic contractions, skyrocketing unemployment, deficit spending for both health-care costs and the development of vaccines. Biden used the pandemic issue to win the presidency. Trump complained that he did not get credit for rolling out quick and effective vaccines against the virus. He accused Biden of hiding in his basement from the virus because of his frailty and also his fear of campaigning.

Biden won the 2020 election by more than seven million votes and with a sizeable electoral college victory. Biden won 81,283,098 votes, or 51.3 percent of the vote. Trump cast doubt on the election outcome and challenged the election results in several states where close margins made the difference for Biden in the all-important electoral college. After his defeat, Trump became the "post-election chaos president" when he implored Vice President Mike Pence to block certification of the electoral college results. Trump took aim at the legitimacy of the election both before and after the November 3, 2020, vote. Trump told his followers to come to Washington, D.C., to protest the outcome of the election, which he said was stolen and a fraud. He urged his supporters to "be there, will be wild!" at the Capitol on January 6, 2021.

Conspiracy theorist Alex Jones spread that same "stop the steal" message to millions of his *Infowars* followers. "This is the most important call to action on domestic soil since Paul Revere and his ride in 1776," Jones told listeners on December 19, 2020. A little more than two weeks later, Jones joined his followers at the Capitol as a behind-the-scenes organizer.[9] Trump spoke to Jones' followers, a weird amalgamation of his own supporters and alt-right militants like Proud Boys and Oath Keepers. Shortly after noon on January 6, Trump fired up the angry crowd assembled on the National Mall and told them it was time to do battle and stop the election theft. He finished his fiery speech by saying, "We fight. We fight like hell and if you don't fight like hell, you're not going to have a country anymore."[10]

The riot that commenced in short order resulted in the worst attack on the U.S. Capitol since the war with Great Britain. The post-mortems after that bloody day of mob action will go on for many years. Scores of rioters who broke into the Capitol were indicted, tried on felony charges, and subsequently jailed. The January 6 mayhem was a disaster for the Republican Party that far exceeded the defeat of candidate Romney by Barack Obama eight years earlier. Nevertheless, the GOP did not engage in the kind of soul-searching, post-election autopsy that it convened after Romney's defeat in 2012. This is mind-boggling because the Romney loss was far less momentous—and far less turbulent.

The events surrounding the 2020 Trump defeat were, indeed, momentous for the future of the Republican Party, as well as turbulent—and perhaps cataclysmic—for the future of America. Images of the worst attack on the Capitol in more than 200 years are vivid, memorable, and easily the most shocking images imprinted on the American psyche since the 9/11 attacks, the Oklahoma City bombing, the Challenger explosion, scenes from the Middle East or Vietnam wars, or the assassinations of American leaders from John F. Kennedy to Martin Luther King.

The big difference in the January 6, 2021, images is that they were not from faraway wars, or spectacular explosions, or terrible incidents of violence. The January 6 images are scenes of angry American males attacking their own country's sacred institutions. These are scenes of toxic masculinity at its worst, with grown men assaulting law enforcement with animal repellants, heavy projectiles, and flag poles transformed into spears. These are scenes of civil unrest, insurrection, and coup détat. Some scholars and political analysts point out that the angry groups of men on January 6, 2021, were simply foot soldiers on the ground for an insurrection. They were not part of the actual coup d'état plotting that was mapped out elsewhere, and much earlier. This was not a spontaneous uprising.

Trump lost by a wide margin in 2020 to Joseph Biden. There was no concession speech, and Trump's supporters were told not to accept the results. Even after the national disgrace of their assault on the Capitol, there was little remorse. Trump's brand of angry, male populism did not subside. In many instances, it was encouraged to continue, and the violence was celebrated. Trump promised those convicted of felonies that, if elected in 2024, he would see that apologies were issued: "I will tell you, I will look very, very favorably about full pardons. If I decide to run and if I win, I will be looking very, very strongly about pardons. Full pardons," Trump promised on a radio show in September 2022. "We'll be looking very, very seriously at full pardons because we can't let that happen. … And I mean full pardons with an apology to many."[11]

With the next election cycle—the midterm contests of 2022—many Republicans doubled down on new promises of "making men great again." They insisted that liberal elites and woke feminists were waging war on males. During the 2022 election cycle, Republican U.S. Representative Madison Cawthorn of North Carolina declared that the liberal culture was succeeding in its avowed effort to "demasculate" all young men "because they don't want people who are going to stand up." Cawthorn pointed to supposed evidence that testosterone levels in young males were at historic lows. He urged mothers to raise their sons to be "monsters" to counteract the epidemic of feminized boys.[12]

Senate candidate J.D. Vance in Ohio sounded a similar alarm and defended Kyle Rittenhouse, an 18-year-old acquitted of all charges in the shootings of three men in Black Lives Matter demonstrations in Kenosha, Wisconsin. Republican Vance said the Rittenhouse trial filled him with "indescribable rage." He charged that "we leave our boys without fathers. We let the wolves set fire to their communities. And when human nature tells them to go and defend what no one else is defending, we bring the full weight of the state and the global monopolists against them."[13]

GOP Governors Ron DeSantis of Florida and Glenn Youngkin of Virginia declared war on schools that they said were pushing a "transgender ideology" on youngsters. They argued that liberal history curriculum in schools was designed to make young white males feel shame, rather than pride, in their gender. The success of DeSantis and Youngkin in mobilizing the Republican base with their attacks on "woke" schools and teachers was contagious. Candidates in other states immediately took up the battle cry against the "demasculating" educational establishment in their states in the 2022 elections.

In political races across the country, GOP candidates also took up the cause for arming men to fight liberal treachery. There was no attempt to lower voices or to calm the rhetoric after the violence against the U.S. Capitol one year earlier. During the 2022 football Super Bowl, Republican candidate Jim Lamon aired an advertisement that was styled to look like an Old West movie about manly heroes ready to fill all villains full of lead. Lamon posed in the political ad as a gun-twirling sheriff firing fast and emptying his weapon on a cowering actor dressed to look like President Joe Biden.[14]

In a U.S. House race in Georgia, Republican Mike Collins also took up arms against treacherous Democrats. Collins pushed a wheelbarrow full of documents into the forest and then shot the paper stacks full of holes. The brave candidate was supposedly targeting "Nancy Pelosi's Plan for America" and transforming it into a smoky cloud of confetti.[15] The political ad was tone deaf to the destruction that took place in Pelosi's U.S. House of Representatives office during the January 6, 2021, riots in Washington, D.C. The video violence was also tone deaf to the break-in at Pelosi's home in San Francisco where her husband's head was bashed in by an assailant's hammer.

In a heated Republican primary in Missouri in 2022, candidates for U.S. Senate tried to outdo each other in demented television advertising with displays of over-the-top manliness. Attorney General Eric Schmidt described President Biden as a "total disaster" in his Senate primary ad and then took a blowtorch to his "socialist agenda." Schmitt referred to his many lawsuits filed as attorney general as noble fights against the Biden administration on U.S.-Mexico border policy. He cited his lawsuits against schools and local governments with their mask mandates to protect against a pandemic that, at that point, had taken close to one million American lives. Schmitt did not forget to add that he stood with President Trump to stop election fraud alleged in baseless claims.

Two other candidates in the Missouri race did not rely on a measly blowtorch to turn the heat up on the "Biden socialists," or to prove their manliness, or to scorch liberal perfidy. A disgraced former Governor Eric Greitens used a semiautomatic rifle with which he demolished a body-shaped metal target in a hail of bullets. "Liberals, beware!" Greitens stated after leaving the target in shards.[16] His tone echoed the grim finality of Arnold Schwarzenegger's *Terminator*. Republican Mark McCloskey, another Senate candidate, had previously gained national notoriety for wielding an AR-15 military-style rifle at a Black Lives Matter protest in St. Louis. In his 2022 campaign for the GOP nomination for U.S. Senate, McCloskey toured Missouri in an SUV emblazoned with a giant photo capturing his gun-toting moments of fame along with his gun-toting wife. "Never Back Down," proclaimed the adjacent text.

Missouri's U.S. Senator Josh Hawley was not up for re-election until 2024, so he did not feel compelled to resort to a blowtorch or an automatic weapon in the state's midterms. However, Hawley made a concerted effort in Missouri to make sure that residents knew that he, too, stood for unabridged gun rights and also stood with President Trump to stop the alleged 2020 election steal. In addition to endorsing and advocating for Trump candidates throughout the country in the 2022 midterms, Hawley also promoted his upcoming book, a manual to restore male pride: *Manhood: The Masculine Virtues America Needs*.

In the early days of his successful 2016 presidential contest, Republican Donald Trump campaigned against Barack Obama as much as against his actual opponent, Hillary Clinton (shown here in 1993). Trump labeled Clinton "Crooked Hillary" and insisted that no one wanted a president in a pantsuit (Library of Congress).

Hawley's publisher, the right-wing Regnery Publishing, proclaimed that the U.S. Senator would soon identify "the defining strengths of men, including responsibility, bravery, fidelity, and leadership." In the meantime, Hawley joined the clamor in the 2022 Republican campaigns regarding liberal attempts to tear down manhood and to indoctrinate boys into thinking their masculinity is inherently problematic. Like many Republican candidates, Hawley chose not to honor the responsibility, bravery, and fidelity of the Capitol police whose blood was shed protecting him from the crazed mob at the U.S. Capitol Insurrection.

Hawley chose to condemn the federal investigations into the January 6, 2021, rebellion that shocked a nation and the world. After all, Hawley and his party felt the real problems that needed investigation in America

Although Donald Trump was defeated by seven million votes in his 2020 contest against Democrat Joe Biden, he insisted that the election was a fraud. In the midterm elections of 2022, many GOP candidates stood with Trump against gun restrictions, women's reproductive rights, and a "fraudulent election" in 2020 (Library of Congress).

were drag balls, transgender children, unseemly library books, and all the effeminate liberal men undermining manliness in the land of John Wayne.

4

Manhood

Masculine Virtues America Needs?

Senator Josh Hawley of Missouri is one of many conservative leaders who is worried about the future of men. Not only has he echoed his political peers on the dimensions of the male crisis in confidence, but also he promised in 2022 to publish a manual for restoring male pride: *Manhood: The Masculine Virtues America Needs*. His publisher proclaimed that Hawley was in a unique place to provide a roadmap to the future for confused boys and wayward men. Hawley grew up in the Midwest, which has been especially hard hit in recent decades by the economic dislocation of men in the workplace. Hawley also navigated a treacherous liberal educational environment to become a leader. He was later able to mentor anxious young men at the University of Missouri where he taught in its law school.

Hawley's Missouri has long been home to tough men exemplifying a certain kind of energy and manhood. Some of them were not exactly mainstream. Jesse James was at the top of the heap among sharp-shooting outlaws. There was also the bloody dueler B. Gratz Brown and the ruthless killer William T. Anderson. In Hawley's western Missouri hometown of Lexington, Confederate General Sterling Price led Missouri's southern sympathizers to defeat Union forces at the Battle of Lexington. Other ornery men of Missouri who frequented Hawley's hometown in the 1800s were those in Quantrill's Raiders and those in the James–Younger Gang.[1]

More mainstream masculine men of Missouri's past include "superman" Bernarr McFadden, who, as a bodybuilder, was the perfect specimen of a man and the "Father of Physical Culture" in America. Missouri's Dale Carnegie became a millionaire preaching about self-reliance and techniques to become a wealthy businessman. Perhaps Missouri's greatest entrepreneurs would be Walmart's Sam Walton of Shelbina, Missouri, and another small-town resident of Hamilton, Missouri, named J. C. Penney.[2] Hawley's vision of manly men conforms to Missouri history with its legacy of macho manhood, its hard-boiled outlaws and lawmen, its rugged and savvy business operators, and its often extreme right-wing politics.

Hawley himself has pushed an absolutist approach to gun rights and the Second Amendment. He has fulminated for defense of "religious freedom," for protection of the unborn, and for a business climate free of regulations based on environmental concerns like climate change. Hawley totally "talks the talk" of right-wing masculine values, but some critics on the right question his commitment to "walking the walk." They point out that he actually ran frantically for cover in the U.S. Capitol Building on January 6, 2021, when an alt-right mob invaded the premises—a mob that he had saluted with a fist earlier in the day.

From the beginning of his rise to political power in state and national politics, Hawley did not hesitate to model himself in the Trump mold of populism as both a campaigner and thinker. Many scoffed at the idea that Hawley, an Ivy League-educated son of a banker, could really pose as a tough and brash man of the people. However, they also had to acknowledge that billionaire New Yorker Donald Trump ran successfully for president by presenting himself as a fearless outsider attacking an establishment elite. Hawley has prospered by presenting himself as an evangelical Christian battling the secular perversions of a coastal cultural elite. He also has done well going into bulldog attack mode against his liberal opposition. He has used some of the same harsh language of the consummate bully, but he has never matched the outrageous nicknames and slanders used frequently by his mentor Trump.

Hawley's critics find it ludicrous that he can preach about manhood, while his chief mentor behaves in a licentious manner that runs counter to most conventional thinking on what constitutes manhood. Hawley, at times, has tried to emulate the rough-hewn and loud-mouthed reality TV star—a man with no boundaries. But how can anyone keep up with a bully who calls his friends and enemies names such as "Fat Jerry," "Mr. Magoo," "Cryin' Chuck," "Lyin' Ted," and "Little Hands Marco." It's not so easy to pull off when you've been groomed to be a gentleman at Stanford and Yale. How can Hawley keep up with a mentor who dodged the draft and yet had the unmitigated gall to call his own military appointees "lightweight," "lapdogs" or worse? Hawley has to try. After all, his state of Missouri went for the outspoken Trump by an overwhelming 18 percentage points in 2016 and by almost 16 points in 2020.

When Josh Hawley debated incumbent Claire McCaskill in his successful 2018 U.S. Senate contest, he unleashed the usual right-wing invective against the incumbent Democrat. He told a Missouri Press Association audience that she was a "radical leftist," a hopeless "elitist" and an unredeemable "Hollywood liberal."[3] He had not yet coined his book pejorative, "Epicurean liberal." He would surely have employed it against McCaskill had that searing arrow been available in Hawley's political quiver. He eventually used it to excess against liberal foes in his 2023 exposé on the decline of the American male and the need to recapture an earlier vision of manhood.

As Hawley's book explains it, his "Epicurean liberal" label actually originates with an ancient Greek sage who died in 270 bc. The philosopher Epicurus is the inspiration behind modern liberalism, which, Hawley implies, is now responsible for troubled men in midlife crisis and all the aimless, unemployed young males watching porn and playing video games in their parents' basements. According to Hawley, Epicurus believed the gods are indifferent to man's fate—

In one of the few competitive U.S. Senate races in 2018, incumbent Senator Claire McCaskill faced off against Republican challenger Josh Hawley in Missouri. Hawley painted McCaskill as a radical leftist and a Hollywood liberal elitist and won the election (courtesy *Webster-Kirkwood Times*).

and god may not even exist. Therefore, Epicurus declared that men should find their own reasons for living and devise their own paths to fulfillment. They should put the god obsession aside, then focus "on pursuing pleasure and happiness."

How inconvenient for Hawley's purposes that the "pursuit of happiness" is actually enshrined in the U.S. Declaration of Independence. This Epicurean life pursuit does not have to be a wayward journey full of golden idols, slovenly behavior, and prurient interest. Nevertheless, Hawley writes in his book that men are likely incapable of holding down jobs, and committing to marriage and a family, when they are captive to a craven and depressing secular outlook on existence. Even worse, for young males, the godless "pursuit of pleasure" leads to permanent residence in their parents' musty cellars, where their X-Box controllers are still intact and their laptop computers are bookmarked for Pornhub.

Go to the book index in Hawley's *Manhood* and you find that Epicurus and the term Epicureanism get dozens of entries in his book. Only notables like Adam, Eve, Moses, and Abraham get comparable attention.[4] For God's sake, even Jesus only gets four mentions in the book, as noted in the index. Given the carnage and woe that Epicurus has rained down upon America, perhaps it makes sense that Jesus takes a backseat to the evil Epicurus and his wicked tenets in *Manhood*. After all, Epicurean liberalism is destroying the very character of American men and, as Hawley emphasizes, it's doubtful that any free nation can "survive without the soundness of character" in its men.

One hesitates to harp too much on Hawley's bogeyman of "Epicurean liberalism," but it takes up so many of his *Manhood* book's 214 pages. And so, it's obligatory to offer a few examples of the Greek false prophet's perfidy and of those depraved liberals who now follow him:

- Epicurean liberals relish destroying biblical truth and sentencing man to total meaninglessness. Only a return to the Garden of Eden story can restore meaning because Genesis reveals that: "Your work matters. Your life matters. Your character matters. You can help the world become what it was meant to be. And that is no small thing."[5]
- Epicurean liberals flee from trial and pain. They like life to be easy and free of challenges. They just want to be "nice persons" who won't stand in the way of anyone else pursuing self-gratification. They are spineless and so ignore and never condemn the vices of others.
- Epicurean liberals trash men and their biblical duty to have "dominion over every living thing that moves on earth." They are like the apple-peddling evil serpent in the Garden of Eden who "offered Adam something for nothing—self-promotion without duty, self-advancement without service or obedience."[6]
- Epicurean liberals disparage marriage and fatherhood as condemnation to a life of hardship and sacrifice. They prefer the "cheap sex" available on the Internet. Hawley cites a sociologist who says that men can easily see more flesh in five minutes than their great-grandfathers could see in a lifetime.[7]

Hawley's point about the easy access to sexual stimulation on Internet sites is troubling. He laments that today's young men are now seeing more bare flesh with an afternoon visit to Porn Hub than their great-grandfathers could see in a lifetime. This begs the question: Is marriage to be valued, in part, because it is a more acceptable venue for seeing female flesh than Internet websites that are so readily available? Hawley contends the so-called Epicurean liberals are advocating the cheap sex of the Internet over the more difficult arrangements of marriage. There's something cheap about this entire comparison.

Elephants in the Room

Just as Jesus said there are many rooms in his Father's house, it can equally be said that there are many elephants in Senator Hawley's book of manhood knowledge. However, it's no surprise that Hawley chooses to ignore all the elephants in his reading room. Hawley must not sidestep the elephants if his book is to have a shred of credibility, but he does ignore all the troublesome pachyderms. Hawley spends a considerable amount of time praising the sanctity of marriage and loyalty to one's wife and to one's vows of holy matrimony. The need for good men to avoid the temptation of "cheap sex" is a primary concern of Hawley's.

And yet, Hawley has used much of his political career to champion Donald J. Trump, not exactly a paragon of marital fidelity, or chastity, or character. In his debate with Senator McCaskill, he pledged to whole-heartedly support the self-confessed sexual predator. Hawley has some-how overlooked Trump's sexual dalliances, such as those with porn star Stormy Daniels.

In Hawley's defense, he has endorsed a man who avoids "cheap sex." Trump's adulterous "sexcapades" with women have cost him dearly. The hush money checks and cash paid out to try to keep his affairs under wraps from the American public have been anything but cheap. Despite Hawley's considerable fealty to Trump, the lecherous standard bearer for the Republican Party gets even less notice in *Manhood* than Jesus. In fact, Trump is never mentioned in the book.

Instead, Hawley goes after a little-known, pop culture maven named Andrew Tate. Hawley damns the obscure "celebrity" for his many boasts about bedding women. "Every man who has been in a locker room recognizes the type. The fake bravado, the endless boasting. "[8] Why in the world does Hawley skewer a pitiful pawn like Tate when he could have easily lanced the king of locker-room bravado?

By now, everyone in America has heard of Trump's pussy-grabbing brags on the "Access Hollywood" tape. By now, everyone has heard of his affair with a *Playboy* model and maybe even his past attempts to get *Playboy* to run a nudie spread to be called, "The Girls of Trump." By now, everyone has heard of Trump's legal encounters with New York columnist

E. Jean Carroll, who accused him of sexual assault, defamation, and battery.[9] Yet, Hawley evidently preferred in *Manhood* to obsess on the failings and offenses of Andrew Tate, rather than the more obvious offender Donald J. Trump.

Another weighty elephant missing from Hawley's book on manhood involves his infamous salute to the manly men of the Oath Keepers and Proud Boys. On January 6, 2021, they were shouting right-wing epithets and threats before storming Congress to try to interfere with the U.S. presidential election certification. Hawley saw the rabble and stopped to give them all an earnest look and then a clenched fist pump of support.

Certainly Hawley could have referenced this symbolic fist pump of support for manliness in his book, perhaps in chapter three, titled "A Man's Battle." Instead, Hawley uses that chapter to drone on about his opting out of public high school in Lexington, Missouri, to face homesickness and bravely play prep football at Rockhurst Catholic High School in Kansas City.

The omission of his infamous clenched fist in the *Manhood* book is especially troubling when considering the national reaction to his salute for the angry men on the National Mall. Prominent conservative columnist George Will wrote on the day of the riot that Hawley, Trump, and Senator Ted Cruz "will each wear the scarlet S of a seditionist."[10] David M. Kennedy, who served as Hawley's academic adviser at Stanford University, said he "absolutely could not have predicted that the bright, idealistic, clear-thinking young student that I knew would follow this path."[11] Jack Danforth, a former Republican senator from Missouri and a Hawley supporter, said that backing Hawley for U.S. Senate was the "worst mistake I ever made in my life."[12] Simon & Schuster cancelled publication of his *Manhood* book and Hawley was forced to resort to right-wing book promoter, Regnery Publishing.

The blowback in Hawley's home state over his clenched fist salute was immediate. *The Kansas City Star* called it "the image that will haunt Josh Hawley" for his life and "one of the iconic images to emerge from the day the Capitol was breached by rioters."[13] Pulitzer Prize-winning *St. Louis Post-Dispatch* columnist Tony Messenger said, "the staging was perfect" and recommended the photograph be known as *Hawley: The Face of Sedition*. The Post-Dispatch published an editorial that labeled Hawley an enabler of "Trumpism" and called for Hawley to resign. The Missouri newspaper said, "Trumpism must die before it morphs into Hitlerism. Defenders like Hawley deserve to be cast into political purgatory for having promoted it."[14]

The fist pump seen across Missouri—and the nation—was only half of Josh Hawley's problems documented on "Insurrection Day" in America.

Not long after his salute to the men of the Oath Keepers, Proud Boys, and Patriot Front, the pro–Trump protesters stormed the Congress. Five people died from the violent melee. Congressional offices were seized, human excrement was smeared on the walls of a building many Americans regard as sacred, and U.S. lawmakers were ushered by security officers to safety from the mob. Josh Hawley was seen and recorded high-tailing it back and forth in the building desperately looking for cover.

More than a few reviewers of Hawley's book on manliness have taken time to note the irony of his cowardly actions after the infamous fist pump to the insurrectionists. It's another elephant in the room that Hawley refuses to acknowledge or to explain in *Manhood*. Why did Hawley flee from the insurrectionists and not challenge them, advise them, or join them with some kind of additional fist action? Hawley's critics call his flight in the halls of Congress the most notable act of his four decades of life: running to escape the crowd of militants for Trump. Some of his detractors note the humor in the music set to accompany his "wee scamper" as captured on video and posted on the internet. They range from the dramatic "Chariots of Fire" to a desperate "Stayin' Alive" by the Bee Gees.

The ironic humor of his fleeing from danger is amplified when put into the context of the Missouri Senator's manhood crusade. Hawley likes to brag on the Western ethos of his state, the gateway to the Old West. In Missouri, brave lawmen stood up to ruthless murderers like William T. Anderson, dangerous outlaws like Jesse James, renegade killers like the Bald Knobbers, and bank robbers like Bonnie and Clyde. Hawley is fond of relating the bravery of Civil War soldiers in the battle in his own hometown. In his *Manhood*, Hawley tells the story of a distant relative of his wife, a brave boy named Bud Sumpter, who risked all to help the law capture a notorious cattle rustler.

The mayhem begins when livestock thief William Coe and his gang "descend on a camp of sheep herders pasturing a flock of nearly 1,700 head just a few miles south of Robber's Roost." Three of the herders are killed after they put up a fight, and the bandits make off with the sheep. Coe's killing and thievery only stops when young Bud has had enough and takes a stand: "Bud Sumpter's choice is one faced by every boy who would become a man. This is what men are called to do, to assert themselves and their power to uphold the right. They are called to acquire the character of a warrior. Predictably, that is not how today's Epicurean liberals see it. Instead, they openly condemn male assertiveness."[15]

Reviewers of *Manhood: The Masculine Virtues America Needs* are understandably skeptical of Hawley's attempts to discredit so-called "Epicurean liberals" with his Old West yarn about young Bud Sumpter and the William Coe Gang. They also wonder whether Hawley is the best champion for male assertiveness, given his slinking from danger in the halls of Congress in January 2021. And why didn't Hawley use his manliness book to explain his own actions in the face of peril, instead of hiding behind the tale of Bud Sumpter, his wife's distant relative?

In fact, Hawley flubbed his manhood challenge. He flunked the Bud Sumpter test. "How can Hawley tell us that a man must be 'willing to give his life for others, willing to act boldly, to face death,' yet not say anything about his well-known Sprint of Self-Preservation?" asked Jon Schwarz writing for *The Intercept*. "How can he at the same time condemn 'liberals' because they 'flee from trial and pain?'" Schwarz queried further.[16]

An Insult to Men's Studies?

In providing readers with examples of manly men, Hawley pretty much relies on biblical figures from the Old Testament, rather than more recent figures who may have feet of clay or, at least, some troublesome baggage. Perhaps Hawley feels it's safer to talk about Abraham, David and Joshua. These males are from a distant past and are less vulnerable to exposés on social media.

Still, are these biblical figures the best examples of manly men? Abraham had a wandering eye and was still fathering children at 86. As an Epicurean sex fiend, Abraham shows an unleashed virility that might put Hollywood liberals Martin Scorsese or Al Pacino to shame. Regarding the other biblical manly men: David was guilty of murder and adultery and spent his entire life regretting it. Joshua did not build a wall, but he claimed to have brought one down at Jericho. Scholars argue this was false bravado—maybe locker-room talk. They say an earthquake likely caused the wall's failure.

Men's studies scholars have been researching masculinity and male behavior in America for decades—long before Hawley took up his study. Why doesn't Hawley reference other masculinities experts upon whose shoulders he could have stood? Some of those experts include Michael Kimmel, Susan Faludi, Herbert Goldberg, Gail Sheehy, Lionel Tiger, Susan Bordo, Warren Farrell, James Doyle, Francis Baumli, Ellis Cose, Harry Brod and Michael Messner.

Hawley's book might have benefited enormously from the insights of these previous masculinities trailblazers. Hawley might be surprised to learn that some female scholars have been especially adept at explaining the male malaise, the loss of male identity in America, and the declining status of men—as women now ascend academic and corporate ladders.

Susan Faludi has provided empathetic character studies of distressed industrial workers, combat veterans, football fans, evangelical husbands, suburban and inner-city teenage boys. Her book *Stiffed* uncovers the powerful social and economic forces that have hurt American manhood.[17]

Susan Bordo sheds light on the historic and traumatic paradigm shift from a utilitarian manliness—grounded in hard work, civic responsibility and communal service—to today's ornamental masculinity. This superficial metrosexual masculinity is often shaped by entertainment, marketing, and shallow "performance" values.[18]

Gail Sheehy studied men and their "crises" when hitting midlife. She examined work anxieties, concerns over sexual potency, marital and family stress, and issues of declining power in the workplace. In *Understanding Men's Passages*, Sheehy dealt with "manopause," surviving job change, coping with post-nesting loss of male identity, and defeating depression.[19]

In his 1997 work, *Politics of Masculinities: Men in Movements*, Michael Messner identified a variety of perspectives and men's groups with different approaches to both defining and affirming masculinity. Some men's groups created safe spaces for male identities unalterably at odds with what is offered by Hawley and today's GOP male traditionalists.

Messner examines such men's groups, many of which got their starts in the last century, such as the Promise Keepers, the Million Man March, Robert Bly's mythopoetic men, various fathers' rights groups and male liberationists. Instead of looking at valuable lessons offered by these male identity movements, Hawley gives us parables from the park, the woods and the playground experiences with his son, Elijah.

One of the men's scholars who've taken issue with Hawley's refusal to locate his study in a vast continuum of manhood research is Rob Okun. Okun is publisher of Voice Male magazine, which he has edited for 30 years. Okun says Hawley is tone deaf to shifts in culture that have been going on for a half century or more.

"Like so many others working to protect white male supremacy [see Carlson, Tucker; McCarthy, Kevin], he's driving a gas-guzzling Cadillac on a road increasingly filled with electric vehicles," declares Okun. "Just as women are vigorously resisting returning to a pre–Roe v. Wade America, men aren't going back either."[20]

Okun says there is a kernel of truth in Hawley's assertion that some young men are floundering in school and in the workplace. However, Okun contends the real crisis concerns how many young men have become obsessed with the gun culture and been suckered into a social media echo chamber of vicious ethnic and religious prejudice and hate.

"To see how out of touch Hawley is, there's nothing in his book about perpetrators of mass shooting massacres, primarily young men," observes Okun. "This omission is startling, but not surprising, given right-wing Sen. Hawley's subservice to the American gun lobby."[21]

Manhood *Reviewers' Ripostes*

Most book reviewers have not been especially kind to Hawley's book and his version of the virtues needed for manhood, but in fairness to the senior senator from Missouri, it must be pointed out that most of the reviewers are likely to be the Epicurean liberals whom Hawley detests. Many reviewers take aim at the final chapters of his book, where he outlines how men are physically and mentally designed by a higher power to be husbands, providers, warriors, builders, priests and kings.

In his warrior chapter, Hawley advises men to be confrontational, strong, and ready to protect "the garden of civilization." Why, then, has Hawley, as Kevin McDermott writes, become "among the most prominent voices undermining U.S. support for Ukraine against its brutal Russian invaders"? McDermott, of the *St. Louis Post-Dispatch,* the flagship newspaper in Hawley's state, also argues that as the sole Senate vote cast against the entry of Finland and Sweden into NATO, Hawley seems all alone in trying not to antagonize or confront the Russian KGB war criminal Vladimir Putin.[22]

Slate's Rebecca Onion also seems incredulous about Hawley's warrior credentials: "Why did a man who is probably our leading national pipsqueak decide that promoting manliness was his ticket to political power?" Onion also seems to fall out of her reading chair when perusing Hawley's king chapter, where he describes hollow men who "desperately want authority for all the wrong reasons.... They preen, they abuse, they dominate. They see others as means to their own ends." Onion is utterly flabbergasted that the name of would-be king Donald Trump is nowhere in sight.[23]

Monica Hesse of *The Washington Post* recalls Hawley's confrontations and badgering of Ketanji Brown at

After becoming a U.S. senator, Josh Hawley denounced American liberals for being anti-male and promoting the idea of "toxic masculinity." His 2023 book titled *Manhood: The Masculine Virtues America Needs* was dismissed by critics as reactionary (courtesy *Webster-Kirkwood Times*).

her Supreme Court confirmation hearings. He demanded that she define the word "woman." He scolded her when she was not forthcoming with an answer to his insulting interrogation. Hawley later clarified things. "Someone who can give birth to a child, a mother, is a woman," he told *Huffington Post*. "Someone who has a uterus is a woman. It doesn't seem that complicated to me."

Reviewer Hesse is flummoxed that Hawley never gets to these basics in his own book: "Unlike his anatomy word-cloud definition of women ['uterus,' 'vagina'], there are no biological requirements offered up in *Manhood*. Hawley never mentions that men must have testes, chest hair or Adam's apples."[24]

In Lloyd Green's *Manhood* review in *The Guardian*, Green feels compelled to forward his commentary with a cautionary note about the author: "Josh Hawley is a neo–Confederate at war with modernity. A Republican senator from Missouri, he opposed renaming military bases honoring rebel generals and was the sole vote against a bill to crack down on anti–Asian hate crime."[25]

Green finds it trite and tiresome to learn over and over again in Hawley's book that Epicurean liberals find life to be "meaningless" and "insignificant." Green notes that life is deemed pretty meaningless and inconsequential by right-wing conservatives in Hawley's Red State America. "In Hawley's Missouri, Covid mortality exceeded the national average," observes Green, regarding the state's handling of the pandemic. "The Missouri gun death rate is more than four times higher than that of New York."[26]

Considering all the jesters and satirists who find Hawley's book to be full of blatant hypocrisy, pusillanimous patriarchy, manhood-obsessed nonsense and silly preaching from a pipsqueak, it might be easy to conclude that Missouri's Hawley is ineffective and a national laughingstock. His *Manhood* is not a book to be taken too seriously. Pundits conjecture that Hawley released the book for use as a political platform to boost his potential as a vice presidential candidate in 2024 or as possible presidential material for 2028.

However, Pulitzer-prize winning journalist Jonathan Capehart finds Hawley dangerous precisely because the liberal left finds him innocuous, while the conservative right embraces him and his godly manhood message: "He is selling a vision of masculinity to white America that has much more to do with prejudice than masculinity."[27]

5

The Conservative Right Comes Late to Masculinity Theory

Today's traditional conservatives, the political right, and GOP leaders like Senator Josh Hawley are coming rather late to the American "masculinity crisis." Only now are they writing decrees and declarations on the manhood dilemma. Historians and scholars of American culture have been writing about men's issues for decades. They have argued that the manhood crisis is nothing new. More than a century old, it can be traced to the end of frontier society, the rise of urbanization and bureaucracy, the arrival of the women's suffrage and civil rights movements.

These trends, which have had such an impact on male identity and definition, have accelerated with suburbanization, de-industrialization, globalization, feminism, and the sexual revolution.

Among the many writers and scholars who have engaged in masculinity studies and written related philosophical tracts for more than one-half century are Joseph Pleck, Michael Kimmel, Susan Faludi, Herbert Goldberg, Robert Okun, Gail Sheehy, Lionel Tiger, Susan Bordo, Warren Farrell, James Doyle, Paul Nathanson, Francis Baumli, Richard Haddad, Tom Williamson, Ellis Cose, R.W. Connell, Harry Brod, and Michael Messner. In addition, manhood scholars with the Masculinities and Men's Studies Alliance (MAMSA) include James Alan Temple, Timothy Beneke, David Gilmore, Caroline Bird, Karen Walker, Jennifer Pierce Martin Levine, Don Sabo, Hartmut Heep, Jane C. Hood, Rebecca Carpenter, Merry Perry, Carl Holmberg, David Natharius, Robert Nill, Francis Shor, and Tony Triglio.

Scholars are in general agreement with Messner and Kimmel and their original descriptions of eight major groups or movements in the "terrain of the politics of masculinities." These movements include men's liberationists, men's rights advocates, radical feminist men, socialist feminist men, men of color, gay male liberationists, the Promise Keepers, and the mythopoetic men's movement.[1] This book will devote a chapter to each of four of the most visible of these movements from the last century. The terrain of the politics of masculinities represents a wide array of thought on the meaning of being male and the kinds of issues that should be of concern to American males.

It's doubtful that the conservative right's newfound urgency to address the manhood crisis in America has allowed its thinkers any real time to explore previous men's scholarship, or to examine men's movements spawned by past intellectual discourse. The conservative right's mission seems hellbent on enumerating, restoring, and protecting traditional male privilege. That seems to be the mission, even if the language and argumentation are occasionally more nuanced. Often the language is not subtle at all—the conservative right argues that defending patriarchy and seeking a return to the traditional marriage contract can restore manhood. It's also one of the "best ways to own the libs." In other words, it's all a political tactic with sparse intellectual grounding.

In any serious inquiry into manhood, it's worth examining a rich past of masculinist thought and to take a closer look at the movements that directly or indirectly resulted from previous intellectual efforts. An examination of these decades of thinking on the subject would suggest that there's no turning back to the patriarchal past so championed and idealized by the conservative right. In fact, there is every possibility for increased political polarization—and even societal chaos—with any attempt to turn back the clock, or to try to impose an unworkable paradigm of the past on contemporary America. A much wiser tack, regardless of ideology, would be to examine the views of those who were looking for new directions for manhood a half century or more ago, and to build upon their scholarship for a more informed perspective on what might constitute a new and enlightened masculinity.

Thought Leaders: Radicals, Gays and Feminist Men

The search for a new definition of manhood, and a new kind of man, is often described as an inevitable response to the rise of feminism in the 1960s. However, the crisis of male identity in America predates the 1960s feminist movement. It is certainly accurate to argue that men's studies programs at the university level were in response to 1960s feminist thought on campuses, as well as to the attendant gender and women's studies courses. Men's studies courses followed and are commonly traced to the 1970s. They include explorations into patriarchy, male privilege, matriarchy, feminist theory, queer theory, and new ideas on what might constitute male liberation, as well as the role of nature and nurture in the composition of men.

Thought leaders on the spectrum of radical feminist men would include Michael Kimmel, John Stoltenberg, and Jack Litewka. One of the startling developments with the beginning of the pro-feminist movement by males on the West Coast was their publication of gender-issue newspapers in the 1970s. The first issue of *Brother: A Male Liberation Newspaper* was decidedly pro-feminist. A kind of underground paper, it eventually transformed into a forum for men against sexism.[2] The thrust of the male-authored opinion pieces in these papers is that overt sexism exists and it is a system and a construct to ensure that men dominate women. The societal construct can justifiably be called "male supremacy" and its most extreme expression and common characteristic is rape, according to the pro-feminist men.

Activist Jack Litewka, in his 1977 article, "The Socialized Penis," outlined ways that men continually oppress women—but how they ultimately make their own lives miserable in the process. The reduction of women to mere sex objects makes warmth and natural communication in heterosexual relationships virtually impossible. Males are conditioned to fixate on the erotic portions of the female anatomy with results that are dehumanizing for all involved. Also, the emphasis on males' accruing many sexual conquests is akin to acquiring animal trophies like an elk head on the wall or a bear rug on the floor. The gratification is fleeting and the objectification converts the "prizes" into nothingness.[3] Litewka described a situation that is now changing, but not fast enough for most women, especially for those living outside the U.S. in countries run by patriarchal governments heavily influenced by reactionary religious authorities.

Academic Michael Kimmel, who studied at the University of California at Berkeley in the late 1970s, took his doctorate from the school in 1981. He went on to teach in New York and California and to publish some of the most significant work on gender and masculinities. In the 1990s, he was voted "Best Professor" on campus at Berkeley by *The Daily Californian*. Themes of Kimmel's work are that sexism shortchanges men as much as it oppresses women. Among Kimmel's books are: *Guyland: The Perilous World Where Boys Become Men* in 2008; and *Manhood: a Cultural History* in 2012. Kimmel became a spokesperson for the National Organization for Men Against Sexism (NOMAS) and also became a self-proclaimed feminist.

In the fourth edition of *Men's Lives*, authors Kimmel and Messner open chapter one of their compendium of thoughtful essays with an observation on popular culture. They note that a cursory glance at any magazine rack or television talk show reveals a crisis of confused males asking themselves: What does it mean to be a real man? What are men supposed to feel? How are men supposed to behave? Should they be like

Tootsie or Rambo? Should they be like Clint Eastwood or Phil Donahue? Should they be like Dennis Rodman or Bill Clinton? Reaching back to the archetypal movie blockbuster *Gone with the Wind*, should they be like the dashing and outspoken Rhett Butler or the sympathetic, soft-spoken Ashley Wilkes?

The rules for gender behavior are in constant flux and are part of the modern masculine milieu. According to Kimmel, the social and political culture and the mass media send out contradictory messages: "Some tell us to reassert traditional masculinity against all contemporary challenges. But a strength built only on the weakness of others hardly feels like strength at all. Others tell us that men are in power, the oppressor. But if men are in power as a group, why do individual men often feel so powerless? Can men change?"[4] The answer of the conservative right is that too many men have changed and become less manly, but they should never have changed in the first place.

Playwright and magazine editor John Stoltenberg was an anti-war activist in the Vietnam War period when he met feminist leader Andrea Dworkin at a draft resisters' meeting. The two gender reformers influenced each other's thinking for more than three decades. Stoltenberg wrote essays, speeches, and conducted gender-equity seminars. Several of his groundbreaking essays, such as "Refusing to Be a Man," "Toward Gender Justice," and "Eroticism and Violence in the Father-Son Relationship," can be found in the 1977 collection *For Men Against Sexism: A Book of Readings*. Stoltenberg was most disturbed by a male propensity to engage in violence.[5]

Stoltenberg joined Dworkin's crusade against pornography, and he founded Men Against Pornography in New York City. His dedication to opposing pornography, which he said belittles and humiliates women, is predicated on the idea that exploitative sexual materials tell lies about women, but alternately tell sad truths about men. His study of violence in gender relations inspired him to co-found Men Can Stop Rape, a group that campaigned to educate young men about the importance of consent in sexual relationships. Stoltenberg's view is that men will only be complete when they develop a conscience and a new kind of consciousness with regard to the treatment of women.

The pro-feminist men's movement has its roots in academia and is a half century ahead of the conservative right in thinking about how to be men of balanced ethical behavior and responsible partners to women. Pro-feminist males in search of a new identity were joined by the men of the gay male liberation movement in the 1960s and 1970s. Gay men also began contributing groundbreaking ideas on American manhood about the same time as the pro-feminist men. Among the gay liberationists seeking a redefinition of what it means to be male are Carl Wittman, John "Jack" Nichols, and David Kopay.

Anti-war activist Carl Wittman self-identified as gay when he was 14 in 1957, but he did not come out of the closet until a decade later when he wrote about it for the magazine *Liberation*. He is most remembered for his *Gay Manifesto* of the 1970s, in which he insisted that exclusive heterosexuality is dysfunctional. He called it stifling and indicative of a hidden fear of people of the same sex. He insisted that the heterosexual intercourse of his time was unsatisfying and destructive: "Ask women's liberation about what straight guys are like in bed. Sex is aggression for the male chauvinist; sex is obligation for the traditional woman."[6]

John "Jack" Nichols shocked his parents when he came out as gay as a teen in the 1950s, and his FBI agent father was especially distressed and resentful. By the 1960s, Nichols was leading the first gay marches on the White House and picketing Independence Hall in Philadelphia. Nichols refused to be silent in a society that deemed homosexuality to be criminal and evil and best kept hidden. He wrote columns on gender and sexuality for both straight and gay newspapers and served in editorial positions with *Sexology* and the *San Francisco Sentinel* in the 1970s and 1980s. In the 1990s and into a new century, Nichols was senior editor of the online newsmagazine, GayToday.com.

After his death in 2005, an autobiographical account of his work, *Jack Nichols, Gay Pioneer: "Have You Heard My Message?"* was published. Critics said the book was egotistical, while others praised it as a remedy for right-wing religious types who could benefit by reading it and perhaps gain some insight into the stupidity of gay-bashing. Among his many achievements was his chairing the Mattachine Society of Washington's Committee on Religious Concerns, which helped build a relationship between the gay rights movement and the National Council of Churches. Also notable was Nichols' journalistic coverage of key turning points in gay liberation history, from the Stonewall riots that sparked a movement to the crisis of the AIDS epidemic. Perhaps his most lasting accomplishment was his work in helping to persuade the American Psychiatric Association to stop labeling homosexuality as a "sickness" and a sign of mental illness.[7]

Unlike gay activists Wittmer and Nichols, the gay liberationist David Kopay did not come out as gay to his parents at an early age. In fact, the talented athlete did not come out of the closet until he had successfully played football at the college level and for nine years at the professional level with the National Football League. In college, he was named an All-American and led the University of Washington's Huskies to the 1964 Rose Bowl. He adapted reasonably well to the demands of the NFL, living up to the image of total heterosexual maleness in what some call the toughest game on earth.

Three years after his retirement, however, Kopay came out in a newspaper story in 1975. He followed that with the *David Kopay Story*, and the fallout from his book was immediate. He had hoped for an NFL coaching career after retirement, but he was effectively blackballed from the sport. His parents and siblings did not easily reconcile with Kopay's new identity. In his book, Kopay said it's important for gay men to accept themselves as real men. That's absolutely necessary if society itself is ever to get over its homophobia. Kopay has spent his time in retirement advising and coaching gay students on overcoming their struggles with their identity. In addition, he gave a $1 million gift to the Q Center at the University of Washington in Seattle, which serves the needs of LGBTQ students.[8]

Million Man Marchers and Promise Keepers

The Million Man March and the Promise Keepers movements have attracted males who have very little in common with pro-feminist men

The Rev. Louis Farrakhan is extremely unpopular in many quarters, as is evidenced by this defaced poster advertising a march in New York City. However, his work on behalf of Black men organizing the 1995 Million Man March in Washington, D.C., was widely praised (Library of Congress).

or gay liberation men, except for sharing a similar quest for a new definition of what constitutes manliness. The Promise Keepers and Million Man
movements share the commonality of being at their height in the 1990s.
There have been calls for a revival of both in recent years. The Promise
Keepers cause draws its numbers primarily from born-again Christian
white men and religious evangelicals.

Many of the leaders of the Promise Keepers have been conservative
preachers, authors, and ministers. A number have sports backgrounds.
Among the notable thought leaders are Bill McCartney, James Dobson,
and Bill Bright.

McCartney was head coach for the Colorado Buffalos of the University of Colorado. McCartney left his position as head coach in 1994, four
years after he founded the Promise Keepers. The demands of heading "one
of the biggest movements of God in history" demanded his full attention,
so he left football.[9] By 2020, the Promise Keepers had influenced an estimated 20 million men, prompting many to re-examine their commitments to their religious faith, their relationships with their spouses, and
their approach to raising children.

McCartney's words on manhood have echoed across the country in
sports stadiums where men have assembled to hear a Christian approach
to life and instruction on how to join the Promise Keepers. McCartney
believes that a husband must sit down with his wife and listen to her in
order for her to bloom. A husband must eagerly embrace a responsibility to be the head of wife and family, just as Jesus Christ is the head of his
church. And just as the church submits to the will of the savior so, too,
should wives submit to their husbands. In return, husbands must be willing to lay down their lives for their spouses and sacrifice for their families.

Another voice for this traditional Christian approach to manhood
is that of Bill Bright, who founded a candy company in his twenties and
which he ran during the World War II period. He was in the U.S. Navy
Reserve, but was spared from combat service due to a high school football
injury. In 1946, Bright quit the candy business to pursue biblical studies at
several institutions, including the Fuller Theological Seminaries of Pasadena, California. Bright went on to found the Campus Crusade for Christ
in 1951 with its first of many chapters located at the University of California—Los Angeles. In 2021 Campus Crusade had 25,000 missionaries in
more than 190 countries.

Bright, who died in 2003, wrote more than 100 books and pamphlets
and promoted the document *Evangelicals and Catholics Together*. He
believed evangelicals and committed Catholics had much in common with
their positions against homosexuality and abortion. He co-founded the
Alliance Defense Fund, which underwrites high-profile litigation cases

to defend Christian free speech rights, Christian anti-abortion activities, and Christian advocacy against LGBTQ rights. Bright's message is consistent with that of Promise Keepers and he contributed to the organization's guidebook, *Seven Promises of a Promise Keeper*. In that guide, Bright advised that men of integrity must reconcile differences with each other and find peace through a love of Jesus Christ.

James Dobson is probably the most well-known collaborator in the Promise Keepers venture of the 1990s. Although he was never ordained a minister, he has often been mentioned along with Pat Robertson and Jerry Falwell, as among the most successful evangelicals in the religious history of America. Dobson produced a radio show for his Focus on the Family that ran on more than 7,000 radio stations worldwide and appeared on 60 U.S. television stations. Born in Georgia in 1936, he once told an interviewer that he learned to pray before he could talk and that his life was completely devoted to Jesus.

As a Promise Keepers proponent, Dobson advised the members of the men's movement that marriage is a contract for life between a man and a woman. In such a lawful commitment as marriage, the mother is the homemaker and the father is the breadwinner. These are biblically-mandated roles. Dobson also took the evangelical view that same-sex relationships are an abomination to god and that legalizing homosexual marriage is judicial tyranny and an affront to civilization. Like many other leaders lecturing Promise Keepers members in American baseball and football stadiums, Dobson frequently used sports metaphors to explain the role of fathers in raising their boys and heading their families.

The Million Man March movement has many similarities with the Promise Keepers in being faith-based and drawing tenets from conservative religious perspectives. The Million Man March has recruited participants almost exclusively from the African American community. Also, it has come in for criticism because one of its primary founders was the Rev. Louis Farrakhan, controversial leader of the Nation of Islam. Farrakhan's message has been characterized as Black supremacist and smacking of anti-Semitism. His followers among the Million Man March movement are attracted by his appeals to racial pride, economic empowerment, and accepting personal and family responsibility.

Among those who have propounded the Million Man March philosophy are Maulana Ndabezitha Karenga, previously known as Ron Karenga. Like Farrakhan, Karenga is controversial. He has a number of felony convictions. Karenga has denied wrongdoing and has described himself as a victim of false prosecution and as a former political prisoner. He is most famous for creating Kwanzaa, an alternative to Christmas and a holiday designed to promote African traditions.[10] He argues that a cultural revolution for Black men and their families requires a return to African traditions.

Another voice for the Million Man March movement is that of Cornel West, a prolific writer and faculty member of the religion department of Harvard University. West marched in the massive Million Man March / Day of Atonement on October 16, 1995, in Washington, D.C. According to West, the 1995 event was important to highlight Black suffering to end the general ignorance and indifference to Black sadness, sorrow and social misery. He rapped the mainstream media for wanting to shift the focus from Black pain to white anxiety over an active minority movement. He added that when white supremacy over Black men begins to recede, then patriarchy, homophobia, and anti-Semitism will likewise begin to be reduced.[11]

Men's Liberationists and Men's Rights Proponents

Significant differences and important similarities exist between the men's liberationists and the men's rights proponents, so it can be a questionable exercise to classify scholars or activists in one group or the other. Also, there is a school of thought that holds that male liberationists gravitated to the position of men's rights advocates as feminists became more vocal and strident. Another explanation for this change is that as fathers' rights ideas have gained momentum, the gap between men and women accelerated, and animosity began to develop over domestic issues in the courts.

In the early years of the men's movement, through the 1960s and 1970s, it is safe to say that men's liberationists were represented by such thought leaders as Francis Baumli, James Doyle, and William Farrell. Baumli's 1985 essay collection, *Men Freeing Men: Exploding the Myth of the Traditional Male*, was praised as a "classic in our understanding of human relations" by Karen DeCrow, past national president of the National Organization of Women (NOW). In the more active years of the men's liberationists, Baumli found a home in the Coalition of Free Men and the National Congress of Men. He hosted radio shows on men's liberation topics.

Baumli has totally rejected the conservative religious view that a woman is the homemaker and the man is the breadwinner in the marriage contract. Baumli's view is that those roles are not intrinsic or naturally determined. Little boys and little girls are nurtured for these roles. They are socially constructed roles, not biologically determined roles. So, it's perfectly okay for women to be assertive and for men to be receptive.

It's perfectly okay for men to stay home and for women to go out into the work world. It's perfectly okay for men to take care of babies and to raise the kids. To that end, Baumli was successful in spearheading the drive for diaper-changing stations, normally confined to women's restrooms, to be installed in men's rooms as well.[12]

James Doyle is in the same camp as Baumli in believing that manhood is largely a social construction rather than a matter of biological determination. At the same time, he has acknowledged obvious biological differences between men and women. The founding editor of *Men's Studies Review* and the author of *The Male Experience*, Doyle always has explored what it means to be a man. Doyle found that the American patriarchy has been breaking down and has been challenged in each decade since the 1960s, whether it's in business, the military, or the religious sphere. Women also are more and more of a presence in team sports and the sports world generally.

In an interview in 2000, Doyle did express worry that men are becoming more listless and violent as their traditional roles are cast off. Fewer male role models exist for young males to emulate. Losing the traditional masculinity blueprint can be scary. In a gender-transitional period, Doyle suggested that the intense fascination with violent sports, like professional wrestling, even as parody, can be a way for young men to reach out for something. On the positive side of this transitional period, Doyle contends that it's liberating and appealing for men to now find their own individuality amidst past societal pressures. Man can be

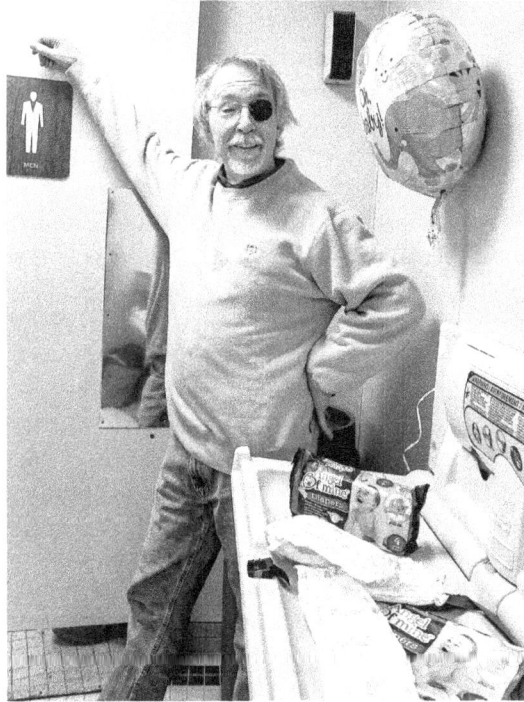

Francis Baumli, author of *Men Freeing Men* (1985), is one of the early men's movement pioneers. He was a force in the National Coalition for Men, and he lobbied for laws to require baby diaper-changing stations in men's rooms as well as ladies' rooms (courtesy *Webster-Kirkwood Times*).

whatever they want to be. "A real man is so individual," according to Doyle, so let that individuation flourish.[13]

It's important to note that male liberationists Doyle, Baumli, and Warren Farrell are all academics who completed doctoral studies. After taking a Ph.D. in political science from New York University, Farrell taught college-level courses in five areas: psychology, sociology, political science, women's studies, gender and parenting issues. Farrell became famous for his role reversal experiments for students and seminar participants. Men were enrolled in a beauty competition to experience "the beauty contest of everyday life that no woman can escape." In the role-reversal date experience, women were asked to "risk a few of the 150 'risks of rejection' men typically experience between eye contact and intercourse."[14]

Farrell and several other male gender scholars transitioned from men's liberationists to men's rights advocates, particularly when the National Organization of Women came out against the presumption of joint custody in divorce cases. According to Farrell, "Everything went well until the mid-seventies when NOW came out against the presumption of joint custody. I couldn't believe the people I thought were pioneers in equality were saying that women should have the first option to have children or not to have children—that children should not have equal rights to their dad."[15]

Men's rights proponents now include Farrell, Herb Goldberg, and Lionel Tiger. From a position that was pro-feminist and men's liberation, Farrell's books became increasingly critical of feminists and their perspectives. From *The Myth of Male Power* in 1993 to *Does Feminism Discriminate Against Men? A Debate* (written with Christina Hoff Sommers) in 2008, Farrell's books took on a sharper edge against feminists with whom he once allied. He became a hero of the fathers' rights movement.

Herb Goldberg studied psychology and received his doctorate from Adelphi University in 1965 and began teaching in the University of California state system. He became famous with his 1976 book *The Hazards of Being Male*, which went into 30 printings and sold almost three million copies. The book became a bestseller with its argument that men deserved a more level playing field in the face of rising feminism. He followed up with several more successful men's-rights activist favorites such as *The Inner Male* and *What Men Really Want* in 1991.

In *The Hazards of Being Male*, Goldberg told men to jettison the illusion that it's a man's world and that they are the privileged sex. Men are only privileged to feel mounting frustration, weariness, and loneliness in their adult lives. And then they have the privilege to die years earlier than their female counterparts. Men need to take off the blinders and redefine themselves in a hostile environment. They need to stop playing a role, often encouraged by women, of lover-husband-parent-breadwinner-strong-and-silent man burdened by unrealistic demands that cripple and kill him.

Lionel Tiger is one of the most controversial men's rights advocates. His works have inspired bomb threats and warnings that he was destined for physical harm. A Canadian born in Montreal in 1937, his university studies led to a position as Charles Darwin Professor of Anthropology at Rutgers University in New Jersey. He is credited with discovering the intricacies of male bonding following studies of primates and other animals in the wild. He has argued that bonds between men often are more significant than male-female relationships.

His controversial books include *Men in Groups* and *Decline of the Male*. Tiger's study, *The Imperial Animal,* has been compared to Adolf Hitler's Mein Kampf by some feminists. Among Tiger's unconventional views are a conviction that women who use birth control have taken away choice from men in their lives and have altered family structure forever. He argues that women working outside the home take power and pride away from their husbands. Working women destroy the function of men to be breadwinners and harm society's established norms. In his *Decline of the Male*, Tiger contends that males face obsolescence with only a small hope of turning their fates around.[16]

Returning to Nature: Mythopoetic Male Philosophers

"Return to nature" can have a twofold meaning when examining the thought of the mythopoetic male philosophers. Returning to nature can mean men gathering with each other in the woods to find their true selves. It can also mean men experiencing the great outdoors together and entering a sweat lodge for contrition, penance, and the purging of impurities. On the more philosophical level of the mythopoetic credo, the return to nature can mean recapturing the essential roots of male identity through myth, folklore, and storytelling. Men must free themselves, the philosophy says, from the artificial definitions imposed on them by society if they are to become truly free, happy, and content.

The core ideas of the mythopoetic men's movement are attributed to poet Robert Bly's text *Iron John*, a 1990 national bestseller of fairy tales and poetry designed to guide men on a spiritual journey to discover their own deep masculinity. The men inspired by poet Bly, who met at lectures and retreats in the woods, were white, well-educated, middle-aged, heterosexual professionals. They did not seem angry like males in some other men's movements, but they did seem frustrated in a world in which feminism was a major focus and in which they were constantly being told to find their feminine side. Their mission was to reclaim their essential masculinity rooted not in their biology but in an archetypal past contained in their souls.

James Hillman, a psychologist who met with Carl Gustav Jung and studied at the C. G. Jung Institute in Switzerland in the 1950s, attempted to guide men on mythopoetic journeys with Michael Meade and other movement leaders. In his 1997 book *The Soul's Code: In Search of Character and Calling*, Hillman described his "acorn theory" of the soul. People already hold the potential for the unique possibilities inside themselves, just as an acorn holds the pattern for an oak tree. Hillman disagreed with the "nature or nurture" argument for how human beings develop feminine or masculine behavior and traits. He proposed a third kind of "energy" within each individual's soul. That energy, which is responsible for much of an individual's character, aspiration, and achievement, can be tapped from the soul to complete the personality.

Soul-searching for the mythopoetic practitioners can be similar to the initiation rituals used by ancient cultures to aid boys in crossing over into manhood. Hillman's theories parallel Bly's ideas on men's needs to rediscover and reclaim their "Zeus energy." In our modern, organized society, the "masculine voice" has been muted, Hillman postulated, and men have become passive, tamed, and domesticated. Men can benefit from the mythopetic movement by reconnecting with the "Zeus energy" that they have lost. The "Zeus energy is male authority accepted for the good of the community."[17]

Mythopoetic advocate Michael Schwalbe has explained how men can explore, examine and reconstruct their inner selves through collective ritual practice and serious discourse. Schwalbe, an author and professor at North Carolina State University, wrote An *"Inside" Look at the Mythopetic Men's Movement by a Sociologist*. Schwalbe wrote that men are floundering in turbulent cultural waters and are filled with guilt. The way to open the cage of guilt and to get free, according to Schwalbe, is to change themselves. They should not waste their time trying to reform society, but they should join with other men and reform themselves.

Schwalbe argued that as the 1970s became the 1980s, the friendly relationship between pre-mythopoetic men and feminist women began to break down. Men felt the sting of a radical feminist critique that saw men as morally irredeemable, and the criticism began to feel like a personal attack, even a betrayal. It was fortuitous that the new mythopoetic activities for men were steeped in Jungian thought developed by prominent teachers. "Mythopoetic activity did change some men's lives. It got them out of their isolation and into fellowship with other men. It raised their awareness of themselves as emotional beings. It helped them find self-acceptance. It brought on bursts of creativity."[18]

Mythopoetic activity changed a number of men's lives by opening their eyes to what they had missed by living in an iron cage of masculinist, bureaucratic rationality, Schwalbe declared. However, he also cautioned mythopoetic men to be aware of the dangers of archetypes celebrating hyper-masculinity. Using stories that are full of sexist imagery and engaging in activities that encourage androcentrism could create monsters and insulate them from their feelings for others.

All of the men's movements discussed in this chapter are rooted in another century and were most active before 2000. However, there have been calls for a revival of the Million Man March and the Promise Keepers organization. In fact, Promise Keepers has been organizing new rallies as of 2021. Men's rights groups have evolved into father's rights groups that are still very much with us. Any attempt by Josh Hawley and the conservative right to now formulate a definition of manhood and manly virtues in response to some "new crisis" shows a lack of knowledge and perspective. It constitutes an ignorance of the legacy of so many scholars and activists who have been on this journey for decades. Ignoring this legacy suggests that "new right masculinists" are exploitative, superficial, and may just be in search of campaign slogans or political platforms that have little to do with bettering the lot of men—or women.

Section II

Manhood in a Previous Century

Into the Wild

A Mythopoetic Manifesto

Imagine a gathering of men in their prime coming together on the edge of a forest in search of something. They are clad in loose fitting clothes, but not in loin cloths, even though they are about to enter a long tent-like structure that has the feel of a Native American tepee. The wood and canvas hovel resembles a kind of huge upside-down canoe. It's a sweat lodge and the men enter it through a flap, one after another. However, they can only enter the primitive shelter after a briefing by a veteran sweat lodge "shaman" who explains what will go on inside.

The anxious sweat lodge neophytes learn that they will experience a purification ceremony. Each of them will be provided a tom-tom drum that they will be expected to beat on as part of an ancient North American aboriginal ritual. There will be flutes, and lutes, and pan pipes, and music, and song, and ceremony. The air inside will be steamy and smoky. It's very likely that participants will suffer some eye irritation. If anyone feels like they are having nausea or are about to pass out, they should raise their right hand high for assistance. River rocks will be heated by a small trench fire and they will be doused with water on occasion to produce a hissing steam with an acrid aroma.

None of these men will ever forget their first sweat lodge encounter and the men with whom they shared the unusual ritual. Neither will they forget some of the storytelling as they participated in a sort of hot vapor bath together. The immersion in the primeval sauna has proven physically refreshing and the sweat from their pores truly seems to purge impurities from their bodies. More important, they come away purified spiritually. It all seemed to culminate in an out-of-body experience that could never be duplicated at a gymnasium, a work-out center, or at the country club. Some of these men will keep coming back for more.

Real men of the John Wayne ethos have never been strangers to experiences at the edge of the forest. Alpha men have always spent time in the woods, where they might take aim at trophy bucks in the fall. In spring, they've been on roaring rivers and frothy streams looking to hook a large-mouth bass or a rainbow trout. In the final two decades of last century, something changed at the edge of the forest. Tamer men, more comfort-able with experiencing rather than exploiting, found their way to the great outdoors. They were not there to hunt game or to hook a fish. Rather than bringing down a beast, they were more intent on becoming the beast. They sought ancient wisdom and a kind of spiritual fulfillment unattainable in suburban backyards crackling with the noise of electric bug zappers and filled with the aroma of beef fillets broiling on hot grills.

In a lengthy 1991 article titled "Drums, Sweat and Tears," *Newsweek* magazine attempted to get a handle on these strange guys and their new movement into nature. The phenomenon of mythopoetic men was strictly for the male gender, for modern men with yearnings for connection. Attor-neys, college professors, computer salesmen, marketing mavens, and more were all coming together to be with each other in the woods. They were convening in dark tepees called sweat lodges, squatting on their haunches amidst steamy smoke from fiery rocks, and re-enacting the sacred rituals of Native Americans. Like the tribal Sioux and Chippewa, they were puri-fying their souls together and finding a new masculine identity in their fellowship of sweat.

"We were chanting and sweating and screaming and hollering. It was fun and uplifting because it involved prayers and a lot of affirmation," a sweat lodge participant told *Newsweek*. Quin Crosbie, a 49-year-old direc-tor of a counseling center in Santa Monica, California, offered details of his first ritualistic sweat experience at a men's retreat in Topanga Canyon.[1] He was one of thousands of men around the country who were attending outdoor conferences, workshops, and retreats, where would-be wild men could be found banging on drums, chanting verse, and attempting to cap-ture ancient male initiation rites.

Newsweek has been covering men's search for manhood ever since the banging drums and chanting began. Its articles have encouraged men to confront new challenges and to stop blaming women for their anxieties. *Newsweek* cited the popular 1990s movie *Falling Down* as providing a clas-sic example of a beleaguered and untethered white male confronting a new multi-cultural world. In the hit film, the Michael Douglas character gives in to white-male paranoia and accuses feminists, the politically-correct crowd, and his uncaring wife for all his mental anguish. *Newsweek* expressed skepticism about unhappy men withdrawing into the woods for treating what ails them, as per the prescription of guru Robert Bly. Most Americans were totally unaware of Bly's wilderness happenings until the 1990 PBS-TV special *A Gathering of Men*, which was put together by Bill

No movie exposed the "masculinity crisis" of the 1990s in a harsher light than *Falling Down* (1993). Michael Douglas portrayed an angry, laid-off, Los Angeles defense industry worker who might have found support in a men's movement but instead succumbed to violence (Photofest).

Moyers. His documentary profiled poet Bly, cited as the founder of the growing men's mythopoetic movement.

Bly's movement was based on his book *Iron John: A Book About Men*, which had become a runaway best-seller. This was a startling achievement for a thoughtful and, at times, dense cross-cultural analysis of male initiation rites. Bly observed a looming crisis of contemporary American manhood and thought it might be addressed through the prism of ancient fables, folklore, and mythology. Bly devised a revised fable about "Iron John." The tale concerned an innocent young son of a king encountering a beastly character who lives in the wilds of the forest. The beast is captured and locked up in the king's castle, but the boy helps the would-be monster escape. Then, afraid of being punished by his father, the boy runs off with the hairy creature to the dark and scary forest, where he grows into manhood. At the end of many learning adventures, the enlightened boy, his royal father, and the weathered beast are reunited and reconciled. The boy has become fully a man. He is much wiser because of his ordeals in untamed nature, and he is prepared for a fulfilling marriage to a princess.[2]

Professor Bly converted this archetypal tale into something for contemporaries. He drew on knowledge of the woods and transformed the sprawling initiation story to meet the needs of all lost men. He weaved in snippets of anthropology and allusions to world literature and turned a piece of rural folklore into something other than a children's fable. It became a vast tale of the loss of something very important in the lives of contemporary men. In the much revered past, young boys profited from crucial passages to a manly life that involved separation from one's mother and initiation into the world of men.

In contrast to this golden past, Bly found that American boys are always under the gaze of mother and her friends, while fathers are away and separate in the sphere of "work" for men. The male elders, who in another time and culture were there to initiate their offspring into the customs of the tribe, are now absent. The consequences, according to Bly, are lives crippled by "father-hunger," lives that are mired in emotional immaturity and chronic unhappiness. They have little to offer the next generation of men.

Assorted scholars and sages latched onto Bly's observations about the hollow lives of modern fathers and young males. These manhood disciples moved forward with Bly's pronouncements, expanded upon them, and formed the philosophical underpinnings for a new men's movement. These philosophers, some of them also mythical poets, stressed that men and women are different, and it's not simply because they are raised differently. They applied Jungian psychology and proposed that deep within the male psyche, there are archetypes buried in the unconscious that can be brought to the fore through tribal ritual and spiritual exploration. These archetypes verify that males of the human species need mentoring by sympathetic fathers who can guide them to their own destinies. The archetypes conjured only confirm that males of the human species require association with other men—not just their female counterparts. An association with whole men is the only way to become balanced, completed, and content.

As a result of Bly's research and his contemplative prose, the new manifesto for mythopoetic men was composed with some of the following tenets:

- Men must reconnect with each other. They must be comrades who celebrate their masculinity together—and no longer act as mere competitors within workplaces.
- Men must spend less time at work and in their houses. Excessive domesticity with their spouses has kept men from realizing the internal needs of their masculinity.
- Fatherhood must be redefined, repaired, and re-established. The separation of sons from their fathers has deprived young males of a true initiation into manhood.
- Men must learn to express their emotions freely. Fatalism, stoicism, endurance, and endless sacrifice are not masculine virtues. Muted, quiet forbearance must end.
- Men can have a softer side that they should proudly cultivate. Gentleness and caring are not feminine. Circumstances may require hidden male virtues to come to the fore.
- Men must summon their "inner warrior" when needed. But there is nothing masculine about being a toxic warrior. Male toxicity manifests itself in exploitation, bullying, and violence.
- Ritual purification can provide the means of escape from toxicity and self-destructive behavior practices. Habits such as unfeeling individualism and unnecessary risk-taking can be broken.

The term *toxic masculinity* is very often dismissed as a pejorative devised by feminists to shame men for their natural, authentic, heroic behavior. It may come as a surprise to learn that the term originated with men and not from radical feminist women. *Toxic masculinity* is a term from the 1980s mythopoetic men's movement and soon found use in academic journals and gradually in the parlance of daily journalism. Men's studies sociologist Michael Kimmel traces the term to mythopoetic trailblazer Shepherd Bliss and writes that it describes a condition that is real and not just a derisive stereotype. Kimmel noted that Bliss rails against toxic masculinity in his writing and believes it is responsible for most of the evil in the world.[3]

Toxic Masculinity Revealed

Many of the men's movements originating in the transformative 1980s and 1990s came to acknowledge both the abstract term and the reality of toxic masculinity. The Million Man March and Promise Keepers movements recognized toxic male behavior that was self-destructive and also harmful to family life. The mythopoetic men's movement, however, did the most to actually define and normalize the term for use in today's journalistic expression. Many conservatives, and particularly the alt-right, shrug off toxic masculinity as an incoherent concept and condescending label. They dismiss it as a propagandist term created by feminists and popularized by academic liberals. In fact, right-wing media will argue that there is no such thing as toxic masculinity. In 2019, political commentators on the right denounced the American Psychological Association's new guidelines that warned about the many damaging effects of "traditional masculinity ideology."

The American Psychological Association consequently responded to the attacks from the right, and conservative criticism generally, by noting that their discussions of violence and harmful competitiveness was not to infer that these negative traits were an inherent part of masculinity. The expert psychologists also stressed that their guidelines accented admirable virtues associated with positive masculinity—including such ideals as courage, leadership, and the willingness of men to be protective in dangerous situations.[4]

Most academics in the social sciences, as well as many feminists, make an effort to explain that toxic masculinity refers to harmful attributes and destructive cultural norms, but they are not to be construed as intrinsic to men or as somehow part of a permanent biological makeup of males. Gender studies expert Raewyn Connell has taken pains to assert that wanton violence and the belittling of women are practices that arise from hegemonic masculinity, rather than from essential male traits. Such toxic behaviors as gratuitous physical violence, used to assert men's dominance over women in many societies, involves features of hegemonic masculinity, but are not the defining features of males as a gender.

Moving from the academic world of mythopoetic theories to the everyday world of media and public discourse, average Americans are now familiar with the use of the descriptive term *toxic masculinity*. It has been used in the media and on television talk shows in reference to the appalling sexual behavior of television celebrities like Matt Lauer, or film industry mogul Harvey Weinstein, or disgraced movie actor Kevin Spacey. The term has found its way into discussions of the reprehensible behavior by politicians like Donald Trump. Trump's bragging that he can kiss and "grab women by the pussy" because he is a star, represents some of the worst and most graphic manifestations of toxic masculinity ever.

Feminist writer Amanda Marcotte, writing on the popular news and commentary website *Salon*, asserts that: "Toxic masculinity is a specific model of manhood, geared toward dominance and control. It's a manhood that views women and LGBT people as inferior, sees sex as an act, not of affection but domination, and which valorizes violence as the way to prove one's self to the world."[5] Ironically, Marcotte notes that the men who aspire to toughness are, in fact, captive to an ideology of living in fear. Men in the thrall of toxic masculinity live in fear of seeming soft, tender, weak, or somehow less than manly. And this insecurity may be the most defining feature of toxic masculinity.

Cultural observer Marcotte is at her best when she provides a grab bag of examples of toxic masculinity and, of course, Trump's behavioral aberrations could—and have—filled numerous books. Marcotte describes how Trump flipped out in political forums whenever someone teased him about his small fingers. Beyond Trump's paranoid style, Marcotte chronicles the ludicrously long, shaggy beards on the *Duck Dynasty* team, meant to stave off any association with dreaded feminine thickets of hair. Marcotte notes the emergence of the term "cuckservative," used by hardline right-wingers to suggest that insufficient racism is somehow emasculating. She even cites the conservatives who "absolutely melt down" about Obamacare ads that suggest men sometimes wear pajamas.

Not all examples of toxic masculinity involve serial predators like the buffoonish Trump. the abusive Matt Lauer, or the Hollywood predator Harvey Weinstein. Nor are they best exemplified by parading white nationalists carrying tiki torches and angrily shouting racist epithets in Charlottesville, Virginia. Sometimes toxic masculinity is evident in smaller and subtler ways—when men insist on taking the largest portions at a dinner; or when they insist on taking up more space than needed on a living room couch or on an airplane flight; or when they engage in "mansplaining" and know-it-all behavior that includes talking over everyone else to make their point.

The mythopoetic men's movement has done gender discussion a great service by creating the term *toxic masculinity*, even as it has sparked some angry commentary on what exactly it means. There are plenty of examples that can be used to illustrate it on the political and entertainment fronts. Even if it cannot be precisely defined, people increasingly know toxic masculinity when they see it, and hear it, and feel it. As attitudes shift about the nature of gender and move away from binary concepts, gender behavior typified by *Mad Men*–era toxicity may begin to wane. Gender education and societal pressures may inspire some men to stop feeling a need to show their manliness by acting out in violent, oppressive, racist, misogynistic, homophobic, and transphobic ways. The mythopoetic men's movement can take some of the credit for any decline in this kind of offensive behavior.

Movement Lessons

At first glance, the mythopoetic men's movement inspired by poet Robert Bly's work, *Iron John*, would seem to be in sync with some of the thoughts that conservatives such as Josh Hawley have expressed about the lost masculinity of American men. Like Hawley, who published *Manhood: The Masculine Virtues America Needs*, Bly has lamented the loss of vigorous masculinity and the "inner warrior" in men. He's attributed the loss to economic dislocation, new societal norms, and distorted cultural imperatives. However, where conservatives like Hawley want men to become more assertive and aggressive, Bly believes that recapturing the "inner warrior" is not at all about a new emphasis on assertiveness or aggression.

The mythopoetic men's movement is not about making American men great again by returning to some "tough guy" ideal of the old frontier, or the 1950s John Wayne era, or the much-mythologized Ronald Reagan era. As a matter of fact, Bly's mythopoetic pioneers of the 1980s and 1990s examined the images of the righteous man, the tough men in cowboy hats, and found them to be superficial and eminently unsatisfying. Bly's followers also concluded that rising fear and paranoia about "feminization" of males in America can result in overly destructive, hyper-hypermasculine chauvinists. Manhood for Bly's movement can actually be about honoring one's feminine side, becoming gentler in relations with women and men, reconnecting with the natural world, and living in harmony with Planet Earth.

That's not to say there are no downsides to the mythopoetic men's movement in the eyes of women, feminists, queer feminists and, of course, conservatives. Conservative males, who are non-believers in the idea of toxic masculinity in the first place, are confirmed skeptics about anything to do with a "mythopoetic movement." They obviously have no use for men seeking cures and lessons for modern manhood in poetry, fairy tales, and arcane mythology. Conservative males are likely to issue a reflexive belly laugh—perhaps utilizing a beer belly—at the idea of self-help books and workshops for men. When real men feel listless or anxious, they buy up tickets for a football game or head out for a round of golf. Like some male Supreme Court justices, real men "really, really like beer." So, when they are feeling empty, they buy a six-pack of their favorite brew to take home to address their emptiness.

It's easy for conservatives to lampoon and poke fun at the therapeutic activities of the mythopoetic men's movement. The idea of men in mid-life crisis gathering in the forest to beat on drums can seem amusing to them. The idea of men with lingering daddy issues gathering in the woods for some primal screaming seems just plain hilarious. The idea of men throwing off their business attire and entering a sweat tent together to purge physical and psychological impurities seems downright hysterical. The sweat tent phenomenon has the added irony in that a number of men trying to find their masculinity have actually lost their lives doing it. They have died from the sweat tent experience due to severe dehydration, heat exhaustion, and suffocation.

An added irony is that some Native Americans have taken offense to the appropriation of their sweat lodge practices. They have threatened lawsuits over theft and misuse of their practices by fraudulent New

Sweat lodge use is a tradition among First Nation tribes of North America, but less common among Eskimo and Inuit peoples. Some indigenous peoples oppose sweat lodge practices by the mythopoetic men's movement as a misappropriation of their sacred rituals (Library of Congress).

Age shamans. Native American leaders maintain that the sweat ritual is intended as a spiritual ceremony—it is for prayer and healing, and the ceremony must be led by elders who know safety protocols. Otherwise, the ceremony can be dangerous. When rocks are used as a heat source, they must have air pockets inside them and be completely dry before heating. Otherwise, there are risks of cracking, shattering, and occasional explosions. Even people who are familiar with sweat therapy can suddenly experience problems due to underlying health issues. Lakota spiritual leaders recommend that people only attend lodges with authorized, traditional spiritual leaders.

Although many feminists are favorably disposed to some tenets of the mythopoetic men's movement, others find it regressive and exclusionary. Many progressive women do take comfort in the idea of men on a quest to rediscover positive masculinity that is less domineering and prone to violence. On the other hand, there is something misogynist in the notion that men can only find their meaning and self-worth in the company of other men—out in the woods and together in a sweat lodge. Some women take insult from the idea that sons suffer inordinately from being brought up primarily by women or by single mothers. There's more than a whiff of sexism in this idealization of a father-son initiation ritual as providing the only satisfactory route for boys to psychological health and an ability to cope with real world challenges.

Some of the leading voices in the mythopoetic men's movement seem all too willing to continue pointing the finger at females for their malaise and crisis of meaning. A mythopoetic figure from the 1990s, Frank Pittman, declared that men have been taught to sacrifice their lives for their masculinity, even as women take more of their masculine privileges away from them with their new-found feminism.[6] The result is that men are suffering doubly with obvious deleterious results. Men live an average of seven fewer years than women, and men suffer higher rates of suicide, homicide, lung cancer, cirrhosis of the liver, and other illnesses. Women won't accept responsibility for all these male problems and see the complaints as the same old women-blaming as practiced by the reactionary traditionalists.

Queer feminists can be especially at odds with the movement of mythopoetic men and are not afraid to say so. Queer feminists bring a unique perspective to the table of gender relations discussion. They argue that almost all women have had their encounters with bullying, entitled, hurtful, toxic men. These men lash out at females who refuse to make themselves smaller to accommodate them. However, queer women contend that they get a double dose of toxic masculinity from bullying males because of their inability to even attempt to "perform femininity" to the satisfaction of frustrated men.

Queer feminist writer Erin Innes argues that the new mythopoetic masculinity is not much of an improvement over the old style traditionalism. Mythopoetic masculinity is still narrow, they say, and still totally defined by an inability to separate sex from gender, and masculinity from straightness. Mythopoetic men "speak only of binary genders and universal straightness, where masculinity is immutable, monolithic, and definable only in opposition to a similarly monolithic (and always heterosexual) femininity. The story this movement weaves constantly comes back to heterosexuality as the basic organizing principle of all peoples' lives. It erases first of all queerness of any kind, and second any ways that humans can live full and rich and deeply loving lives outside of hegemonic straight marriage and the trappings of white middle-class respectability."[7]

Mythopoetic men realize that traditional maleness is dysfunctional, but they are sometimes handicapped by many of the old, reactionary assumptions of the past, according to feminists like Innes. Nevertheless, mythopoetic philosophers are still at work trying to find the holy grail of manhood, more than three decades after Bly published *Iron John*. The gurus following in Bly's footsteps are not afraid to try new approaches to achieving manliness, whether in a sweat lodge, a conference room, or a Zoom meeting. They are not deterred by harsh censure from feminists on the left or by the belly laughs of ridicule emanating from the "real men" on the right.

Marchers Take a Vow

Million Man Manifesto

Visualize a throng of Black college men walking onto the National Mall in Washington, D.C. They're at the biggest demonstration specifically for them since the Rev. Martin Luther King, Jr., gave his "I Have a Dream" speech on August 28, 1963. The man now at the dais on the mall was there when Dr. King was murdered by an assassin on April 4, 1968. The Rev. Jesse Jackson witnessed the last breaths of the fallen civil rights leader on the balcony of the Lorraine Hotel in Memphis.

Now, Jackson was giving a speech at the 1995 Million Man March, and the young men on the mall were listening intently as Jackson's words filled the air above a sea of Black faces in the nation's capital. The college activists considered Jackson's declaration: "America will benefit and ultimately be grateful for this day. When a rising tide for racial justice, and gender equality, and family stability, and inclusion, and fairness, lifts the boats stuck at the bottom—all boats benefit....

"Why do we march? We march because our dignity and our destiny are at stake. What must we do? We cannot wallow in our pain. We must turn to power. We can't get a victim's complex. That's a central message of Jesus the Christ, who was born in the slum, but the slum was not born in him."[1]

The 1995 Million Man March on Washington, D.C., was a life-changing event for a multitude of Black American males from all over the country. The national gathering was inspired by a call to Black men to come to seek atonement for their past indiscretions. The event was meant to encourage the Black participants to become better husbands, fathers, sons, brothers, and friends. Perhaps the overriding goal for this budding men's movement for African Americans was to show unity, and to allow husbands, fathers, sons, brothers, and friends to join hands and show solidarity. "It's time for us to come together and be as one," Cyrus Colbert told *The Atlanta Constitution*, as he boarded a bus from Atlanta to attend the March in the nation's capital. He said he never thought he would see such a day as that of October 16, 1995.[2]

"This was the most powerful movement I'd ever witnessed in my life. Never have I ever felt so proud to be a Black man," said Earl Nelson, a college junior student at Richard Stockton College in Pomona, New Jersey. He and other Black young men loaded onto 14 buses for the trip to Washington. When they arrived at JFK Stadium for the walk to Capitol Hill, they heard people shouting and chanting: "Freedom for the Black man!" It was awesome, and humbling, and uplifting for them to witness.

"The March was outstanding, powerful and ordained by god. Who would have ever believed that over one million Black men would assemble together for a positive cause, despite all the negative rhetoric that had been said about the Black men and their behavior. There were not any fights or violent acts throughout the duration of the March," observed Nelson. "This was without question, the largest and most powerful movement in America. I am so proud that I was a part of this history."[3]

Organized and headlined by Nation of Islam leader Louis Farrakhan, the Million Man March had a reach far beyond Washington. Black Americans, unable to make the March, were encouraged to stay home from their usual school, work, and social engagements in favor of attending teach-ins and worship services. The intent of the local gatherings was to focus on the challenge of achieving a vibrant and self-sufficient Black community. To that end, local organizers described October 16 as a "Day of Absence," when normal life activities would be suspended in favor of watching the March on television or engaging in neighborhood voter registration drives.

Those staying home to watch the March event on television listened to prayers, songs, poetry, and notable speakers from the nation and across the globe. Speakers included the Rev. Jesse Jackson, the Rev. Louis Farrakhan, the Rev. Clay Evans, the Rev. Al Sharpton, the Rev. James Bevel, the Rev. Joseph Bevel, the Rev. Benjamin Chavez, the Rev. Joseph Lowery, the Rev. Wendell Anthony, the Rev. Al Sampson, and more. Tributes were made to prominent Black American heroes such as Booker T. Washington, W. E. B. Dubois, Marcus Garvey, Paul Robeson, Martin Luther King, Jr., Elijah Muhammed, Medgar Evers, Malcom X, Mary McLeod Bethune, Sojourner Truth, and Harriet Tubman. Poets and lyricists participating in the event included Steve Cobb, Useni Perkins, Maya Angelou, and more.

The many prominent speakers invited to address the Washington marchers were given the charge by event organizers to "convey to the world a vastly different picture of the Black male" and to unite in self-help and self-defense against the social ills and economic travails plaguing the African American community. Organizers included civil rights activists from the National African American Leadership Summit and the

Nation of Islam, in coordination with local chapters of the National Association for the Advancement of Colored People. Together they formed the Million Man March Organizing Committee. Benjamin Chavez, Jr., founder of the National African American Leadership Summit, served as national director of the Million Man March.

The Million Man March had many prescriptions and elevated goals for Black men to find themselves and to define their manhood. Male participants were asked to atone for their past failings and to reconcile with their wives, their families, their Black community, and their Christian God. Leaders asked that Black males throw off the hackles of victimhood and settle disputes, overcome conflicts, put aside hatreds. Above all this, there was a manifesto calling for personal responsibility

Civil rights leader Jesse Jackson (shown here in 1983) told the men at the Million Man March that they must not wallow in their own pain. Jackson said they must remember that Jesus Christ was born in a slum "but the slum was not born in him" (Library of Congress).

and self-sufficiency as the essence of Black male pride and for achieving manhood.

"The Million Man March / Day of Absence Mission Statement" is a sprawling document that covers a lot of ground, but which takes note of the political climate for Black Americans in 1995. In the aftermath of Republican Party's so-called "Contract with America" and its victory in the 1994 Congressional elections, many Black leaders felt the country was poised to backslide on civil rights protections and the social and economic issues facing the Black community. March organizers believed that conservative politicians were reverting to the usual "blaming the victims," pointing the finger at urban Blacks for "domestic economic woes that threatened to produce record deficits, massive unemployment, and uncontrolled inflation."[4]

One of the primary motivating factors for the Million Man March was, undoubtedly, to put important Black issues back on the nation's political agenda. However, independent observers were taken aback at how much the March's mission statement, and the speeches directed to Black males, were reflections on defining manhood and calls on the participants to find strength, dignity, and unity. The mission statement put emphasis on atonement, reconciliation and responsibility. In particular, there was surprise by onlookers at how much attention was paid to the subject of "atonement," and not just the usual political grievances often expressed by National of Islam's Farrakhan.

Among the mission statement points was a declaration asking the creator and all other parties to forgive the personal failings of repentant Black males. The precise wording asked participants to dare to atone:

- For over-focusing on the personal at the expense of the collective needs of our families and our people.
- For collaborating in our own oppression by embracing ideas, institutions and practices which deny our human dignity, limit our freedom and dim or disguise the spark of divinity in all of us.
- For failing to contribute in a sustained and meaningful way to the struggle of our people for freedom and justice, and to the building of the moral community in which we all want to live.
- For failing to do as much as we can to protect and preserve the environment through practicing and struggling for environmentally friendly patterns of consumption and production.
- For any time we have turned a blind eye to injustice, a deaf ear to truth or an uncaring heart away from the suffering and pain around us.
- For not resisting as much as we can sexist ideas and practices in society and in our own relations and failing to uphold the principle of equal rights, partnership and responsibility of men and women in life, love and struggle.
- For lacking the moral consideration and human sensitivity towards others that we want for ourselves.
- For not always practicing the Seven Principles: unity, self-determination, collective work and responsibility, cooperative economics, purpose, creativity and faith.[5]

In addition, the Million Man March mission statement's atonement declaration advised confession and contrition for "all our offenses, intentional and unintentional, against the creator, others and the creation, especially those offenses caused by our accepting the worst and weakest conceptions of ourselves; for not always following the best teachings of our spiritual and ethical tradition of Islam, Christianity, Judaism (Hebrewism), Maat, Yoruba, Akan, Kawida and all others, and sacrificing and ignoring the spiritual and ethical in pursuit of material things."[6]

As the years have passed, reactions to the Million Man March movement have become increasingly positive—perhaps because, at the time, there was an inordinate fear in the white community about the March as a prelude to strident Black nationalism and racial violence. The memories of chaos and destruction in American cities after the 1968 assassination of the Rev. Martin Luther King, Jr., came to mind. Riots took place in 110 cities with 13 people killed, more than 1,000 injured, and 6,100 arrested. Some of the worst rioting and arson incidents took place in Washington, D.C. The riots devastated Washington's inner-city economy.[7] Along with the upheaval, businesses were burned to the ground, and thousands of jobs were lost. Made uneasy by the violence, "white flight" from urban cores of U.S. cities accelerated.

The Million Man March did not trigger the expected violence, and there was no cause for all the paranoid visions. March leaders offered positive ideas for Black men to take back home after the event, and some of the suggestions were acted upon. A massive and ongoing voter registration drive resulted. In the past, Louis Farrakhan had few kind words for the democratic system, and he shunned both Democrats and Republicans. At the March, Farrakhan urged Black people to register as Democrats, Republicans, or Independents—and to get involved in the political process.

Farrakhan also encouraged Black men to return home and to join organizations working on behalf of African Americans. Some of the groups he suggested were the moderate National Urban League and the National Association for the Advancement of Colored People. Neither the Urban League nor the NAACP had endorsed the Million Man March. His message was that Black men should not stand on the sidelines and criticize what other brothers are doing, or not doing. The message was one of unity among Black men, and the sense of brotherhood was apparent at the October 1995 event.

A reporter for *The Washington Post*, Terry Neal of Reston, Virginia, could not suppress his very favorable reaction to the Million Man March experience as he covered it on assignment: "It was my story that ran on the front page of the *Post* the next day. I recall the complex emotions I felt trying to negotiate my role as an objective observer with my role as a human and a Black man, who was so proud of that glorious moment of brotherhood and revelry."[8]

Henry Johnson of Alexandria, Virginia, was impressed by the peaceful nature of the Million Man March and the brotherly attitudes of those in attendance. Johnson was able to attend the event with his two sons, ages 8 and 14. As a father, he was pleased by the examples being set. "I remember the passion and pride I felt from being in a crowd of positive Black men from all over America. My sons stood and sat with me all day and never complained. The key point for me was the warmth I felt from all these normal men like me coming together for a common cause with peaceful results."[9]

Critics of the Movement

Certainly the Million Man March and the resulting Black men's movement had many vocal detractors among those in both Black and white communities. The fact that Louis Farrakhan was a central figure in the March event was problematic for the Jewish community, which viewed him as anti-Semitic, and also for women who viewed him as a religious patriarch and misogynist. He was accused of being a Black supremacist by many conservative political voices. Black conservatives urged all Blacks to avoid participation in the March because any useful message of the event could not be separated from the messenger. Civil rights icon and Atlanta congressman John Lewis skipped the March because he said Farrakhan preached racial, religious and sexual divisiveness.[10]

Jews have had issues with Farrakhan and his sermons and statements for many years. He has blamed Jews for the international slave trade, plantation slavery before the Civil War, Jim Crow laws, sharecropping and general Black oppression. Farrakhan has suggested that a small handful of Jews control the movement of the great nation of America like a radar controls movements of great ships in the waters. Black journalists like George Curry of *Emerge Magazine* suggested that Farrakhan's statements often were misconstrued or taken out of context, and that the Million Man March was bigger than any one man.[11] He said Black male March participants were focused and attracted to his message on racial pride, on economic empowerment, and on personal and family responsibility.

Many critics of the March and the Black men's movement found it offensively patriarchal because it was exclusionary. In excluding women from the Million Man March, Black women accused it of gender apartheid and a nostalgia for a time when men ruled the roost. Black women were frightened that the movement heralded a dramatic resurgence in Black male sexism. *Emerge Magazine* editor Curry defended the all-male event and said he found it ironic that some female critics were taking aim at an all-male gathering upon returning from the United Nations Conference on Women in Beijing, China.

The Million Man March in Washington, D.C., filled the National Mall in 1995 with Black men who joined hands in solidarity. Most reviews of the March were positive, but some Black women found the March offensively patriarchal (Library of Congress).

Angela Davis, Barbara Ransby, and Evelynn Hammonds were among Black feminists who formed an alliance called the African American Agenda 2000 in their effort to oppose the Million Man March. Others who contended that the exclusion of women was counterproductive included Jewel Jackson McCabe, Michelle Wallace, and Clarence Mitchell. Activist Mitchell was skeptical as to whether the March was grappling with real issues, rather than just a feel-good activity. "Yes, it is time to march, but we must march for something tangible—for jobs, decent wages, for decent housing, and quality public education and single payer health care," Mitchell declared. "We cannot afford the division between African-American women and men. If we ever needed each other we certainly do now."[12]

Mitchell found a kindred spirit on the gender issue with the Million Man March in a prominent male poet, Amiri Baraka, previously known as LeRoi Jones. Baraka denounced the March and noted, "First of all, I wouldn't go to war and leave half the army at home."[13] Writer Herb Boyd suggested that Baraka was making an ironic commentary on Farrakhan's pre–March military metaphor, "You don't take your woman into the foxhole with you."[14]

Many defenders of the March sought to disarm these critics by pointing out that March organizers enlisted many female voices to speak to and to counsel the Black men at the March. Perhaps the best defense of the March and movement as a predominantly male activity came from Charshee McIntyre, a retired professor and the first woman President of the African Heritage Studies Association. McIntyre said feminists needed to accept that the March was male-oriented, just as there are groups of women lawyers, women doctors and women professors who meet together to enjoy each other's company and converse about mutual interests.

"Among the sisters bonding occurs all the time," McIntyre observed. "We pick up friends from our early years to our nineties. Such is not the case with our young men, who are often isolated and left to struggle alone. You see, Black (women) did not lose the roles they had in Africa, but our brothers did, and anything they do to improve themselves I support."[15] In some manner, McIntyre echoed the mythopoetic perspective on men generally. Men used to be moored to the ancient patterns and rituals of previous tribal organization, but now they are untethered and have been cast adrift. They are now seeking comfort in the old connections.

MMM Movement Lessons

The Million Man March, a predominantly Black men's movement, has been favorably compared to the largely Caucasian male movement of the Promise Keepers. Both movements are heavily influenced by conservative Christian tenets on how men are to conduct themselves. The Promise Keepers were founded and initially led by well-known men with ties to evangelical faith orientations. Their principles and pronouncements frequently mention Jesus Christ by name and also refer to biblical passages as a basis for their beliefs. There has been some controversy and debate over whether Louis Farrakhan is a Christian minister or a Muslim cleric, but the leader of the original Million Man March also frequently calls upon the guidance of Jesus. In his lengthy speech at the 1995 Washington, D.C., event, Farrakhan quoted from spirituals as well as the from the Old and New Testaments, and he termed himself a prophet.

There is no question that the men of the Promise Keepers and the men of the Million Man March are overwhelmingly conservative Christian in orientation. Both groups espouse anti-abortion viewpoints and a disapproval of homosexuality and alternative sexual lifestyles. Both groups are disposed to believe that a man's rightful place is as head of the household, while his female spouse is charged with domestic duties and family matters at home. Both male groups take a dim view of feminists and their support for the Equal Rights Amendment. Promise Keepers are unlikely to quibble with Minister Farrakhan's advisories for women on the importance of homemaking, especially cooking and cleaning. "You're just not going to be happy unless there is happiness in the home," Farrakhan has counseled women. "Your professional lives can't satisfy your soul like a good, loving man."[16]

Although the men of the Promise Keepers and men of the Million Man March will contend that their primary interest is for the next world and not in the affairs of the present world, both groups' leaders are hardly aloof or apolitical. Many have leaned decidedly Republican in recent years. During the 2016 GOP presidential primaries, Farrakhan praised Republican candidate Donald Trump as the only candidate "who has stood in front of the Jewish community and said, 'I don't want your money.'"[17] While Farrakhan did not endorse Trump outright, he did say of the Republican candidate that he liked what he was seeing. Farrakhan praised Trump in 2018 for his attacks on past actions of the U.S. Department Justice and the FBI. Many evangelical religious leaders associated with the Promise Keepers have had no reservations about endorsing Trump in his presidential bids.

The similarities in the religious and political orientations of the Promise Keepers and the men of the Million Man March would appear to bode well for conservative Republicans now as they seek to redefine manhood for the 21st century. Both groups of men would seem to offer a ready pool of recruits for a new men's movement based on much the same conservative Christian religious doctrine. However, the Million Man March men may actually be at odds with the latest conservative manhood formulations and their premises. The new manhood philosophy, as drawn up by Republican U.S. Senator Josh Hawley, takes the position that today's rudderless men can attribute their decline to failed liberal policies promoted by Democrats.

In contrast, the Million Man March manifesto champions many of the liberal policies and raises the alarm that Republicans will abolish hard-won civil rights gains enacted by Democrats whenever such opportunities arise. Among those advancements are voting rights protections, affirmative action programs, and redistricting measures to maximize Black political participation in the legislative process. The manifesto also argues for the enactment of more liberal programs, including affordable universal health care guarantees, support for affordable housing developments, and an economic "bill of rights" to rebuild deteriorating urban core areas inhabited by minorities.

Promise Keepers find much to agree with in the Atonement section of the lengthy Million Man March manifesto. Promise Keepers, who indicate they desire closer ties to minority communities, find much to like in the calls for Black men to strive to be better persons, to make the world a better place to live, to take on more individual responsibility, and to commit to their families' welfare. However, two major sections of the manifesto beyond the Atonement pledge are more problematic for the conservative right. They are titled "The Challenge to the Government" and "The Challenge to the Corporations." Each offers a long list of demands.

"The Challenge to the Government" outlines the need for long-awaited monetary reparations and apologies: "Historically, the U.S. government has participated in one of the greatest holocausts of human history, the Holocaust of African Enslavement. It sanctioned with law and government the genocidal process that destroyed millions of human lives, human culture, and the human possibility inherent in African life and culture. It has yet to acknowledge this horrific destruction or to take steps to make amends for it."[18]

"The Challenge to the Corporations" demands that companies quit shipping jobs overseas and to end destructive policies of deindustrialization, disinvestment, and corporate relocation: "Moreover, we call on corporations to reinvest profits back into the communities from which it extracts profits; to increase support for Black charities, contribute more to Black education in public schools and traditional Black colleges and universities; to open facilities to the community for cultural and recreational use; and to contribute to the building of community institutions and other projects to reinvest in the social structure and development of the Black community."[19]

The Million Man March manifesto, under the influence of Louis Farrakhan, took the view that much of the difficulty for Black men in achieving their manhood can be laid at the feet of white society. The Million Man March was an opportunity to air grievances at a time when Blacks faced unemployment rates nearly twice that of whites, a poverty rate of more than 40 percent, and a median family income far less than that of the country's white households.[20] Also noted were the excessive numbers of Black men in prisons and a continuing struggle against abuse by law enforcement. There was an indictment of the majority culture for the destructive impacts of environmental racism.

The Million Man March movement was about atonement and self-improvement, but also was very much about grievance against white nationalism and a legacy of oppression. For that reason, it's unlikely that the conservative Black male movement would ever find much common ground with the conservative movement of the predominantly white male groups like the Promise Keepers. What's more, the far right conservative Caucasian movements of recent times have grown outwardly hostile to Black males. New alt-right organizations of white males have even taken up paranoid visions that Jews intend to use Blacks as tools to replace white hegemony in American society. Any reparations and addressing Black grievances are far off the table with the predominantly Caucasian organizations on the right.

Making Promises

Promise Keepers Manifesto

Behold a vision of well-groomed men striding through the vast parking lots surrounding Arrowhead Stadium on the northeast border of Kansas City. Hundreds of enthusiastic men are chatting with each other; they seem oblivious to the steady drone of traffic heading east and west on nearby Interstate 70. Across America similar scenes are playing out at stadiums for professional baseball and football. These men are used to attending major league sporting events, but tonight there is something different happening at Arrowhead—different, but still major.

This is a giant congregation of men enlisting in the Promise Keepers movement. The evening will begin with songs of praise to almighty God, to be followed by exhortations from Tony Evans. He is a senior pastor at a Dallas Bible Fellowship Church attended by legions of Texas Christians. Pastor Evans is a familiar figure at Promise Keepers rallies. He asks the men to come forward and reaffirm their commitment to Jesus Christ. Wave after wave of men answer his emotional appeal and tearfully rededicate their lives to Jesus.

Evans is followed by several more heavy hitters in the new religious movement for men. There's Gary Smalley, author of numerous books on family relationships from a Christian perspective, whom many of tonight's attendees have just discovered. There's Bruce Wilkerson, who launched "Walk Thru the Bible." He has personally trained in the "Teaching for Life Change" and is himself a trainer in the Christian "Dream Giver" methodology. There is Pastor Haman Cross, Jr., who strives to break down the color barriers in Christianity and calls for an end to Sunday morning segregation in the big box churches of America.

It's Wilkerson who delivers the most passionate admonishments to the men assembled in Arrowhead Stadium. All have fallen short in so many different ways in their dedication to their Christian faith and family, and they readily admit it. Wilkerson beseeches them to draw a line in the sand

*against temptations to evil. He tells them that they must put away pornogra-
phy. He tells them to reject adultery. He tells them to end the coveting of one
another's wives. They must confess their shortcomings and embrace a new
Christian life. "How long you gonna wait?" Wilkerson bellows, demanding
answers from the shaken men. "How long? Do it now! This very night! Draw
a line in the sand!"*[1]

In 1997 the Promise Keepers men's movement filled more than 20
sports stadiums like Kansas City's across the country. Christian males
filled the stadiums looking for a life-changing event and an opportunity
to reaffirm principles of their faith. They found evangelical orators ready
to meet their needs and the opportunity to join all the men in a movement
of common purpose. The Promise Keepers began in 1990 as an evangelical
para-church organization with the goal "to bring about revival through a
global movement that calls men back to courageous, bold leadership."[2]

Tim Pettus of Columbia, Missouri, was among the men in the Midwest who answered the Promise Keepers' call in greater Kansas City. The
husband and father of three youngsters willingly headed to Arrowhead
Stadium along with 75,000 of his brethren. They raised their voices in unison with a promise to be better examples of faith, to be better husbands, to
be more responsible heads of their families.

"As the sound floated into the night air over Arrowhead Stadium, men
from diverse backgrounds, occupations and races came together in joyous
celebration of unity in the body of Christ," wrote Pettus in a subsequent
opinion piece about the rally. He noted that at the same time that he was celebrating Christian manhood in the home of Kansas City Chiefs football,
65,000 more men were congregating for the same purpose on the West Coast
in Seattle. Pettus and others marveled at the ability of the religious organization to rally so many kindred spirits. Pettus also used his newspaper opinion
piece to tamp down criticism of the active religious men's movement.

First, he took aim at those who branded the Promise Keepers as sexist
because women were not allowed to participate. Pettus refuted this charge
as coming from "left-wing feminist groups, such as the National Organization for Women, which are hostile to men wherever they find them."
Pettus said the radical feminist critics ought to ask wives of participants
what they think. He said the naysayers would find overwhelming support
from wives of Promise Keepers, because the group encourages their men
to be better husbands and fathers. He brushed aside the sexism charges,
stating that Promise Keepers is a ministry to men, by men, urging men to
be more responsible to their god, their church, and their family.

Promise Keepers could not be racist as critics charge, according to
Pettus, because three of the seven speakers at Arrowhead Stadium were
Black. Minorities also were evident in the stadium crowd. Pettus conceded

The late John Wayne has been an idol of men's groups such as the Promise Keepers, but those who brand him as sexist and racist want his statues removed. A statue at his birthplace museum in Winterset, Iowa, will likely remain intact (Library of Congress).

that the Black numbers at the stadium rally were not representative of their presence in the general populace. However, he stressed that the organization had made a concerted effort to reach out to all minorities and to make racial reconciliation a major theme of gatherings. Pettus said participants were urged to cross color lines and to extend their hands in friendship and solidarity to all men.

Pettus also took on the accusation that Promise Keepers acts as a political front for the "religious right." Pettus insisted that throughout the April 26–27 event in 1997, elections and politicians were never mentioned, neither liberal nor conservative, neither Democrat nor Republican. Everything was politics-free. However, Pettus himself contradicted his own non-partisan contention for Promise Keeper when he strayed into familiar conservative rant territory at the end of his opinion piece. He concluded his article with a tirade against fatherless families caused by big government: "We have spent trillions of dollars on government programs designed to make our nation a better place. Much of this money, if not most, has been wasted. Many of the programs have made the problems worse. We have more crime, more fatherless children, more separation, more bitterness, than when they began."[3]

Never mind any underlying political agenda, most of the stated goals of the Promise Keepers are difficult to object to when it comes to its message of love, respect, and responsibility. One speaker at the Arrowhead event, Stu Weber, told attendees that 40 percent of children in America go to bed each night without a father. Weber said all studies show that children in this predicament are more likely to be troubled. Single-parent households are looked on as a scourge upon America. A key tenet of Promise Keepers is that men must become more responsible for their children, more concerned with family, and they must reach out to aid other children without fathers.

The organization has a list of seven important promises for men in the movement. A strong devotion to marriage and family is of primary importance. Promise Keepers adherents pledge to honor the seven commitments as follows:

- A Promise Keeper is committed to honoring Jesus Christ through worship, prayer, and obedience to his Word, through the power of the Holy Spirit.
- A Promise Keeper is committed to pursuing vital relationships with a few other men, understanding that he needs brothers to help him keep his promises.
- A Promise Keeper is committed to practicing spiritual, moral, ethical, and sexual purity.
- A Promise Keeper is committed to building strong marriages and families through love, protection, and biblical values
- A Promise Keeper is committed to supporting the mission of the church by honoring and praying for his pastor and by actively giving his time and resources.
- A Promise Keeper is committed to reaching beyond any racial

and denominational barriers to demonstrate the power of biblical unity.
  * A Promise Keeper is committed to influencing his world, being obedient to the Great Commandment (Mark 12:30–31) and the Great Commission (Matthew 28:19–20).[4]

The seventh promise, "committing to influence the world," draws on Apostle Mark's directive to all of Jesus Christ's followers to "love the Lord your God with all your heart, and with all your soul, and with all your mind, and with all your strength" and "to love your neighbor as yourself." The seventh promise also underscores the Apostle Matthew's directive for Jesus Christ's followers to "go forth therefore and make disciples of all nations, baptizing them in the name of the Father and of the Son and of the Holy Spirit, teaching them to observe all that I have commanded you; and lo, I am with you always."

Promise Keepers practitioners often protest that they are not in the business of proselytizing or of attempting to convert other men from one religion, belief, or opinion to another. Rather, they are interested in leading by example. However, the emphasis on Matthew's directive for followers to go out "and make disciples of all nations" would appear to contradict this contention. The men of the Promise Keepers are clearly commanded to reach out to their fellow men, to bring them into the fold, and to guide them on the path to Christian manly virtues. They have a history of proselytizing, although it is not a required duty as with Mormons or Jehovah's Witnesses.

In a 1997 story, *Time* magazine expressed concern over the phenomenal growth of Promise Keepers in a very short time, with an average of 50,000 men at each of 22 sites in 1996. *Time* reported that the seven-year-old organization boasted annual revenues of $87 million with a large brick headquarters in Denver and 360 paid staff members. Theologians told *Time* that Promise Keepers seemed intent on reinforcing the idea that God is male and that male religious leadership is the solution to poverty, illegitimacy, drug abuse, juvenile delinquency and the destruction of the family.[5]

What's Not to Like?

New converts to Promise Keepers are befuddled by its various critics and will even wonder aloud: "What's not to like?" What is objectionable about an enlightened men's movement that is spreading a message of friendship for one's fellow man, faithfulness to one's marriage, responsibility for raising one's children, and total devotion to one's god? Interestingly enough, some of the Promise Keepers harshest critics are not from dyed-in-the-wool secularists, hostile atheists, or the so-called "woke, left-wing mob." A surprising number of other Christian denominations are willing to step forward to challenge the gospel according to the Promise Keepers.

The *Christian Courier* has summarized some of the religious objections to the Promise Keepers as based on what the *Bible* and the *New Testament* tell us about Jesus and the prophets. Some of the objections, they argue, concern what the *New Testament* tells us about the unity of the Christian faith and the true path to redemption. An examination of a few of these doctrinal objections reveal accusations against the Promise Keepers for disingenuous superficiality. For example, the *Christian Courier* argues that the Promise Keepers emphasis on male togetherness and solidarity, as a formalized male movement, has no scriptural sanction whatsoever and is clearly at odds with the teachings of Jesus Christ.

The *Christian Courier* posits: "What if someone aspired to establish an all-white movement, designated as the Caucasian Covenant Keepers? The outcry would be vociferous—and rightly so! If a para-church movement, segregated along racial lines, is unacceptable, where is the value in gender exclusion in pursuing spiritual goals? 'PKism' is a fad with no biblical basis."[6]

The *Christian Courier* also questions the Promise Keepers' dogma on how to achieve redemption and forgiveness of sins. The Promise Keepers' approach is tagged as facile and false, and completely at odds with *New Testament* teaching relative to salvation and to forgiveness by the deity. The Rev. Wayne Jackson of the *Christian Courier,* a pastor of the Church of Christ and author of 20 books on the Christian faith, asks how anyone who possesses even a modicum of biblical knowledge could endorse or support the men's movement of the Promise Keepers.

According to the *Christian Courier's* Jackson: "Advocates of 'PK-ology' promote the so-called Sinner's Prayer. They allege that salvation occurs the instant the following words are mouthed: 'God, I confess to you that I am a sinner. And, through faith, I invite your Son into my heart this very moment, to save my soul.' Though many who offer such a petition are unquestionably sincere, there is no *New Testament* precedent for this sort of prayer." Moreover, Jackson maintains, in spite of explicit biblical evidence to the contrary, that Promise Keepers perpetuates the ignorance that immersion in water has nothing to do with one's salvation (cf. Mark 16:16; Acts 2:38; 22:16; 1 Peter 3:21). "This is nothing short of heresy," Jackson insists.[7]

Many Christian denominations have joined Church of Christ theologians to dismiss the Promise Keepers as lacking any genuine biblical authority. Leaders of the Lutheran Church–Missouri Synod describe the male group as full of doctrinal compromise and inconsistent doctrine. They suggest that it all seems to be a ruse to appear ecumenical and to draw in a large audience. The tactic of using biblical teaching in a simplistic manner to attract followers is labeled as a disservice to Christianity.

Although it took some time for Christian religious denominations to examine the Promise Keepers playbook for apostasy, secular women's groups wasted no time to denounce the religious men's movement. Patricia Ireland of the National Organization of Women provided examples of how the Promise Keepers dogma was a threat to women's rights. The oft-repeated phraseology, that just as "the church submits to Christ, so also should wives submit to their husbands," grew tiresome for feminists. On the other hand, these same feminists certainly agreed with admissions by Promise Keepers that Christian men had serious failings as absentee fathers and for lapses in their commitments to family.

Ireland of NOW saw the new Christian men's movement as little more than a Trojan Horse to carry a fresh phalanx of "Christian soldiers" into battle for old right-wing causes, particularly those espoused by the Moral Majority and the Christian Coalition.[8]

The Moral Majority, founded by Baptist minister Jerry Falwell, Jr., in 1979, bound the Christian right with the Republican Party in support of such causes as public school prayer, the sanctity of heterosexual marriage, the personhood of fertilized zygotes, and prohibitions on content considered lewd coming out of the American music industry and in Hollywood films. The Christian Coalition, founded by Marion Gordon "Pat" Robertson in 1987, also allied conservative Christians with the Republican Party. Robertson appointed Ralph Reed for day-to-day operations and for coordinating coalition members on such issues as opposition to abortion, to gay rights, to federal welfare programs, as well as support for gun rights, for an unwavering alliance with Israel, and a staunch advocacy of a strong, well-funded military.

It was not much of a stretch for Ireland and other feminist leaders to assert that Promise Keepers was in the same vein as the Moral Majority and far from apolitical. They made the case that the men's group was simply a rehash of right wing politics and toxic masculinity. So many of Promise Keepers leaders were outspoken right-wing conservatives from decades prior to the group's emergence. Examine the credentials of the writers in the seminal manual for Promise Keepers published in 1999, and most are found to have been aligned with hyper-conservative causes for years. The 1999 manual titled *Seven Promises of a Promise Keeper* includes essay instructions from such politically-connected scribes and spokesmen as Bill Bright, founder of Campus Crusade for Christ; James Dobson, founder of Focus on the Family; Jack Hayford of National Religious Broadcasters; and, and Bill McCartney, sports legend and activist for Christian masculinity in sports, schools, and legislative bodies.

Dobson and Bright stand out especially as spokesmen for Christian masculinity in the political arena. Far from being non-partisan religious men, both Dobson and Bright had long track records of rubbing shoulders with conservative politicians and candidates for high office. Most of the more than two dozen authors contained in *Seven Promises of a Promise Keeper* were firmly in the Ronald Reagan camp in 1980, despite the fact that his Democratic opponent in the presidential election, Jimmy Carter, was a born-again evangelical and Sunday school teacher. Dobson became a regular consultant on pro-family issues for the White House once Reagan was elected president. Dobson even recorded one of his famous "Focus on the Family" radio broadcasts with Reagan in the Oval Office. Reagan appointed Dobson co-chair of the Citizens for Tax Reform and to the National Advisory Committee to the Office of Juvenile Delinquency Prevention.

The leaders of the Promise Keepers and the men's organization's conservative allies had pasts in right-wing politics. It was not a difficult task for feminist critics such as Ireland to refute Promise Keepers' contentions that the group showed no political favoritism toward conservatives or liberals but was only interested in nurturing better husbands and family men. A full decade before Promise Keepers had its genesis, many of its big name mentors and supporters could be found playing key roles in conservative politics. Tim LaHaye, a Baptist minister and author of best-selling fiction on the Rapture, was another favorite of the Reagan Administration. In 1981, he founded the influential Council for National Policy, a secretive organization purposed to align Republican leaders with the goals of the religious right.

Leaked membership directories from LaHaye's organization revealed a network of conservative religious political activists, a number of whom would assume roles a few years later with the "apolitical" Promise Keepers. Some of the names revealed in the leaked directories from the Council for National Policy included: James Dobson, Jerry Falwell, Gary North, Pat Robertson, D. James Kennedy, Tony Perkins, Bill Bright, Richard DeVos, Wayne La Pierre, Grover Norquist, Gary Bauer and Oliver North.

Promise Keepers' Schism

Although the message of the Promise Keepers attracted Christian men to the organization throughout the 1990s, the strident criticism of its leaders and their mission began to take a toll. Membership started to plateau and then declined. Sports stadiums were not filling as easily as the millennial year of 2000 approached. Despite leaders' assertions that the group was apolitical, it was not hard for skeptics to pull back the curtain on its directors to show that many of its spokesmen were in the thick of hardcore, right-wing politics. Nor was it hard to pick up on the misogynist tendencies in some of the basic messaging regarding the requirements for manhood in the gospel according to Promise Keepers.

Not all of the complaints about Promise Keepers' ideology came from outside the organization—from feminists, political liberals, the gay community or competing Christian denominations. Within the Promise Keepers, there also was discord and differing interpretations of manliness and manhood. Some members became disenchanted with the declarations anointing men as the rulers of the homestead, as the commanders-in-chief of house and spouse, as the key deciders of family fortune and fate. In her study, *Jesus and John Wayne: How White Evangelicals Corrupted a Faith and Fractured a Nation,* author Kristin Kobes Du Mez describes departures from the orthodoxy within the Promise Keepers. Some of the internal estrangement can be located in the concepts of "soft patriarchy" and male "servant leadership." Both involved a move away from the ideal of "macho" masculinity and traditional views of manhood that were inherent to the Promise Keepers creed.[9]

Servant leadership as a general concept is the idea that the best leaders always prioritize serving the greater good. Leaders with this style serve their team first and avoid prioritizing their own objectives. In a servant leadership environment, all the subordinates are likely to feel that their voices are heard and that they are not less important than the man at the helm. In the context of family life, the man of the family does not "lord over" his wife and children. Instead, he lives to serve and support the family's needs with his hard work, dedication, and example. Within the context of Christian life, the servant leadership model not only allows men to maintain some leadership within the home, but also requires humility and a recognition of new economic realities impinging on the ability of men to be the sole breadwinners for the family.

Soft patriarchy became an antidote to the belief that manhood must always involve strength, tenacity, confidence, and the will to achieve and dominate. With soft patriarchy, men can be men even while exhibiting gentleness, sympathy, understanding, and sensitivity. Meekness can replace militancy. Quiet compassion can replace unbridled passion. The contrast of soft patriarchy versus an autocratic masculinity was in many ways reflective of an old debate over who was Jesus Christ. Was Jesus a soft-spoken and gentle man who looked like a hippie? Or was Jesus a hard and uncompromising leader ready to unleash the power of his almighty father against evil forces?

Advocates for the soft patriarchy approach within the Promise Keepers movement argued for men and fathers to take their counsel from the humble teacher and philosopher Jesus. This would be the Jesus from the Sermon on the Mount, advising his followers to comfort the afflicted, to open their eyes to the blessedness of the meek, who were destined to inherit the earth. This would be the Jesus espousing mercy and forgiveness, even when hanging from the cross: "Father forgive them, for they know not what they do." This would be the Jesus who championed peace and living in harmony—the Jesus who blessed all peacemakers as the children of god. Religious thinkers from Leo Tolstoy to Mahatma Gandhi to Martin Luther King have admired Jesus' sermon, and it has been an oft-quoted source for Christian pacifism. The traditionalists in the schism within this religious men's movement were more disposed toward the angry Jesus in the temple than the Jesus preaching peace and circulating among the poor, the prostitutes, the persecuted, and the outcasts.

The story of Jesus driving the money changers from the holy temple is the best known account of Jesus' anger. The context of the clearing of the temple is well-known, and the pictures and graphics depicting the temple event show a strong and virile Jesus single-handedly driving out a cowering group of religious hypocrites. His anger is palpable, and he appears to be wielding a small leather whip. Since Promise Keepers was founded by men with military and sports backgrounds, it was predictable that they would embrace an image of Jesus in which toughness and righteous indignation win the day.

According to the *New Testament* account, Jesus' outrage was at Passover. Many of the Jewish faithful had come to make an animal sacrifice at the temple in Jerusalem during this holy time. The authorities at the temple rejected the offerings brought along as failing to meet kosher law. So, the travelers were urged to buy a suitable sacrifice, but then there was the currency problem. Different currencies had to be handled and changed into useable legal tender. The travelers were exploited by exorbitant exchange rates. The authorities in the sacred temple were getting rich with filthy lucre. It became exceeding expensive for tired and travel-weary worshipers who simply wanted to honor their god in an appropriate manner. The sad spectacle of pious profit-takers exploiting exhausted worshippers enraged Jesus. He vigorously attacked and lashed out at the religious authorities and drove them from the temple.

The debate within Promise Keepers between those who championed a vigorous man-of-action Jesus and those who favored a more thoughtful and serene Jesus was never hashed out or decided openly. There was

Actor Mel Gibson became the hero of the Promise Keepers with his ardent faith in Christian masculinity. Members adored his *Braveheart* (1995) and *The Passion of the Christ* (2004) movies. Here, Gibson advises James Caviezel, who played Christ (Photofest).

no spirited theological discussion over whether the ideal man should be a loving father in the mode of "soft patriarchy," a man who lived by the *Beatitudes* enunciated on the "Sermon on the Mount." However, there were conservative thinkers and writers associated with the Promise Keepers movement who were outspoken against the "pussification" of young Christian men. Young men were biologically designed to be like the battling Scotsman William Wallace as portrayed by Mel Gibson in *Braveheart*; they were designed to be like the fearless fighter Col. Davy Crockett in John Wayne's paean to patriotism, *The Alamo*; they were designed to be like the unflinching "blood and guts" General George S. Patton of World War II as portrayed by George C. Scott in the film classic *Patton*.

In the end, cataclysmic events at the turn of a new century played the biggest role in determining the direction of the Promise Keepers—and the many evangelical males tied to this men's movement. The new century would take a tragic turn into a perilous and uncertain future with the terrorist attacks upon America on September 11, 2001. Calls for retribution against radical Islam, for the neutralization of an alleged nuclear threat from Iraq's Saddam Hussein, and for an unwavering response to "axis of evil" countries required Christian warriors ready to defend a Western civilization under assault. Strident voices arose from the smoke and ashes of the twin towers in New York City's Lower Manhattan. They called for a vision of American masculinity that did not countenance servant men, soft patriarchy, or loving one's enemies.

A Promise Unfulfilled?

Leaders of the Promise Keepers might have justifiably anticipated a revival after the traumatic events of September 11, 2001, and the subsequent U.S. military actions in Afghanistan and Iraq. Many right-wing commentators framed the terrorist challenge to American world dominance as a clash of civilizations: an emerging Islamic radicalism versus an uncertain, but awakening Christian empire of the West. Promise Keepers was attracting energetic Christian men interested in understanding and living out the credo of their religious affiliation. These were men who were once motivated to find their rightful place in the family and who now could be expected to seek out their proper place in a world at war in which the very existence of their family and country was on the line.

After an earlier period of discussion about the meaning of masculinity and the identity of the real Jesus, the post 9/11 Promise Keepers now sent a message that the warrior Jesus and the macho male were, in fact, the real deal for Christian men. Ryan Dobson, son of Focus on the Family and Promise Keepers leader James Dobson, espoused a more militant manliness than his father. He preached that man is the absolute and undisputed leader in the Christian family, and it was time now for men to be undisputed warrior leaders. And it was time for those manly leaders to step up and put a stop to raising a generation of sissified boys. To that end, the younger Dobson promoted the Mixed Martial Arts Academy, where young boys could be toughened up in MMA fight cages. By 2010, an estimated 700 white evangelical churches had embraced MMA as a means of youth outreach.[10]

In spite of a newer and more uncompromising message about tough men and their warrior roles after 9/11, the Promise Keepers did not seem to gain any new ground. Perhaps that's because it looked like a bad case of revisionism to many Christian men who had since moved on to something else. Also, the U.S. invasions of Afghanistan and Iraq did not go so well. After auspicious starts, America's warriors became bogged down in two Mideast quagmires exacting a heavy toll in soldiers' blood and the U.S. citizenry's national treasure. The purposes of the wars, first to track down

Al Qaeda terrorist leader Osama bin Laden and then to find and destroy Saddam Hussein's weapons of mass destruction in Iraq, somehow got lost. The missions were not being accomplished. By 2008, the "decider" and war president George W. Bush made jokes at a Washington, D.C., dinner about not finding Iraqi WMD. He said he no longer cared whether Osama bin Laden was caught or not.

To add insult to injury in 2008, the American banking system crashed and brought on one of the worst recessions in U.S. history. The staggering economy paved the way for the first Black president, Barack Hussein Obama, to be elected in November 2008. The demoralized evangelicals, and lapsing Promise Keepers, were shaken, but not especially tearful over the election loss of Republican John McCain to Obama. They considered McCain to be too milquetoast for the times. Nor were they at all surprised when Republicans lost a second time to Obama in 2012. The standard bearer in 2012 was another U.S. Senator just like John McCain. Mitt Romney, too, was viewed as a milquetoast, a middle-of-the-road double-talker who could not even answer Democrat accusations that he strapped the pet dog, Seamus, to the top of the family van on a vacation trip. By 2016, evangelicals and the lapsed Promise Keepers were looking for something dramatically different in a national leader.

The reasons the Promise Keepers were unable to make a comeback after 9/11 involved both its past message and its now-dated image from the halcyon days of the 1990s. Evangelical Christian men were no longer in tune with an organization that once had purported to be "inwardly-looking" and not concerned with partisan viewpoints or political affiliations. There also was more to being a man now than learning how to be good father or how to honor one's spouse. For conservative men, the National Rifle Association and the World Wrestling Federation had far more interesting messages about what being a man is all about. New, more perilous times did not call for men in plaid shirts and creased khakis shuffling together into stadiums to ask God's forgiveness for their failings at fatherhood. The times seemed more appropriate for men determined to tote an AR-15 to the gun range while sporting a red Make America Great Again hat to cover thinning pates.

9

Men's Liberation and Fathers' Rights Groups

Picture an angry group of fathers, some accompanied by their young children, carrying signs to protest a movie that they feel is sexist against men. They're marching outside the local Cinema 14 in suburban St. Louis. According to the protesters, there are plenty of women who abuse, attack, blackmail, and commit various acts of fraud against husbands, dads, and male employers. Yet, the films out of Hollywood always show the men as the bad guys, whether it's 9 to 5, Legally Blonde, *or* First Wives Club.

The men at the protest are members of men's rights groups like the National Congress of Fathers and Children. They carry signs that say, "Hate Isn't Funny" and "Hollywood Hates Men." Steve Wilson tells a local reporter that he joined the fathers' support group a year ago after a divorce turned his life upside down. He said the other divorced fathers opened his eyes to the fact that the media and the courts are biased against men. Besides, he said, it was significantly cheaper to talk to supportive men in this group than to pay to talk to his divorce lawyer.[1]

Brian Lockwood came to the protest with his nine-year-old son, Max. He said his ex-wife probably would not approve of the protest for Max as "quality father-son time" with dad, but he didn't care. He said he was tired of movies, and society generally, portraying men as complete jerks. At the same time, he said, it seems that women are always given a pass and are supported as completely justified in anything that they do to men. Lockwood said he was also tired of newspaper stories about deadbeat dads who don't pay alimony. He said women want equal pay in the workplace, but still want to be subsidized by men in their role as single mothers.[2]

David Usher, a board member of the National Congress of Fathers and Children, said film producers need to be on notice—men have had enough. He said the October 1996 cinema demonstration marked the first time in history that the men's movement was making a national statement with similar protests across the country. He said it was the sexist movie, First

Wives Club, *that galvanized men into a cohesive and determined national movement.*

Usher explained that it's difficult for men to get together and to feel comfortable airing out their grievances. He said men are getting past feeling that such gatherings are whining and unmanly: "I think we are beginning to see a movement by men that takes a very rational approach," said Usher. "I don't think the emerging men's movement will have anything like feminists burning their bras like in the 1970s."[3]

Fathers' rights groups were on the march in the final decades of the 20th century. At the same time, mythopoetic men discussed whether it was time to get out from behind their work desks to rediscover the outdoors—and nature's plan for fathers and sons. The men of the Million Man March discussed whether racial progress for Black males was dependent on their taking more responsibility for their children and the state of their marriages. The Promise Keepers debated whether men needed the anchor of Christian faith to do their best as providers and as loving partners of their spouses.

Fathers' rights groups, on the other hand, were grappling with the more immediate concerns over who gets the kids, how much alimony is going to get paid out, and whether a second marriage was healthy for a new direction or just an opportunity to crash and burn again. The men got a boost in the 1990s thanks to the backlash against Hollywood portrayals of American males. Newly-formed men's groups protested outside cinemas showing movies ridiculing men. Female stars were railing against the patriarchy, but newly-liberated men were not amused by Jane Fonda, Dolly Parton, Kathleen Turner, Goldie Hawn, or Sarah Jessica Parker. These ladies were no friends of men dealing with real life, according to the men's rights groups. The men took particular umbrage with the popular feminist film *First Wives Club*.

What was it about *First Wives Club* that set men off to protest the film in more than 25 cities? The movie begins when the reunion of characters played by Goldie Hawn, Bette Midler, and Diane Keaton, at the funeral of a college friend who killed herself after her husband left her for a younger woman. As they catch up on each other's lives, they come to the realization that they have also been discarded by their husbands for younger women. The three form the First Wives Club and commit themselves to seeking vengeance against their ex-husbands.

The male protesters at the cinemas expressed outrage that the women abuse, kidnap, blackmail, and commit various acts of fraud against the men. They said it was even more outrageous that the women in the movie donate their financial gains to open a battered women's center, ostensibly to empower more women to engage in their same activities against men.

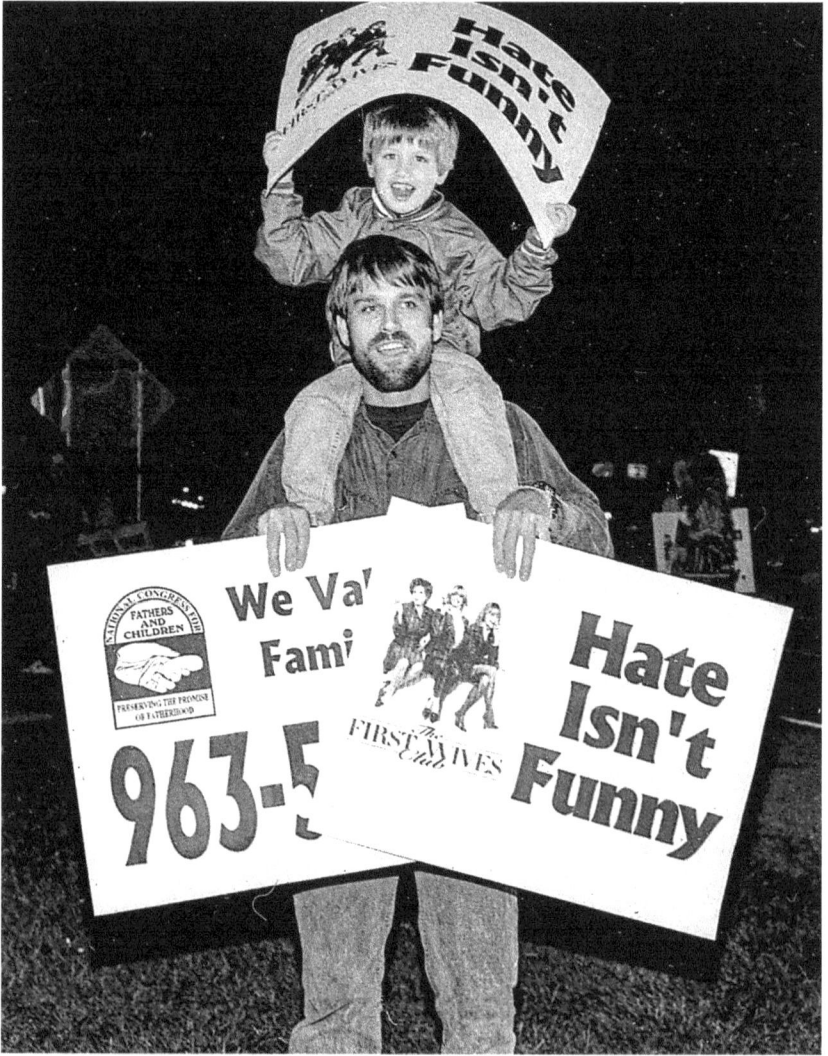

Fathers' rights groups in the 1990s protested outside courthouses, cinemas, and TV stations over what they perceived as sexism against men. Men's liberationists and fathers' rights groups felt the judiciary favored women in court cases (courtesy *Webster-Kirkwood Times*).

Interestingly enough, the cinema protesters were inspired to have their new spouses form The Second Wives Club to protest the sexism perpetuated against men by the *First Wives Club* film.

The men's rights groups and fathers' rights groups also took to protesting TV portrayals of family men, which seemed to only depict them as unfeeling louts or consummate buffoons. Media analyst Marshall McLuhan pointed out in the 1950s that many of the first television shows disrespected family men right out of the box.[4] McLuhan was one of the first to point out that mass culture emasculated men. He said there was no better exhibit for this problem than Dagwood Bumstead from the television series *Blondie*. Dagwood is an aimless bumbler whose life is devoted to long baths, long naps on the couch, consumption of large sandwiches, and fending off the nagging and nitpicking of his wife, Blondie. Dagwood was just the beginning of the ubiquitous televised male buffoon, which is a staple of the medium to this day.

Dagwood was the first in a long succession of miserable male TV characters including Ralph Cramden, as played by Jackie Gleason in *The Honeymooners*; Chester A. Riley, as played by William Bendix in *The Life of Riley*; and Archie Bunker as played by Carroll O'Connor in *All in the Family*. Bunker portrayed the classic toxic male with his constant ethnic, racist, and sexist slurs, slurs which always backfired on him. He came to symbolize the narrow-minded and prejudiced working-class dad whose redemption only came through lessons imparted by younger betters of the Bunker household. Those youngsters would be Gloria and her husband, nicknamed "Meathead." *All in the Family* was one of TV's most watched sitcoms during its eight-year run from 1971 to 1979.

Bunker was capable of occasional glimpses of illumination and enlightenment, but not so with the character of Al Bundy in *Married... With Children*, which aired from 1987 to 1997. Bundy, played by Ed O'Neill, was consistently boorish, beer-swilling, cheap, and misanthropic. The most controversial episode in *Married... With Children* occurs when Al Bundy becomes founder of NO MA'AM, a men's rights group which stands for the National Organization of Men Against Amazonian Masterhood. NO MA'AM has potential, but degenerates into a mere social club for neighborhood males to drink, fart profusely, bowl, visit strip clubs, talk about porn, and crab about their nuisance wives.

Compared to Al Bundy of *Married... With Children*, the life of the most influential male character in American television history, Homer Simpson, is downright edifying. A cartoon master of buffoonish masculinity from the amazingly popular *The Simpsons*, Homer is a crude, obscene, incompetent, lazy, donut-eating, and booze-guzzling ignoramus. However, he is devoted to his family and is mostly sincere, if categorically stupid. As with other television fathers, his children, Bart and Lisa, frequently have to correct him. His wife, Marge, must bail him out of jams. According to series writers Matt Groening, James Brooks and Mike Scully, a constant debate among them was just how far to go in portraying Homer's stupidity. One suggested rule: "He can never forget his own name."[5]

As if TV sitcoms don't provide enough opportunity to bash males as buffoons, television advertising has always gotten in on the act as well. Men have been portrayed as ding-dongs in advertisements for Kentucky Fried Chicken, Federal Express services, Tide laundry soap, lots of snack food commercials—and much more. A controversial Huggies diaper commercial begins: "To prove Huggies can handle just about anything, we put them to the toughest test imaginable: dads, alone, with their babies, in one house, for five days." The assumption that dads can't take care of their own children was offensive to many stay-at-home dads, who protested.

Fathers' rights groups and male liberationists note that advertising is a more insidious tool against male interests and fatherhood because it is 24–7, it's everywhere all the time, and it's often created by women whom they characterize as confirmed gender feminists. "Ad after ad makes doltish dads the butt of all jokes," according to Seth Stevenson of the web magazine, *Slate*. "He's outwitted by his children. He's the target of condescending eye rolls from his wife. He's dumb, incompetent, sometimes even a selfish oaf—but his family loves him anyway."[6]

Despite all the alleged family love available to manly buffoons, men in the 1990s had had enough of getting beat up as incompetents by the mass media. By Father's Day 2001, groups like American Coalition of Fathers and Children, Fathers Are Parents Too, Men's Freedom Network, Full Time Dads, and the Fathers Rights Association of New York were marching against media gender bias, abuse of sexual harassment laws, and discrimination against men in the workplace, in the courts and, of course, in the news industry. Protests were held in states from California to New York. St. Louis, Missouri's David Usher got some ink in a *Time* magazine article titled "Hell Hath No Fury" in its October 7, 1996, issue. Usher went after "the sweet revenge" of the scorned women in the *First Wives Club* movie. "It's raw sexism," commented Usher about the Hollywood production. "We stereotype men and women, and they act out these stereotypes, and it goes straight into the divorce court."[7]

Usher said it was time for men to just say "no" to the gender bias that pervades U.S. media outlets. When men are constantly depicted as complete jerks, it makes them very easy to hate and easy to side against in any dispute or altercation. When women are constantly portrayed as victims of male violence and abuse, it makes them appear as justified in any vengeance that they wreak upon men. The situation is made all the worse when children are brought into the picture to act out against their fathers, according to Usher. He said the vast American populace was conditioned to view sexism from only one perspective—the perspective of feminists.

Just Say No: Men's Rights Manifesto

Men's rights and fathers' rights manifestos contrast sharply with those of other male groups such as the mythopoetic men, the Million Man March males, and the Promise Keepers. While these groups put together a slate of concerns that are inwardly-looking and tend to focus on how men should change themselves, the men's rights groups are laser focused on complaints against gender bias, child custody laws, and discrimination against men in the mass media, in the workplace, and in the courts. The indignation apparent in their checklist of grievances reflects the overt anger in two important movement books with titles that reflect a deep consternation with a system and a culture purportedly stacked against males.

Herb Goldberg's book, *The Hazards of Being Male: Surviving the Myth of Masculine Privilege*, offers a thesis about the falsehood and emptiness of "male privilege." He accomplishes this by piling up startling statistics from the 1970s era. The statistics, compiled during the time he wrote his treatise, involve many issues such as men's chronic health problems, men's vulnerability to severe workplace injuries, and men's presence in the criminal justice system. They are alarming statistics, and some have not changed appreciably in the decades since Goldberg wrote his book.

On the medical front, males make 25 percent fewer visits to doctors and dentists than females, and this is due in part to their conditioning to be stoic about their problems and even chronic conditions. They are four to five times more likely to die from emphysema and bronchitis than females. Death rates from cirrhosis of the liver and cardiovascular diseases are twice as high. Men die from pneumonia and influenza 64 percent more often and from hypertension almost 40 percent more often than women. Rates for lung cancer and esophageal cancer also are more than 40 percent higher.[8]

Suicides are astronomically higher among males than females. For divorced males the suicide rate is more than three times the rate of divorced females. Goldberg attributes this discrepancy to the higher trauma men endure in divorce situations, because of loss of children and the economic burden placed upon them. Also, there are the tragic effects of the male resistance to reaching out and asking for help with the emotional problems that plague them. Hence, according to Goldberg, they are more vulnerable to self-destructive behavior.

On the criminal-justice front, Goldberg notes men are six times more likely to be arrested on narcotics charges; thirteen times more likely to be arrested for drunkenness; nine times more likely to be arrested for offenses against children; fourteen times more likely to be arrested for weapons offenses. Goldberg also notes an inequity in how the criminal justice system treats men in felony cases compared to women, according to a 1967 UCLA analysis. The study revealed: "Women were found to receive much better treatment than male offenders"—the judges showing "something of a chivalrous attitude toward women,"—and that "a substantially higher percentage of women offenders receive sentences involving non-imprisonment than do their male counterparts."[9]

Warren Farrell's book, *The Myth of Male Power*, makes many of the same points as Goldberg's study. However, Farrell makes recommendations for organizing and taking political action at the conclusion of his take on the mythologies of male power in American society. He also does an effective job summing up the powerlessness of men. He notes that men are subject to overwhelming violence via the law (the draft); via custom and religion (circumcision); via violent sports and the attendant approval of attractive women (cheerleaders cheering men who bash heads and smash faces); via taxpayer money (high school wrestling, football, ROTC, the military); via our entertainment dollars (boxing, football, hockey, rodeos, car racing, war movies, and westerns).

Farrell even goes after parents and grandparents who subject young males to violence by offering their love and approval at the Thanksgiving high school football game at which high-performance sons commit to battering each other. Of course, there also is the approval of violence that comes from telling young men, who are the best at bashing heads against eleven other young males, that they have "scholarship potential." Goldberg does concede there is compassion for men in North America on one count: "North Americans do refrain from subjecting men to violence via bullfights—we feel it's cruel to the bull."[10]

Farrell cites the mythopoetic men's movement as a sign that men are tired of competing with each other and victimizing each other. He writes that it is healthy to see men giving themselves permission to talk with each other about a "socialization" system that injures and even kills them. Part of that social system, according to Goldberg, involves being deprived of the attention and sexual favors of women unless the man guarantees economic security in return. Another part involves status, praise, respect, and other "bribes" conferred on men in exchange for risking their lives to defend women, the family, and the country in conflict.

Angry men's rights books and manifestos have brought together a long list of grievances. The pronouncements counsel stalwart male defiance on a range of issues and make clear it is time to just say no:

- Say no to the chivalry trap: It's time for single men to stop opening doors and paying the tab for women to be entertained and lavishly fed when out on the town.

- Say no to the macho trap: Men die years earlier than women because they feel they must be providers, must be the risk takers, must be stoic when they're hurting inside.
- Say no to the war machine: Men do most of the dying in military service and get the most dangerous assignments: Any military draft must conscript women as well as men.
- Say no to workplace humiliation: Women have unfairly put men on the defensive over issues of sexual harassment and gender equality in the workplace.
- Say no to judicial unfairness: Men must protest gender bias in family courts that seem to always favor women on custody issues, visitation hours, and child support.
- Say no to media bias: Men must demand the media cover misandry and oppression of men, and end the constant focus on men behaving badly, mistreatment of women and general misogyny.
- Say no to the war on boys: Men must stand up for their sons, who face discrimination at school because of their natural tendency toward outspokenness, feistiness, and daring behavior. Boys are suffering from academic institutions that are making them the "second sex" with continual attempts to reform and feminize them.

Not all of these male grievances identified at the end of the last century have had staying power. An all-volunteer military in America has eliminated some of the major complaints about men facing the draft and having the overwhelming responsibility for defending the nation. Also, there have been changes in customs and mores about dating rituals because of the introduction of the internet, but also because of an increase in the economic power of women. One particular grievance that has had staying power involves the "attack on boys" and alleged attempts to reform their rough edges and to "feminize" them. Indeed, magazine covers and books today come with titles about "a war on boys" and societal contempt or disregard for boys.

A number of female intellectuals have denounced the situation for men and the treatment of boys, which has hurt them in grade school and high school and diminished their numbers in college and university programs. Christina Hoff Sommers wrote as much in *The War Against Boys: How Misguided Feminism Is Harming Our Young Men.* Sommers argues that boys are being pathologized, criminalized, and demoralized. She has high praise for another female taking up the cause of boys and men: "When the fashion of male-bashing reached a new high in the early nineties, Camille Paglia alone had the courage to remind the male-averse

Suzanne Venker, a former Fox news contributor, supports fathers' rights groups with her books on the mistreatment of men and boys by a "liberal, feminist culture." Her 2012 editorial "The War on Men" remains one of the most consulted op-eds in the network's history (courtesy *Webster-Kirkwood Times*).

feminists that masculinity is 'the most creative cultural force in history,'" Sommers declared.[11]

Author Suzanne Venker is another pro-male writer never afraid to ruffle a few feminist feathers. She has described feminism as a war on men and boys. She insists that feminists have destroyed the institution of marriage, which helps civilize young males and stabilize society. Without marriage, young men are still acting like they're 18 when they are in their 30s. They are without responsibility, purpose—rudderless. "Men just try to get along, but they have a lot to be angry about," according to Venker. "Feminist ideas have led to so many failed marriages, and then the divorce laws have all been written in favor of women—feminists have made sure of that."[12]

It should be pointed out that many of the anti-feminist writers who defend boys and men are not necessarily on the same page as men's rights activists like Goldberg and Farrell. The anti-feminist writers often defend the traditional male roles and champion a return to chivalry, unimpeded male competition, an admiration for male sports heroes and for male sacrifice in war time. In contrast, Goldberg and Farrell see many of the traditional roles of boys and men as a straitjacket and an impediment to males achieving true liberation and self-fulfillment. They see males' traditional roles as toxic to society and to men themselves.

Men's Rights: Action and Reaction

The books of Goldberg and Farrell have often been cited by angry fathers' rights protesters, like those demonstrating outside the cinemas showing female-centric movies like *9 to 5* and *First Wives Club.* Throughout the 1990s, fathers' rights groups committed to many actions that achieved visibility and media coverage. Among the various men's rights' activities:

- Picketing outside the homes of judges who, according to members of the National Congress of Fathers and Children, have an established record of "ruling to make fatherhood against the law, if the wife so decides."
- Lobbying in state capitols to oppose laws, supported by any number of women's groups, range from tougher child support enforcement measures to domestic violence legislation aimed at men.
- Demonstrating outside newspaper offices or TV stations over gender bias in their news stories. The National Congress of Fathers and Children expressed anger at a newspaper that was endorsing child support legislation in a statehouse without "any attempt to consider the father's perspective on the issue."
- Unfurling banners on a pedestrian bridge over an interstate highway that let drivers know that dads have family rights, too. These roadway actions were taken on Father's Days for maximum effect.
- Passing out handbills at supermarkets to protest the sale of women's magazines like Cosmopolitan in a "family shopping environment." Their handbills declared that Cosmopolitan "presented a terrorist training article about 'getting even' with your boyfriend, which taught women how to destroy his vehicle, get him fired from his job, and destroy his current relationship."

Men's rights writer Farrell cautioned men that it's not enough to just protest down at the local cinema or outside the home of a divorce court judge. In his *The Myth of Male Power*, Farrell said men need to do the hard work of getting involved in politics and formulating and writing legislation that could further their goals. He argues that men need to devise a counterpart to the Equal Rights Amendment (ERA) written for women. He also argues for affirmative action for men in professions or family constructs in which they are often underrepresented or face discrimination.

Farrell proposes an ERRA or Equal Rights and Responsibilities Amendment. The amendment would "outlaw male-only responsibility for draft registration; it would prevent men in the armed services from being required to enter combat unless women were required to enter combat; it would permit community property only in conjunction with community responsibility; it would give incentives to schools to educate females to be equally responsible for taking sexual initiatives and risking sexual rejection rather than lecturing only males on how not to do it wrong; it would replace discussions of sexual harassment in the workplace with discussions of how both sexes make sexual contact in the workplace."[13]

An ERRA would allow affirmative action programs for recruitment and training of the underrepresented sex in a profession, but not for the hiring of less qualified members of that sex, according to Farrell. An ERRA would deprive congressional districts of AFDC funding if judges assigned the children to women more than 60 percent of the time in cases of contested child custody; it would deprive universities of public moneys as long as there were significantly more women's studies courses than men's studies courses; it would deprive TV stations of federal licensing if the FCC found a consistent pattern of male bashing or consistent attention to women's issues and neglect of men's issues.[14]

Men's rights writer Farrell argues in *The Myth of Male Power* that women have worked hard to identify the "glass ceilings" that have held them back from achieving economic security and appropriate status in society. Men must emulate women and increase the awareness of the "glass cellars" which confine them and make them disposable. While women have benefited from the Equal Employment Opportunity Commission (EEOC), men need to be developing an Equal Life Opportunity Commission (ELOC) because, after all, men's issues are problems of life and death. An ELOC would address problems such as the high rates of male suicide, male incarceration, male homelessness, male disease, male executions, and the factors that lead to the earlier deaths of males—loneliness, performance pressures, financial responsibilities, divorce, discrimination, and more.

The men's rights and fathers' rights movements had many intellectual advocates at the turn of the century in America and were much more visible at that time. Nevertheless, they have never completely gone away.

These men's movements share some commonalities with mythopoetics, Promise Keepers, and the Million Man March activities. However, the men's rights and fathers' rights movements tend to be less abstract and closer to the day-to-day living challenges facing men. For this reason, they are likely to have a more active presence in a new century. They also have the potential to address the current "men's identity crises" and to identify obvious places where men in groups have "gone off the rails" in American life now.

Men's rights groups and fathers' rights groups can be difficult to classify ideologically. In some areas of American life, they appear to be embracing liberalism when they argue against the burdens of being the chief family breadwinners or the subjects of military drafts in wartime. On the more conservative side of the gender equation, these groups can be seen taking a more conservative stance when it comes to battles over workplace equity, sexual harassment lawsuits, affirmative action, and perceived bias in the courts and mass media. With the rise of more angry and extreme men's groups in the Age of Trump, the male agenda shifted decidedly rightward. And male militancy often replaced anything that might smack of plaintive whining on gender issues.

Section III

MANHOOD IN THE NEW CENTURY

10

Proud Boys

Standing Back, Standing By

He called himself a Western chauvinist. He wanted to remain anonymous at the big March, so he wore black clothing instead of the signature black-and-yellow polo shirt of the Proud Boys. He did insist on wearing his customary Make America Great Again red baseball cap. He was an initiate, what they called a first-degree Proud Boy. But on this day, November 14, 2020, he just might ascend up the ladder to become a third-degree member of the all-male organization.

This was the day of the Million MAGA March, not to be confused with the Million Man March of October 16, 1995, in Washington, D.C. On this November day, the marchers were 978,000 demonstrators short of the predicted one-million number that the "Stop the Steal" protesters had hoped for. The Proud Boys were at the March in solidarity with their president, who refused to concede the 2020 election, despite its being certified in all 50 states, and despite all the failed legal objections in numerous courts.

This participating "Western chauvinist" was inspired to join the Proud Boys March thanks to the announcement on the website proclaiming: "As We have done throughout Our Great History. We will Stand Together, as United Citizens, in the face of Evil, Censorship, Suppression, and Manipulation. We will defend Freedom against the forces of Fascism, Socialism, and Communism that are working to tear this country apart…. We Will Not be Stopped!"[1]

The Proud Boy MAGA marchers basked in a November sun to listen to their mentors. Alex Jones of Infowars told the rally about the Deep State, and evil forces bringing down President Trump and the country. "We declare independence from that communist Chinese agent Joe Biden and his demonic pedophile family," Jones shouted.[2] To signal his acknowledgment and support, Trump's presidential motorcade detoured to go past the rally on the way to deliver him to a Virginia golf course.

Later that November evening, the Proud Boys made good on their earlier

127

threats against the dread Antifa, a group that sometimes counter-protested Proud Boys. The Proud Boys waded into the counter-protesters, fists flew, blood flowed. Two police officers were injured, a stabbing took place, weapons were confiscated and there were 21 arrests. No doubt, a Proud Boy or two achieved the ultimate recognition of manhood on the evening of November 14, 2020. One or two could ascend to the fourth and final degree of Proud Boy membership just by getting bloodied in a "fight for the cause." Two months from now some of these Proud Boys would be indicted for an assault on Congress, but on this November day, it was time to march.

Most Americans were totally unaware of the right-wing extremist group, the Proud Boys, until the presidential election debates of September 2020 between Joe Biden and Donald Trump. The Proud Boys became famous when Trump gave the group a shout-out at the TV debate moderated by Chris Wallace. Wallace offered Trump a chance to condemn white supremacists like the Proud Boys. Instead, the defiant President enigmatically instructed them: "Stand back, and stand by."[3] The Proud Boys enjoyed the recognition of the President and the membership ranks grew exponentially. Their rallies and violence culminated in the 2021 attack on the Capitol when threats were made on the life of Vice President Mike Pence for his refusal to act to overturn the 2020 election results.

The Proud Boys constitute a kind of emerging men's group for a twenty-first-century America. Sometimes described as a street gang, Proud Boys argue that manhood is best achieved through physical violence against Muslims, Black Lives Matter, radical feminists, communist agitators, or immigrants. There are plenty of targets to go around. The Proud Boys are adamantly against race-mixing, gender-bending, gay rights, and political correctness. Unlike men's groups of the 20th century, there is very little self-scrutiny or soul-searching—or time for atonement. There is a fight-club ethic—a respect for using one's fists. Spilling blood is the total rite of passage and a means for achieving the highest level of organization membership.

The Proud Boys were founded at the time of the 2016 election between Hillary Clinton and Donald Trump by a digital communication maven named Gavin McInnes. Details on McInnes's early life are sketchy, but he was born to Scottish parents in England. The family migrated to Ontario, Canada, which is ironic given McInnes's antipathy for immigration. In Canada, he studied English at Carleton College and at Concordia University.[4] He was involved in publishing in Montreal and later moved to New York City. Canada has never seemed too eager to claim McInnes or the Proud Boys, which the country has branded as a terrorist organization—along with the Atomwaffen, The Base, Boko Haram, and the Russian Imperial Movement.

In the Williamsburg area of Brooklyn, where McInness settled, he was something of a hipster, but decidedly out of step with the lefty politics of a locale that he began to mock. He launched a successful online talk show, *TMGS* or *The Gavin McInnes Show*, a sort of shock-jock offering for the alt-right. For some listeners, he managed to make sexism, misogyny, homophobia, and hate for immigrants swank and cool. The show attracted a dedicated audience and some advertisers. That dedicated audience was undoubtedly a factor in McInnes's conviction that Proud Boys could become a thing.

A Proud Boys' mission statement or manifesto can be pieced together by excerpting from McInnes's various online pronouncements, although the group itself has not formulated any kind of formal white paper or strategic plan on its own. That kind of cerebral exercise would run contrary to the group's anti-establishment and anti-intellectual credentials. If the Proud Boys have engaged in any kind of serious analysis or theoretical deliberation, the Boys have conducted this kind of thing with plenty of alcohol and cocaine as mental lubricants. Proud Boys will admit to discussing right-wing conservative Patrick Buchanan's writings at length, particularly his 2002 book, *The Death of the West: How Dying Populations and Immigrant Invasions Imperil Our Country and Civilization*, and his 2006 book, *State of Emergency: The Third World Invasion and Conquest of America*.[5]

Most of the Proud Boys' discussions of Buchanan's *Death of the West* book have taken place in seedy bars. Buchanan maintains that white Western civilization is dying. Collapsing birth rates in Europe and America, coupled with population explosions in Africa, Asia and Latin America are causing terrible upheavals in the world order. Unchecked immigration is swamping every Western society. The *Death of the West* reveals how a civilization, culture, and moral order are passing away right in front of our eyes. A new world order sanctioned or accommodated by our naïve political leaders has terrifying implications for our liberties, our religious faith, and the preeminence of American power.

The Proud Boys have adopted the canon of Buchanan's *Death of the West* book and have decided to answer the call in a militant fashion. U.S. leaders in Washington, D.C., lack the political will to uphold the rule of law, so it is up to the Proud Boys to show up at the Mexican border, or at Black Lives Matter, or at Gay Pride demonstrations to restore some civilized order. Comparing the immigrant invasion of America from across the Mexican border to the barbarian invasions that ended the Roman Empire, Proud Boys want to smash what they see as a liberal devotion to diversity and political correctness. It must be smashed violently with a little blood, maybe a lot of blood, if necessary.

Although the Proud Boys have not fashioned a formal manifesto for

Patrick Buchanan is an intellectual hero of the Proud Boys, whose members champion his books on the decline of Western civilization. Conservative pundit Buchanan ran unsuccessfully for the 2000 Republican presidential nomination (courtesy *Webster-Kirkwood Times*).

their organization, they are perfectly willing to borrow from the xenophobic playbook and the cultural war rhetoric of Buchanan, who never really recovered from the drubbing he took from George W. Bush in the 1992 Republican primary. A Proud Boys manifesto also can be constructed by excerpting from the many episodes of McInnes's TMGS or his Facebook or blog posts. Other Proud Boys leaders, especially Enrique Tarrio and Kyle Chapman, also make observations that belong in any manifesto mix. Chapman left Proud Boys to establish FOAK (Fraternal Order of Alt-Knights), meant to be a sort of tactical arm for Proud Boys.

McInnes derived the name for his organization from the *Aladdin* movie song "Proud of Your Boy."[6] After an evening of bloodletting or insurrection, members will sometimes post on their Facebook sites:

"Proud of Your Boy." Proud Boys clearly have a set of beliefs and aren't shy about making declarations, as they:

- Proudly declare themselves as "Western chauvinists," who will never apologize for creating the modern world. For the Proud Boys, Western civilization needs no apology for its inherent superiority.
- Proudly declare their intolerance for all minorities that engage in what they see as victimhood and who blame others for their shortcomings and their inability to find a seat at Western civilization's table.
- Proudly declare their misogyny if, in fact, refusing to allow women to join their organization constitutes discrimination or contempt. The membership is pleased to allow women to join an auxiliary that can help service members' needs.
- Proudly swear off porn and "wanking addictions." Masturbation should be limited to once a month, so members are motivated to interact, to have sex, and to procreate with women.
- Proudly define and identify themselves in contrast to those whom they hate, mock, and fight. Proud Boys are not Marxists, socialists, communists, jihadists, Antifa, feminists, homosexuals, globalists, or multiculturalists.
- Proudly oppose all liberal policies, except the liberal use of alcohol. Alcohol promotes fraternal discussion of the decline of Western Civilization and the use of violence to restore Western dominance.
- Proud Boys believe in the cleansing power of violence and its use to identify real men among the group's membership. Members engage in vigilantism and self-deputize to support societal law and order. Violence solves everything in any Proud Boy manifesto.

Founder Gavin McInnes has expressed all these tenets of the Proud Boys at one time or another. On his New York–based show, on shows where he himself has been interviewed, McInness has enjoyed being outrageous like many right-wing operatives who get behind the microphone. However, it's the Proud Boy actions and events that really tell their story.

Events Tell Their Story

The many declarations of the Proud Boys are sophomoric at best, as if formulated in the bowels of a demented fraternity house on social probation somewhere on the Great Plains. Their prohibitions against the depravity of "wanking," and their self-professed admissions of chauvinism on behalf of Western civilization, would seem to border on silliness. However, there is nothing especially silly or amusing in regard to their catalog of invasions and disruptions of gatherings by those with whom they disagree—violently.

The Proud Boys' sad history of bloodying their philosophical opponents is felonious and pathological. They are especially obsessed with countering "Antifa." The Proud Boys understanding of history, as explained by their mentor Patrick Buchanan, is far more in-depth than any knowledge that they have of anti-fascism and a group that was born out of resistance to Mussolini and Hitler. Antifa has its roots in Europe during the 1920s and 1930s. Like so many on the right, their much-hated Antifa is synonymous with communists, socialists, fascists, pederasts, progressives, leftists and Democrats in the mind of the Proud Boys. When the news media report the enmity of Proud Boys and other alt-right groups for Antifa, reporters seldom ask any questions on how anti-fascists can also actually be fascists, or communists, or even progressives.

Nevertheless, with Proud Boys, it's all about the action, the hooliganism, the bloodied lips and split noses and broken appendages. The great philosophical underpinnings of the Proud Boys can be left to such seminal thinkers as Patrick Buchanan, or Steve Bannon, or Stephen Miller, or to Roger Stone, who was once Richard M. Nixon's brain trust and who became Donald J. Trump's brain, particularly on immigration and on safeguarding the republic. Among some of the many Proud Boy bloody interventions:

Berkeley Protests. In the spring of 2017, "March for Trump" rallies seemed to be popping up every other week in Berkeley, the "home of free speech." The Trump rallies were soon an invitation to youthful political brawling. Proud Boys joined Oath Keepers to take on the feminists, progressives, anti-fascists, and local campus liberals. Dueling rallies devolved into a large mob of 1,500 people fighting all over the place. Arrests followed, but the police were outnumbered. Proud Boys claimed Berkeley for the alt-right. That was not going to happen, though, and the battling continued throughout 2017.

Unite the Right. In early August of 2017, the university town of Charlottesville, Virginia, braced for the worst after groups of neo–Confederates, Klansmen, white nationalists, and Proud Boys descended on the town to stand up for Confederate iconography. The so-called Unite the Right Rally opposed the plans for removal of the Statue of General Robert E. Lee from former Lee Park. Americans watched TV news accounts in horror as white supremacists marched, demonstrations turned violent, and serious injuries mounted. On the afternoon of August 12, a self-identified white supremacist rammed his car into a crowd of opponents of the right, killing Heather Heyer and injuring 35 people.

President Trump earned plaudits from former Ku Klux Klan Grand Wizard David Duke after Trump said that there were "very fine people on both sides" of the Charlottesville mayhem. Proud Boys took comfort from Trump's assertion, although they tried to cover their tracks after the bloody violence. "But the fact remains that these rallies were organized by a second degree member of the Proud Boys named Jason Kessler," wrote Andy Campbell in his book *We Are Proud Boys*. "He was a white supremacist author and former UVA student who spent much of his time writing and whining about 'white genocide,' Islam, and what he called 'disproportionate Jewish influence.'"[7]

Portland Violence. Also in August of 2017, Portland Mayor Ted Wheeler urged demonstrators "to choose love" at a virtual press conference before people were assembling at the downtown waterfront. His message seemed ironic and hopeless as Proud Boys were seen carrying batons, chemical spray, and baseball bats. One man carried a pickaxe handle emblazoned with the Proud Boys insignia. The right-wing militants and the anti-fascists faced off and soon bullets were flying, vehicles were vandalized, and hundreds clashed.

Reporter Robert Evans of *Rolling Stone* magazine interviewed an Antifa fighter who said the street fighting mirrored that of the fights between the communists and Nazis in the Weimar Republic before the rise of Adolf Hitler. Evans wrote: "And it is here that Portland may once again be ahead of the nation. August 22, 2021, marked Portland's first exchange of gunfire between right-wing and left-wing activists. It will not be the last one. And if it happens here, it will happen elsewhere in the country soon. Because what happens in Portland never stays in Portland."[8]

NYC GOP. In 2018, the Proud Boys made an attempt at political legitimacy when leader Gavin McInnes was invited to New York City's Metropolitan Republican Club to give a speech. The Proud Boys already were being given jobs providing security for several Republican heavyweights. Ann Coulter, who wrote a book, *In Trump We Trust: E. Pluribus Awesome!*, referred to the Proud Boys as brawny brutes who could be spread among hostile audiences to tamp things down in case of pandemonium.[9]

MacInnes embarrassed some Republicans at the New York City event with his expletive laced rant against political correctness and his brandishing a Samurai sword. Nevertheless, GOP bigwig Roger Stone continued to thank Proud Boys for their service for right-wing politicians and declared himself to also be a "Western chauvinist." The Proud Boys waited outside the Metropolitan Republican Club for things to get dark. Following the dictum of their "Late Night, Alt-Right" Moon Man insignia, the group was ready to pounce and pummel Antifa and liberal demonstrators when night fell.

Immediately after the GOP event, Proud Boys' fists began to swing at the protesters outside the venue. Following McInnes's advice to the GOP that it was okay to accept some bigotry, the Proud Boys fighters outside the Republican happening let loose with homophobic slurs as they beat some demonstrators to a bloody pulp. Police arrested them and charged them with riot and assault. The adverse publicity from the violence resulted in several social media platforms removing Proud Boys from their Internet sites, which actually served the group's interests for recruitment and organizing more rallies.

Counter Terrorism Rallies. In 2019, Proud Boys organized a series of large rallies and declared that they were designed to end domestic terrorism by leftist agitators. Organizers included Proud Boys chairman Enrique

As a militant alt-right group, the Proud Boys enjoy sporting extremist regalia, shoulder patches, and fatigues. The "Late Night, Alt-Right" Moon Man insignia reflects the group's love for late-night, bloody fights with Antifa and liberals (photograph by the author).

Tarrio and former *Infowars* lieutenant Joe Biggs. The events carried into 2020 with the usual amounts of violence and bloodletting as part of the Proud Boys effort to counter "socialist terrorism" in America. On the far-right website *Gateway Pundit,* based in St. Louis, Tarrio promised to come back month after month in Portland until Mayor Wheeler freed his city from the grip of Antifa.[10]

Trump Campaign Events. In 2020, the Trump presidential campaign followed the advice of right-wing writer Ann Coulter and welcomed Proud Boys to stifle any dissenting voices at campaign rallies. Proud Boys also threatened the news media on several occasions, singling out journalists whom Trump had branded as the "Enemies of the People." Some of the violent incidents went public as cable television outlets covered the rallies continuously. Trump was witnessed advising Coulter's "brawny brutes" to just punch out demonstrators because that was "a beautiful thing."

Million MAGA March. In 2020, the November 14 march in Washington, D.C., protested the outcome of the presidential contest in favor of Joseph Biden. This proved to be a dry run for storming the Capitol in early January. Proud Boys united with several thousand Trump supporters acting in defiance of the election results and with calls for fraudulent votes to be thrown out. White nationalist Nick Fuentes was a keynote speaker, along with the usual lineup of right-wing legislators and bloggers. When the fighting began, journalists were singled out for smackdowns by the Proud Boys. Several were injured seriously resulting in charges. Suspected Antifa members also were severely beaten.

Proud Boys wore garb declaring "Pinochet Did Nothing Wrong!" That was one of many Proud Boys' war cries referencing the South American military junta leader, who in 1973 overthrew a democratically-elected government in Chile. Pinochet dispatched his leftist critics in Chile with arrests, prison, torture, and free flights over the ocean where they were thrown out of airplanes. Proud Boys approved. Proud Boys like Joe Biggs posted blog declarations announcing a new civil war, the ultimate triumph of Trump forces, and the end of the liberal media: "…they keep spewing lies to their base, knowing that when the race is called for Trump, there will be mass chaos.… Buy ammo, clean your guns, get storable food and water. Be prepared!"[11]

Insurrection: Oath Keepers Convictions

January 6, 2021, was the day many Trump supporters expected the election to be nullified thanks to Vice President Mike Pence's refusal to certify the electoral votes in Congress. Many in the 2021 mob were aware of Trump's call for Pence to block the count in Congress and to pave the way for alternate slates of state electors to be installed so that the race could be called for Trump. When Pence did not cooperate with this scheme, because he insisted he had no such authority, Trump supporters called for Mike Pence to be hanged. A noose and gallows were put together in the midst of frenzied rioters.

President Trump expressed disappointment with Pence to the crowd on January 6. He made an appeal to his angry followers with the exhortation: "We won in a landslide. This was a landslide. They said it's not American to challenge the election. This the most corrupt election in the history, maybe of the world.... And we fight. We fight like hell. And if you don't fight like hell, you're not going to have a country anymore.... So we're going to, we're going to walk down Pennsylvania Avenue. I love Pennsylvania Avenue. And we're going to the Capitol...."[12]

Proud Boys, Oath Keepers, Three Percenters, members of Patriot Prayer, Patriot Front, the Fraternal Order of Alt-Knights, and other right-wing groups begin their march to the Capitol, while Trump retreated to the White House to watch what might unfold on television. The Proud Boys stood together and marched with a large throng of Trump followers behind them. When they reached the barricaded checkpoints, they pushed them apart and rushed past police. They sprayed bear mace on officers who tried to stop or slow them down. They turned American Flag poles into spears aimed at law enforcement. Protesters on the east side of the Capitol plaza, led by Proud Boys, overran the police. Protesters on the west side of the plaza were led by Proud Boy Dominic Pezzola, who seized a police shield in the chaos.[13]

Pezzola hammered a window of the congressional building with the police shield until the glass finally shattered. This may have been the first breech which allowed the insurrectionists to pour into the building. Jacob Chansley, tagged as the QAnon Shaman, was one of the first 100 rioters to enter the building. He became the face of the January 6 attack because of his painted face, his bare chest and sweat pants, and his fur headdress with horns. This is unfortunate because the criminal trespass of the Capitol was deadly, costly, traitorous, and a felonious, but the focus on Chansley made it all appear as some kind of clownish Halloween prank that simply went a little wrong.

Other activities by the invaders, which allowed the right-wing media to dismiss January 6 as mere pranking, included a video of their chanting, "Nancy, Nancy, Nancy," outside of the House Speaker's office; or footage of a rioter sitting at her desk and leaving notes calling her a "bitch"; or coverage of Nancy Pelosi expressing disgust at the amount of human feces smeared inside the Capitol by defecating intruders; or rioters taking selfies of themselves, as if in amazement over the accomplishment of their break-in. QAnon Shaman Chansley took selfies on the Senate floor and sitting in the chamber seat Mike Pence had occupied an hour earlier. Chansley scrawled out a note condemning Pence: "It's Only a Matter of Time. Justice Is Coming!"[14]

According to an FBI affidavit, "a government informant said that members of the far-right militant group the Proud Boys told him they would have killed Pence 'if given the chance.' The rioters on January 6 almost had that chance, coming within forty feet of the Vice President as he fled to safety."[15]

President Trump has apparently resisted any temptation to apologize to Mike Pence for the threats made on his life by his followers on January 6. During the Insurrection, he could not be persuaded to send out a message on social media to Proud Boys or Oath Keepers asking them to stand down and stop their menacing words aimed at Pence—instead he told his staffers that his vice president probably had it coming regarding the physical threats made against him.

After police reinforcements cleared the Capitol and the carnage inside and on the grounds came to an end, Trump did offer his supporters another message: "I know your pain, I know you're hurt. We had an election that was stolen from us. It was a landslide election and everyone knows it. Especially the other side. But you have to go home now. We have to have peace."[16]

Within days of Trump telling the Insurrectionists that he loved them, and that they should go back to their homes, federal authorities began knocking on doors at the residences of the Proud Boys in order to serve warrants. In the initial identification of rioters who were sought out for committing crimes on January 6, almost 80 turned out to have links to the Proud Boys. The group coming in a close second as criminal suspects were the Oath Keepers, followed by the Three Percenters.[17] Proud Boys leaders went to trial in 2023 on seditious conspiracy charges. Proud Boys founder Gavin McInnis avoided legal trouble, as he has separated himself from the group's violent activities, disavowed plans for January 6, and advised Proud Group members not to go to Washington, D.C.

Securing the conviction of Enrique Tarrio in July 2023 was a major victory for the Justice Department, in part because Tarrio himself was not present for the riot at the Capitol. Tarrio was charged with directing the attack of the Proud Boys from a remote location. Three other Proud Boys leaders convicted of seditious conspiracy are Joseph Biggs, Ethan Nordean, and Zachary Rehl. The Proud Boys brawler wielding a police shield to smash in a Capitol building window, Dominic Pezzola, was cleared of the sedition charge, but was convicted on other serious charges.

Although the convictions and stiff prison sentences may lead some to think the Proud Boys have been dealt a mortal blow, there are plenty of local chapters with new leaders ready to step up. Also, jailed leaders will be released at some point or even pardoned if a sympathetic, right-wing GOP president takes charge of the nation later this decade.[18] An Associated Press story in July 2023 revealed that Proud Boys chapters had moved on from "Stop the Steal" rhetoric to other issues near and dear to most men in the right-wing fold.

Proud Boys have been spotted disrupting school board meetings over issues such as whether critical race theory or slavery is being taught in school curriculums. In some cases, their harassment and threats have driven school administrators, board members, and teachers to quit education all together. Proud Boys also have been seen at anti-abortion rallies to act as "security" for evangelical protesters. They also have shown up at other demonstrations for gun reform and engaged in "open carry" in states where lax gun laws give a nod to their threatening behavior.[19]

Research into other Proud Boy events by *Vice News* reveals more than 100 uniformed appearances by the group in 73 cities and 24 states in 2021. The Proud Boys have hardly been reined in, despite some setbacks in court proceedings over the Insurrection violence. In his study *We Are Proud Boys*, Andy Campbell argues that the activities documented by *Vice News* and others shows the men of the Proud Boys are already fighting on for another day. They may be the most successful political extremist group in the digital age in America.

"The urgent truth is that we're looking at a snowballing extremism crisis in America, growing and changing so rapidly that our institutions are having a hard time keeping up," said Campbell. "The Proud Boys, now veterans and teachers in the extremist space, have figured out how to game the few systems in place that would thwart them—police, media, and top-tier politicians—giving them more power and influence than any of their far-right peers in America."[20]

Oath Keepers

"Not on our watch!"

He called himself a peacekeeper, a trained and armed volunteer to protect lives and property at any location where regular law enforcement was
deemed incapable of quelling civil unrest. Ferguson, Missouri, was considered such a place. St. Louis and national news media knew him only as John,
but they were happy to get some quotes from him for their broadcast reports.
John was one of four heavily-armed white men patrolling the dark streets of
riot-torn Ferguson in August 2015, on the one-year anniversary of the death
of Michael Brown.

The unrest, which became known as the "Ferguson Uprising," began on
August 10, 2014. That was the day after the fatal shooting of Michael Brown
by Ferguson Police Officer Darren Wilson. As the details of the shooting
emerged, police established curfews and deployed riot squads. Along with
peaceful protests, there was a significant amount of violence and looting in
the vicinity of the site of the shooting, as well as across Ferguson. Protesters
said they were angry because of the killing of an unarmed shoplifting suspect, and because of a pattern of overzealous policing and discriminatory
city policies.

On this anniversary of the Brown shooting and the Ferguson riots,
two groups of suspected looters began firing at each other during a memo-
rial demonstration, and more violence followed. John and his three friends
arrived carrying military-style rifles and sidearms. They said they were part
of a group known as Oath Keepers. John insisted his organization was a
well-intentioned association of current and former U.S. soldiers, police, and
first responders ready to protect businesses and law-abiding citizens from
mayhem.

"We're just keeping an eye on activities down here," John told two
MSNBC reporters. He and his three other unofficial militia men moved
among a crowd of demonstrators as if they were negotiating the worst of a
war zone. "We're just keeping an eye on them, making sure they stay safe."[1]

The crowd wasn't having it. They yelled out obscenities at their would-be protectors. They asked what would happen if they, as Black people, came into a white community and began strutting around with automatic weapons. They called it just another manifestation of white privilege, because in Missouri there is one rule for white gun owners and another for Black gun owners. And if you're Black, you can be shot and killed with impunity, even if you're not carrying a weapon, crowd members argued.[2]

Local police said the Oath Keepers were not helping matters and were not welcome in Ferguson. They had no authorization by law enforcement. Their actions simply increased distrust and anger in a wounded community. St. Louis County Police Chief Jon Belmar said that the Oath Keepers' presence was both "unnecessary and inflammatory."[3]

Larry Kirk, an Oath Keepers' member and a police chief in rural Old Monroe, Missouri, told reporters that even if people were uncomfortable with the heavily-armed members of his group in Ferguson, they should know that the Oath Keepers' presence was all about keeping the peace. They were protecting people with their Second Amendment right to carry heavy weapons openly, as defined and guaranteed by the conservative lawmakers in the Missouri statehouse.

Kirk told the news media: "Whether we are comfortable with somebody exercising their right, we still have to be able to have them exercise that right so we don't lose it."[4]

Residents of eastern Missouri learned a lot about the Oath Keepers due to their militia activities in the distressed St. Louis suburb of Ferguson in 2014 and 2015. Later, in 2018, residents of southern New Mexico learned a lot about the Oath Keepers due to a "call to action" for members to engage in paramilitary activities to stop an invasion of immigrants into America. In 2020, residents of Minneapolis learned a lot about the Oath Keepers due to "interventions" in Black Lives Matter protests after the police killing of George Floyd. The entire nation learned a lot about the Oath Keepers in the aftermath of the January 6 insurrection in Washington, D.C. That's when members were involved in storming the Capitol and taking over U.S. Congressional offices.

The Oath Keepers organization was officially started in Lexington, Massachusetts, in 2009 with a rally opposing the election of Barack Obama as America's first Black president. Members put the emphasis on the new president's middle name "Hussein" and contended that Obama was an undocumented Kenyan and a Muslim and not qualified to be U.S. President.

The non-profit group was founded by Yale Law School graduate and former U.S. Army paratrooper Elmer "Stewart" Rhodes. The group denied charges of extremism and a propensity for violence, but members were openly racist, misogynist, and anti–Islamic. Oath Keepers seemed the quintessential extremist men's group for a new century in America. Its members are encouraged to take up arms, if necessary, to defend fundamental rights against an increasingly oppressive government.

Members have been instructed to disobey any orders by elected politicians, police, or military officials that, in their view, violate constitutional guarantees. Fully two-thirds of Oath Keepers are ex-military or law enforcement, and 10 percent are active duty military or law enforcement. Oath Keepers often show up at their border actions, or their "peacekeeping" activities, or at demonstrations, in their military fatigues. Credible resources put the official membership of Oath Keepers at 5,000, while the group's own rosters suggest the membership may be as high as 35,000 or more.[5]

Oath Keepers embrace a number of conspiracy theories to explain the deadly outcomes of confrontations with the government at Ruby Ridge and Waco. They believe an effete government and an intelligence "deep state" have secretly planned to impose martial law, seize all Americans' guns, force resisters into re-education camps, and install a one-world totalitarian "New World Order"—with a heavy assist from the United Nations. It's obvious why most U.S. Senators would never declare solidarity with such a subversive group. However, some congressmen representing extremely red districts in the U.S. House have had no problem echoing the wild claims and calls to action of the Oath Keepers. These legislators give verbal "aid and comfort" to conspiracy theorists.

FBI investigations have found the Oath Keepers to be a "paramilitary organization" that is large, but loosely organized as a militia. The armed citizens are convinced the federal government has been overtaken by a shadowy conspiracy of socialist totalitarians. The Southern Poverty Law Center has described the group in similar fashion as extremist and conspiratorial, but prefers to let top Oath Keepers' leaders, like Stewart Rhodes, speak for themselves. Among Rhodes' alarming pronouncements:

- "It is the height of Orwellian perversion of language and logic to say that disarming you of the most effective arms for combat that you still have is somehow not really disarming you, because you still have hunting rifles and shotguns. And you can bet that if you let them take away your military semi-autos, next on their list will be bolt action rifles, which they will call 'sniper rifles' (and By God, that is certainly what they are good for!)."[6]
- "This is a military invasion by the cartels and a political coup by the domestic Marxist controlled left, which sees open borders and mass-illegal invasion as their ticket to permanent illegitimate

political power. This is a matter of national security and also a matter of national survival. This invasion/coup must be stopped, and with the ongoing failure of the RINO dominated Republicans to finance a wall, stopping it will now require full scale military action, which we strongly encourage President Trump to take under his authority as Commander in Chief."[7]

- "Frankly, we're concerned about a Benghazi-style attack. That's why Oath Keepers will be posted outside of D.C. We've got some of our best men working on the plan right now for where we're going to be. But we'll make sure that we're within range because I don't trust the Pentagon, I don't trust the brass, I don't trust even the Secretary of Defense to stand behind the President [Trump] and don't be surprised if you don't get the same kind of standdown order you saw with Benghazi."[8]

- "You must act NOW as a wartime President, pursuant to your oath to defend the Constitution, which is very similar to the oath all of us veterans swore. We are already in a fight. It's better to wage it with you as Commander-in-Chief than to have you comply with a fraudulent election, leave office, and leave the White House in the hands of illegitimate usurpers and Chinese puppets. Please don't do it. Do NOT concede, and do NOT wait until January 20, 2021. Strike now."[9]

- "Well, I think what we have to realize is that, you know, Trump actually failed. … He had a duty and responsibility to step up. But he failed to do that and he allowed a ChiCom puppet into the White House and I think we now need to just declare that to be illegitimate and refuse to comply with anything that comes out of his mouth, anything he signs, anything passed as so-called legislation. Label it 'pretend legislation' like the Founding Fathers did."[10]

The militia groups that began emerging in the United States in the 1970s and 1980s were not as overtly political or belligerent as the Oath Keepers of a new century. The men in the earlier militia groups tended to be "weekend warriors" who enjoyed getting together for drill practice and to talk about weapons and gun rights. With a few terrible exceptions, they did not engage in violent activities, shrilly denounce porous U.S. borders, or engage in conspiratorial attacks on ChiCom puppets in the White House.

Rhodes' inflammatory quotes speak for themselves. Although the Oath Keepers have not devised an organizational manifesto of principles, they do abide by a so-called, "Declaration of Orders We Will Not Obey."[11] Oath Keepers always insist that they are a non-partisan association of

Preparing for real combat are two members of a Midwest militia group known as the 1st Missouri Volunteers. Militias contend they are sanctioned by the Second Amendment. Critics of such militias say they're too heavily armed, too unregulated, and too prone to political extremism (courtesy *Webster-Kirk-wood Times*).

currently serving military, reserves, National Guard, peace officers, fire-fighters, and veterans.

All have sworn an oath to support and defend the U.S. Constitution against all enemies, foreign and domestic. With that pledge in mind, the Oath Keepers will not follow orders, especially those given by liberal administrations. They will defy U.S. leaders whom they feel are part of a Deep State that has perverted constitutional norms.

Oath Keepers have enunciated a declaration of 10 orders not to be obeyed because they believe them to be patently unconstitutional or unlawful—or because they are immoral infringements upon the natural rights of the people. In fact, Oath Keepers maintain such orders constitute acts of war against the American people, and as such, they are acts of treason by governmental authorities. Oath Keepers declare that they will defend the republic in such cases, but not make war against the American people. And so, they affirm and declare the following:

- Oath Keepers will not obey any order to disarm the American people, assist or support any such attempt to disarm the people by other government entities, either state or federal. Oath Keepers stand by the Second Amendment to preserve the power of the people to have effective final recourse to take up arms in the face of tyranny. Accordingly, Oath Keepers oppose any and all infringements on the right of the people to keep and bear arms, particularly a renewal of the "assault-weapons" ban or attempts to register and track gun owners.
- Oath Keepers will not obey any order to conduct warrantless searches of the American people, their homes, vehicles, papers, or effects, such as house-to house searches for weapons or persons. Oath Keepers believe that in the future, "we expect that sweeping warrantless searches of homes and vehicles, under some pretext, will be the means used to attempt to disarm the people."
- Oath Keepers will not obey any order to detain American citizens as "unlawful enemy combatants" or to subject them to trial by military tribunal. The only constitutional form of trial for an American, who is not serving in the military, and who is accused of making war on his own nation, is a trial before a civilian jury, not a tribunal. Any government attempt to apply the laws of war to American civilians, such as against domestic "militia" groups the government brands "domestic terrorists," is an act of treason.
- Oath Keepers will not obey orders to impose martial law or a "state of emergency" on a state, or to enter with force into a state, without the express consent and invitation of that state's legislature and

governor. The power to impose martial law—the absolute rule over the people by a military officer with his will alone being law—is nowhere enumerated in the Constitution. The imposition of martial law by the national government over a state and its people, treating them as an occupied enemy nation, is an act of war and treason.

- Oath Keepers will not obey orders to invade and subjugate any state that asserts its sovereignty and declares the national government to be in violation of the compact by which that state entered the Union. In response to the obscene growth of federal power and to the absurdly totalitarian claimed powers of the Executive, upwards of 20 states are considering, have considered, or have passed courageous resolutions affirming state's rights and sovereignty.
- Oath Keepers will not obey any order to blockade American cities, thus turning them into giant concentration camps. One of the causes of the American Revolution was the blockade of Boston, and the occupying of that city by the British military, under martial law. Such tactics were repeated by the Nazis in the Warsaw Ghetto, and by the Imperial Japanese in Nanking, turning entire cities into death camps. Any such order to disarm and confine the people of an American city will be an act of treason.
- Oath Keepers will not obey any order to force American citizens into any form of detention camps under any pretext. Such vile orders to forcibly intern Americans without charges or trial would be an act of war against the American people, and thus an act of treason, regardless of the pretext used. Oath Keepers will not commit treason, nor will we facilitate or support it—"Not on Our Watch!"
- Oath Keepers will not obey orders to assist or support the use of any foreign troops on U.S. soil against the American people to "keep the peace" or to "maintain control" during any emergency, or under any other pretext. Oath Keepers will consider such use of foreign troops against Americans to be an invasion and an act of war. Oath Keepers will oppose such troops as enemies of the people and we will treat all who request, invite, and aid those foreign troops as the traitors they are.
- Oath Keepers will not obey any orders to confiscate the property of the American people, including food and other essential supplies, under any emergency pretext whatsoever. Deprivation of food has long been a weapon of war and oppression, with millions intentionally starved to death by fascist and communist

governments in the 20th Century. Accordingly, Oath Keepers will not obey orders to confiscate food and other essential supplies from the people, and we will consider all those who issue or carry out such orders to be the enemies of the people.

• Oath Keepers will not obey any orders which infringe on the right of the people to free speech, to peaceably assemble, and to petition their government for a redress of grievances. Oath Keepers will not obey or support any orders to suppress or violate the right of the people to speak, associate, worship, assemble, communicate, or petition government for the redress of grievances.

According to Oath Keepers, the above list is not exhaustive but members consider their bullet points to be "clear tripwires." They form a "line in the sand" involving government orders that will not be obeyed. Oath Keepers say they will know when the time for another American Revolution is nigh. Apparently, that time was nigh with the January 6, 2001, insurrection in Washington, D.C. Oath Keepers leader Rhodes provides reassurance that when a revolution comes, his members will not fire upon fellow Americans who resist government violations of their God-given rights. Oath Keepers will even join them in the battle against all those who desire to enslave them.

The rhetoric of the Oath Keepers is overheated and apocalyptic, but it appeals to a certain breed of men who desperately seek a mission and dedication to a cause beyond themselves. These are men who also seek manly camaraderie and loyalty to "principles." The Oath Keepers' "Declaration of Orders We Will Not Obey" provides these principles, which can in no way be compromised. In the conclusion to the declaration, a solemn promise and mutual aid agreement is articulated: "And for the support of this Declaration, with a firm reliance on the protection of Divine Providence, we mutually affirm our oath and pledge to each other our Lives, our Fortunes, and our sacred Honor."

Events Tell Their Story

Declarations, promises, and pledges provide the philosophic glue that can serve to hold a movement together on a cerebral level. However, the true test of a movement is revealed by the physical actions that declarations, promises, and pledges inspire. In the case of the Oath Keepers, there are plenty of incidents that tell the story of the organization in the time since it was officially started in the year 2009 in Lexington, Massachusetts. Leader Rhodes insisted that Lexington was the appropriate birthplace for the group with its history in the War of Independence. Even so, most of the Oath Keepers' early activities did not occur in that birthplace of America, but rather in Western outposts—home to militias, white supremacy groups, and the posse comitatus.

Among some of the Oath Keepers many activities:

Bundy Ranch. In 2014, Rhodes and his fellow Oath Keepers traveled to Cliven Bundy's Nevada ranch. They were responding to a request Bundy had made asking militias to join him in facing off with federal officials. Authorities were seeking to confiscate his cattle because Bundy had neglected to pay federal grazing fees for a score of years. The federal authorities finally stood down because of armed threats from Bundy's defenders and sensational national television news coverage. The Oath Keepers men could not take credit for any "win" by Bundy and his allies because they evacuated the scene upon hearing reports that President Obama was allegedly going to swarm the Bundy ranch with armed drones.[12] That supposed air attack never happened.

Sugar Pine Mine. In 2015, Oath Keepers showed up at several controversial actions in the Pacific Northwest that involved the federal Bureau of Land Management and local mining operations. Federal authorities ordered the mines shut down because of disputes over miners' claims. Oath Keepers and other armed volunteers organized "security operations" to surround and protect the mines from federal intervention. In the end, the federal authorities allowed operations to continue until the claims were resolved in court. As in the Bundy ranch case, the defenders claimed victory over the federal authorities, and this time the Oath Keepers could claim a piece of the action.

One reason the Oath Keepers leaders went to isolated areas of Nevada, Idaho, and Oregon to engage in actions against federal authorities is because these locales represent fertile recruitment grounds. The Oath Keepers organization could be a magnet for white supremacists, anti-government conspiracy theorists, and members of the Posse Comitatus. The Posse Comitatus started in the 1960s as a rural anti-tax movement but also found alliance with extreme, right-wing Christian Identity groups. Federal authorities often are vastly outnumbered at confrontation sites.[13]

Gay Marriage Fight. In 2015, Kim Davis garnered international media attention as county clerk for Rowan County, Kentucky, when she refused to issue marriage licenses to same-sex couples. She subsequently refused to comply with a federal court order to issue licenses. Oath Keepers announced that members would travel to Kentucky to protect Davis from federal contempt-of-court citations and possible arrest. Leaders denounced local authorities for not protecting Davis. Although some Oath

Keepers made a presence, Davis herself declined their offer to provide a security detail.

Voter Protection Acts. In 2016, Oath Keepers leader Rhodes announced "Operation Sabot 2016" that would prevent Hillary Clinton and Democrats from stealing the presidential election from Donald Trump. Rhodes encouraged members to dress "to NOT impress"—no military garb or weapons—and to then do surveillance at polling places. He told the *Huffington Post* that their monitoring operation was inspired by an undercover video published by James O'Keefe's Project Veritas. A video put out by the organization featured a supposed Democratic operative talking theoretically about how a voter fraud operation could work. That video was a "smoking gun," Rhodes said.[14]

Stop Sharia Law. In 2017, Oath Keepers participated in "March Against Sharia" rallies and also organized actions against immigrants. The rallies against sharia were predicated on paranoid suspicions that Muslims hope to replace the American legal system with their own Islamic sharia law.

The rallies against an "invasion of illegals" were meant to give moral support to Americans living along the southern border. Oath Keepers volunteered to go to the border to protect ranch families, and they demanded that Trump declare a national emergency to hasten the building of a border wall.

Stop Health Safety Mandates. In 2020, during the pandemic and the initiation of public health safety measures, Oath Keepers responded by offering to protect and to advocate for individuals who defied mask mandates, social distancing requirements, and later vaccination requirements. Oath Keepers received support from politicians who joined them in opposing such mandates. In May of 2020, leader Rhodes spoke at a rally in Palestine, Texas, to trash pandemic safety mandates, and he followed with similar event in Austin, Texas.

Oath Keepers responded to requests for protection by owners of salons, fitness centers, restaurants, and more. The owners asked for support against government authorities who might want to shut them down for defying mandates. Oath Keepers went into tactical militia mode at a number of business locations. Oath Keepers invariably claimed that authorities "backed off" from any owner arrests or business shutdowns because of their actions to defend people from dictatorial mandates.

Million MAGA March. In 2020, after the results of the 2020 election were announced, Rhodes urged Trump to use the Insurrection Act to hold onto his position of power and to defy the election outcome. His group argued the election was stolen from Trump and rallied in several "Stop the Steal" events. On November 14, Oath Keepers attended the Million MAGA

The tactical militia patch is a favorite of alt-right men's groups like the Oath Keepers. It's consistent with the "III Percenters" creed that it took only 3 percent of colonists to oust the British and that only 3 percent of U.S. citizens are needed for an American revolution now (photograph by the author).

March in Washington, D.C. They were goaded by U.S. House members Marjorie Taylor Greene, a Republican from Georgia, and Louie Gohmert, a Republican from Texas, to not give up the fight against the stolen election. More speeches in downtown Washington followed, with former deputy assistant to the president, Sebastian Gorka, asking the assembled to "never let them steal our republic."[15]

Alex Jones of *Infowars* gave the most inflammatory speech by insisting that "the pedophile globalists and their attempted election steal and the Clinton blackmail rings have only summoned the sleeping giant that is America." He likened the day to July 4, 1776, and a Second American Revolution. When night fell on November 14, bloody confrontations began. Most of the conflict was between Trump supporters and counter protesters. Ron Schaffer, a member of the Oath Keepers from Indiana who attended the Million MAGA March event, was later indicted for his role in the January 6 assault on the U.S. Capitol.

Schaffer spoke to the news media that Saturday in November: "A group of thugs and criminals hijacked this country a long time ago. And now they're making their big move, and it's not gonna' happen," he said. "They're messing with the wrong people here, trust me on that.… We're not going to merge into some globalist, communist system, it will not happen. There will be a lot of bloodshed if it comes down to that, trust me.…

If somebody wants to bring violence, I think there's a lot of us here that are ready for it … they're pushing us to a point where we have no choice."[16]

Insurrection: Oath Keeper Convictions

The January 6, 2021, Insurrection that followed just weeks after the Million MAGA March might be described as the ultimate exhibition of toxic masculinity. Called to action by President Trump, Schaffer exhorted his supporters at the National Mall to oppose the 2020 election "stolen by radical-left Democrats." The mob then sought to keep Trump in power by storming the U.S. Capitol building and preventing a joint session of Congress from formalizing the election victory of president-elect Joseph Biden. Oath Keepers were in the forefront of the angry crowd as events spiraled out of control.

At the Ellipse, Oath Keepers donning black hoodies with prominent logos left Trump's rally of outraged speakers and changed into military combat uniforms. They put on helmets, grabbed implements for hand-to-hand fighting, and made their way to the Capitol steps and poorly-defended police barriers. By early afternoon, rioters reached the doors and windows of the Capitol and breached the building. U.S. lawmakers were rushed to safety by security just before the mob swarmed the building and seized several Congressional offices, including that of House Speaker Nancy Pelosi. Angry males made no secret of their contempt for the woman leader with their "PELOSI IS SATAN" printouts and slogans.

Rioters caused serious injuries and several deaths among Capitol defenders, as well as several million dollars in damages to the building. It took several hours for police reinforcements to clear the building and restore calm, so the joint session of Congress could resume its business later in the evening. Crowd control experts commented that the mob did not seem to have a clear plan once they were in the headquarters of the nation's business. Some Oath Keepers lamented that they did not have access to a cache of weapons stored nearby in Virginia in the event of a successful breach.[17]

Months after the bloody insurrection that shocked the nation and the world, trials began for many of the lawbreakers and some of the ringleaders of the January 6 spectacle. The Capitol had not endured such an assault since the War of 1812 when the British Army raided and set fire to the White House, along with the Capitol. As of June 2023, more than 1,033 rioters had been arrested, with approximately 485 federal defendants receiving sentences. About 277 defendants were sentenced to time behind bars and roughly 113 defendants were sentenced to a period of home detention.[18]

At his trial in May 2023, Oath Keepers founder Rhodes took the witness stand and told the jury that he was an American patriot attempting to remedy an unconstitutional election. Rhodes described his military experience, a stint in the Army that was cut short by a training accident. Rhodes also described his group as peaceful, disciplined and dedicated to putting a nation right that had lost its way. Unlike some other Oath Keepers on trial, Rhodes was not contrite.

Prosecutors told jurors that Rhodes was head of a terrorist group that spent thousands of dollars on ammunition and training. The Oath Keepers stashed a massive cache of arms to be used by a quick reaction force at a Virginia hotel. In a meeting with another man after the riot, Rhodes was secretly recorded saying the Oath Keepers should have brought rifles to the melee: "We should have fixed it right then and there. I'd hang [expletive] Pelosi from the lamppost."[19]

Rhodes was subsequently found guilty of seditious conspiracy sentenced to 18 years. While Attorney General Merrick Garland commented that the Justice Department would continue to do everything in its power to hold accountable those who attacked democracy, Rhodes could take some comfort in the words of Trump. Donald Trump and other Republican candidates for the 2024 presidential nomination announced that they would consider pardons for those who were sentenced to prison for the events of January 6, 2021.

Not all of the Oath Keepers sentenced to prison time were as defiant as Rhodes in their trials. U.S. Army veteran Kenneth Harrelson, who was identified as a "ground team leader" in the assault on the Capitol, said he was not interested in politics and had never voted for a president in his life. Harrelson said he was lured to Washington, D.C., with promises of a "security job." He said he should have never been involved: "I am responsible, and my foolish actions have caused immense pain for my wife and our children."[20]

Many top Oath Keepers leaders have had their day in court for the bloody insurrection and have received substantial sentences. During their trials, some blamed President Trump for leading them into violent insurrection on January 6, 2021. They pointed a finger of blame at Trump, even though on several occasions he promised that he would pardon them if he attained a position to have that power again. Oath Keepers can blame Donald Trump all they want for their legal troubles and prison time, but they were involved in thuggish and violent activities before Trump entered politics and was elected U.S. President.

Some conservative commentators have dismissed the January 6 events as an aberration and a rally that just got out of control for a few hours. They also contend that most of the men who joined groups like the

Oath Keepers have learned their lesson and most likely will not to be seen or heard from again. In his study, *Oath Keepers: Patriotism and the Edge of Violence in a Right Wing Anti-government Group*, Sam Jackson argues that the group obtains its legitimacy with some Americans by always likening contemporary political disagreements with incidents from the American Revolutionary War with the British. Oath Keepers want to make the point that they are not frivolous and that the wrongs that they seek to address are as serious as those that spurred a War of Independence.

Jackson, a professor in the College of Emergency Preparedness, Homeland Security, and Cybersecurity at the University at Albany, State University of New York, insists that the extreme right Oath Keepers are not going away. Jackson contends the ever-present danger of the group's philosophy is that it shifts the normal understanding of appropriate political behavior. "It suggests that Americans should act as vigilantes—whether by monitoring polling places for voter fraud or volunteering with civilian paramilitary groups on the U.S.-Mexico border."[21]

A clear majority of those vigilantes are going to be men who find their existential legitimacy and political power from the barrel of a gun, to rephrase the famous axiom of communist China's late chairman Mao Zedong. For the foreseeable future, this kind of men's movement will be most comfortable handling deadly weapons and spewing hostile political rhetoric. Professor Jackson maintains that the Oath Keepers will be with us for the foreseeable future, despite the trials and prison sentences meted out for the January 6 Insurrection. That's because these angry men will find purpose and meaning in having a bogeyman to resist.

When the likes of a Trump is in power, Jackson contends, militant right-wing extremists will be there to counter progressives, gay people, immigrants, Muslims and other religious and ethnic minorities. When liberals are in power, they can always revert to their anti-government stance with their resolve to prevent the next Waco, Ruby Ridge, or Bundy Ranch. They will adamantly oppose what they see as dictatorial mask mandates, or school "brainwashing programs" emanating from Washington, D.C., or elite universities. Above all, the Oath Keepers will be vigilant against any and all attempts to restrict their gun ownership, no matter who is in power. After all, this is written into their "Declaration of Orders We Will Not Obey."

12

"Deplore-a-Balls" and Accomplices

In one of the many memorable moments from the 2016 presidential debates between Donald Trump and Hillary Clinton, Democrat Clinton took her Republican opponent to task for enlisting racist, sexist, homophobic, and Islamophobic men as spokespersons and operatives for his campaign. She criticized Trump for choosing the notorious Steve Bannon as his chief executive officer, especially given Bannon's role as the executive chair of the far-right website *Breitbart News*. Clinton read headlines from the site, including "Would You Rather Your Child Had Feminism or Cancer?" and "Hoist It High and Proud: The Confederate Flag Proclaims a Glorious Heritage."[1] She also said Trump needed to disavow the support of former Ku Klux Klan leader David Duke.

During an August 2016 campaign fundraiser, Clinton explained how Republican voters could be placed into two baskets: moderates whom she might approach for votes and the hopeless alt-right crowd. In a September 8, 2016, she modified that comparison with a new explanation for basket content. Clinton said: "You can take Trump supporters and put them in two big baskets. There are what I would call the deplorables—you know, the racists and the haters, and then the people who are drawn because they think somehow he's going to restore an America that no longer exists."[2]

Trump's alt-right supporters were pleased to take ownership of the Clinton "basket of deplorables" term and began using it at many of their actions to counter gay, feminist or Black Lives Matter demonstrations. In planning some of their bloody confrontations with leftist groups, the extremists began referring to their activities as "Deplore-a-Balls." Trump supporters at the 2018 Conservative Political Action Conference arrived wearing hats emblazoned with the phrase "Proud to Be Deplorable." Some political pundits declared Clinton's phrase to be a major gaffe, but by the Insurrection of 2021, it was hard not to agree with Clinton's "deplorables" description any longer.

The agitated mob outside the Capitol on January 6, 2021, was truly attending a rabid "Deplore-a-Ball." Trump's "Stop the Steal" basket was filled with an assortment of angry male militia members and dangerous extremist men's groups. The Proud Boys and Oath Keepers were prominent and played major roles in criminal activities at the violent spectacle outside the 2020 election certification meeting of the Congress, and then inside the U.S. Capitol.

Others present and active in the mob action included various state militias, the National Socialists Club, Crusaders, Texas Freedom Force, Woodland Wild Dogs, QAnon groups, Vanguard America, and more. Groups worth examining that were at the riot, besides the Proud Boys and Oath Keepers, include Three Percenters, Fraternal Order of Alt-Knights (FOAK), and Patriot Front. A number of accomplice organizations were not necessarily on the ground or in force for the day's events, but they were a presence, nonetheless.

"Three Fingers Up"

Three Percenters received attention after the Insurrection because almost three dozen members of the group were identified as key participants. They are known for their "Three Fingers Up" salute, and many in the alt-right claim membership. The University of Maryland's National Consortium for the Study of Terrorism and Responses to Terrorism verified the Three Percenters' presence at the January 6, 2021, melee. Also known as the "Threepers," the Three Percenters' creed claims that only 3 percent of American colonists joined together to throw off the yoke of British Imperialists, and it will take only 3 percent of the real U.S. patriots now to end the encroachment of the American left on white Christian America.[3]

After the disturbances meant to stop Congress from certifying the results of the 2020 election, the Three Percenters' activities garnered attention in courtrooms and in the news media. The group received renewed attention for member participation in the plot to kidnap Governor Gretchen Whitmer of Michigan in October 2020. The kidnapping plot was hatched primarily by a paramilitary group calling themselves the Wolverine Watchmen. After their arrests and convictions for the kidnapping plot, a number of them were identified as Three Percenters. Some of them received lengthy sentences.

Wolverine militia leader Barry Croft, Jr., was sentenced to 19 years and seven months in December 2022 for felonies, including kidnapping conspiracy, conspiracy to use a weapon of mass destruction, and possessing an unregistered destructive device.[4] Croft regularly wore insignias associated with the Three Percenters and was later identified as the second-in-command of its Wisconsin branch. Adam Fox of Grand Rapids, Michigan, was the mastermind who whipped up the plotters with talk of hog-tying "the bitch" and laying the governor out on a table like they had made a drug bust.[5]

The Three Percenters had a lengthy list of grievances against Governor Whitmer as well as with the Michigan statehouse. They believed Whitmer was destroying businesses and the state economy with her handling of Covid-19. Three Percenters believed that the state's mask mandates were just the beginning of dictatorial government demands on the citizenry. They also believed Michigan liberals in state schools were indoctrinating children to believe that only Black lives matter.

The right to own and open-carry guns was under serious threat from Whitmer and her party, according to the Three Percenters and Wolverine Watchmen. Wolverines had no use for Whitmer or her opposition to military-style automatic weapons. At their get-togethers, they did speak highly of Kyle Rittenhouse, who shot at leftist demonstrators in Kenosha, Wisconsin, killing two. The Wolverines also had high praise for a St. Louis couple who received national attention when they armed themselves to confront Black Lives Matter demonstrators in their west St. Louis neighborhood.

Unfortunately for Wolverine Watchmen members, their organization was heavily infiltrated by the FBI and wired informants, so their conversations and plotting were frequently recorded by law enforcement.[6] They were known to follow the conspiratorial accounts of Joe Biggs of the Proud Boys and Alex Jones with his extremist *Infowars* website. Incidents like the failed Capitol Insurrection, and the foiling of the Whitmer kidnapping plot, brought associates of the Three Percenters to national attention, but they were involved in many unsavory incidents from the group's inception in 2008.

In 2008, Mike Vanderboegh conceived the idea for the Three Percenters as a small militant group of volunteers, who could counter odious government regulations and their enforcement. Vanderboegh had the creds to start an anti-government movement as he had previous experience with militia movements like the Sons of Liberty. Vanderboegh also claimed to be a commander of an Alabama militia group, the First Alabama Cavalry Regiment. He was involved with the anti-immigrant Minutemen in the mid–2000s, but he gained the most attention when he created the Sipsey Street Irregulars as part of the Three Percenters, which helped popularize and expand the American militia movement.

Vanderboegh maintained that Three Percenters was more of an idea than a top-down organization. Members identifying themselves as Three Percenters would simply "come out of the woodwork" whenever government intrusion into ordinary lives became apparent. He said that is exactly what happened at the Bundy Ranch confrontation when righteous men showed up to ward off federal law enforcement. The rally cry was, "No More Free Wacos," a reference to the government confrontation with the Branch Davidians in Texas, which resulted in the fiery deaths of 76 cult members led by David Koresh. At the Bundy Ranch, Vanderboegh said the Feds backed off from their persecutions because patriot resistance made a showing.

Since Vanderboegh founded the Three Percenters in 2008, its militia group members have been involved in any number of conspiracy creations and confrontations with government. The group was involved in numerous firearms violations and the firebombing of an Islamic center in Illinois. It also was behind a plot to blow up a residential compound housing Muslim workers of Somali descent in the state of Kansas.[7] Three Percenters also were apprehended stockpiling pipe bombs and other illegal incendiary devices for use against the offices of various Democratic politicians.

Concerns about the Three Percenters' dangerous activities prompted the Canadian government to label the extremist men's group as a dangerous terrorist entity in 2021.[8] In July 2023, a court found that Three Percenters' hero Ammon Bundy, his close associate, and three of his allied groups, must pay more than $50 million in damages for accusing a hospital of child trafficking and harassing its medical staff.[9]

Meet the FOAK-ers

The Fraternal Order of Alt-Knights (FOAK) members are closely associated with the Proud Boys. The FOAK group was conceived as a kind of tactical arm for the Proud Boys with a mission of silencing liberal left demonstrators and fomenting violence against protesters at rallies. The group's founder, Kyle Chapman, apparently desired to be more militant and outspoken than was acceptable for Proud Boys' founder Gavin McInnes. Chapman dismissed McInnes as not manly enough to lead the militant group and dissed him as too frightened by legal problems to direct the Proud Boys in their violent operations. Enrique Tarrio took the reins from McInnes.

Chapman later vowed to overthrow Tarrio from Proud Boys leadership, saying that he showed cowardice on the battlefield in confrontations with leftist demonstrators. Tarrio remained the chairman of the Proud Boys up until his incarceration for his role in the January 6 Insurrection. Tarrio has said he does not think Chapman's attempted takeover of Proud Boyds could ever succeed. He said he was convinced Chapman was either inebriated or joking when he made the posts on the internet saying he would topple Tarrio.

As head of FOAK, Chapman has held himself up as a model warrior. According to the Southern Poverty Law Center, he ascended to the top of the alt-right heap with the distribution of a meme in 2017 in which he was sporting a gas mask, ski goggles, bike helmet and a battle shield with a design derived from a Ron Paul campaign logo. He was in full regalia mode when a video of his attack on a demonstrator at Berkeley was taken in March 2017. The attack account spread online and soon he became known as the "Based Stick Man," a label and image he willingly embraced.[10]

Acting as the "Based Stick Man," Chapman was a vigilante who carried a big stick and used it to beat up demonstrators from Antifa and Black Lives Matter. He instructed new FOAK initiates to make shields like his from wooden tabletops secured from Home Depot. Sticks for beating enemies should be of hickory or ironwood. The newly-created FOAK was not for the faint of heart, but for pro–Western knights willing to use their armor and implements in the battle against Muslim infidels or neo–Marxists. Chapman fashioned himself as a selfless warrior dedicated to leading FOAK fighters to protect the naïve white citizenry. This dedication frequently got him and his manly knights in trouble.

Chapman was arrested in April 2017 on charges of assaulting a person in Berkeley while filming a promotional video for a rally. In August 2017, Chapman pleaded no contest to the charge of felony possession of a leaded cane and was sentenced to five years of probation. Also in August 2017, Chapman helped organize and speak at a "Make Men Great Again" rally, where he said white men were under assault and being demoralized by anti-white guilt. In July 2018, Chapman was charged with being a fugitive and extradited to Texas for charges related to a brawl in Austin where he hit a man in the face with a wooden bar stool. A witness to the attack recognized Chapman on television when he was advertising a "Texans for American Freedom March" outside the Texas capitol. Chapman pled guilty to aggravated assault.

Chapman has been heavily influenced by the English Defense League, and he views its Islamophobic leader, Tommy Robinson, as a hero and model. Robinson's British males share many of the grievances of the white men of FOAK, as well as their tactics in intimidating immigrants and residents of Muslim neighborhoods in England. The English Defense League organized about a dozen demonstrations per year between 2009 and 2015, and some of those actions resulted in clashes with the police in London and elsewhere.[11] Robinson's criminal record has prevented him from entering the United States or consorting with FOAK and other alt-right forces in North America.

FOAK's Chapman, like the English Defense League's Robinson, has a record and has been in and out of jail. Analysts of right-wing extremism trends note that Chapman has a lot to fear, not only from the prospect of more prison time, but from violence resulting from internecine rivalries within the alt-right movement. In his 2022 study on the Proud Boys, Andy Campbell makes the point that militant leaders like Chapman and McInnes may be idolized by some followers, but they are just temporary icons and are not essential to the movement. Also, these leaders generally spend relatively short times in incarceration for their disruptive acts, and they emerge as martyrs. This offers them more opportunities for media attention and for mobilizing unlawful right-wing actions.

Patriot Front Manifesto

Although most right-wing militant groups do not operate with well-articulated mission statements and manifestos, that cannot be said of Patriot Front. Its leader, Thomas Rousseau, has writing skills seldom found among right-wing militia members or alt-right headbangers. While working on his Texas high school newspaper, *The Sidekick*, Rousseau wrote opinion pieces supporting "campus carry" for firearms and opposing bathrooms for non-binary students. He also supported Trump for President, arguing that the 2016 election was a choice between democracy and a corrupt establishment.

Student journalist Rousseau also engaged in rhetorical flourishes that would later show up in his Patriot Front propaganda. He wrote about frustrated and alienated blue-collar workers who had had enough of being characterized as racist and sexist. He said the "forgotten majority of America" had no use for a liberal, globalist agenda, and despite the decay of the nation, was determined to resist being replaced by tens of millions of immigrants. That word *replace* and the attendant word *replacement* would become key buzzwords in the Rousseau political lexicon for the future.

Less than two years after his high school graduation, Rousseau could be found at the "Unite the Right" rally in Charlottesville, Virginia. He also could be found consorting with members of the extremist Vanguard America, and he was captured in photos in the vicinity of James Alex Fields, Jr., an alt-right activist who was later convicted of killing Heather Heyer. Fields killed Heyer and seriously injured others holding an anti-racism protest when he purposely mowed them down as they tried to dodge his oncoming car.[12] The anti-racism protest was meant to counter the "Unite the Right" rally supporting the South's Confederate legacy and statues devoted to Confederate generals like Robert E. Lee.

Patriot Front members rely on visual propaganda to promote their message and attract new members. Their patch logos and hat slogans include "Life-Liberty-Victory," "Revolution Is Tradition," and "For the Nation, Against the State" (photograph by the author).

Many Americans watched the nightly news in horror on August 12, 2017, when the 32-year-old Heyer was killed by blunt-force trauma in the deliberate use of Fields' car as a murder weapon. They also may have reacted with horror at some earlier coverage of the "Unite the Right" events in Charlottesville when white supremacists paraded with tiki torches and chanted, "Jews will not replace us!"

The conspiracy theory of "replacement" is rooted in white supremacist ideology, which claims there is an intentional effort, led by Jews, to promote mass immigration, intermarriage, and other efforts to promote the "extinction of whites" in America.[13] Reproductive freedom and abortion rights play into the replacement theories and any conspiracies to further white extinction. This has motivated Rousseau's group to sometimes join abortion protesters.

The killing of Heather Heyer was disavowed by both Vanguard America and by Rousseau. In fact, the tragedy of her murder and the resulting negative publicity may have led to the demise of Vanguard America. However, it was an opportunity for Rousseau to pick up some of the defecting members of Vanguard America and to create a new organization, Patriot Front. In many ways, Rousseau's new Patriot Front just picked up where Vanguard America left off. It's very obvious in Rousseau's Patriot Front Manifesto that some form of replacement theory is a key component of his organization's credo.

The manifesto calls for the formation of a white "ethno-state" that can resist those who would dilute the purity and superiority of the original "pan-European" men who settled America. The Patriot Front manifesto constantly makes mention of American historical figures and describes its politics as a renewal of a supposed authentic American identity based on pan–European colonizers. As Rousseau emphasized in his internal announcement of the organization's split with Vanguard America, Patriot Front's rebranding is primarily aesthetic, not ideological. The political stance remains staunchly white nationalist.

At a November 3, 2017, Patriot Front demonstration at the University of Texas at Austin, members gathered around a statue of George Washington on campus with torches and flares. They listened intently while Rousseau delivered a speech declaring that America confronts an existential threat. He denounced a corrupt, rootless, global elite for its plans to enslave white Christian America, and then to replace these natural heirs of America with minorities.

Unlike Proud Boys, or some other hardcore militia groups, Patriot Front seems less interested in creating mayhem, punching faces, or drawing blood. The group seems more interested in getting its message out. The group will anonymously post flyers or drop banners off overpasses or out building windows. The Patriot Front's mission is to get its paranoid warnings out and to get its urgent bulletins mainstreamed for both the masses and for prospective new members. Fox News' Tucker Carlson, since fired from the network, picked up on Rousseau's Patriot Front vibe for his cable broadcasts:

"I know that the left and all the little gatekeepers on Twitter become literally hysterical if you use the term 'replacement,' if you suggest that the Democratic Party is trying to replace the current electorate, the voters now casting ballots, with new people, more obedient voters from the Third World," Carlson said in April 2021. "But they become hysterical because that's what's happening, actually. Let's just say it: That's true."[14]

After the May 2022 mass shooting in Buffalo, New York, when a gunman killed 10 Blacks at a grocery store, Carlson noted: "You've heard a lot about the great replacement theory recently…. We're still not sure exactly what it is…. Here's what we do know for a fact: There is a strong political component to the Democratic Party's immigration policy. We're not guessing this. We know this, and we know it, because they have said so."[15]

Carlson's comments were evidently considered timely, if off-base. The Buffalo shooter was found to be influenced by the white supremacist "Great Replacement" rhetoric of the far right. The attack was described as an act of domestic terrorism and was being investigated as a hate crime motivated by fear of white replacement and "white genocide." The shooter was found to be in possession of his own manifesto on replacement theory written to justify his acts of "political violence."

Although the Patriot Front does not specialize in political violence, it has been involved in activities that have tangled up members in some legal difficulties. Between May 1, 2020, and December 31, 2021, Patriot Front destroyed 35 murals and memorials across America that honored George Floyd and other Blacks killed in police violence. Some of the murals depicted LGBTQ expressions of pride. In Idaho in June of 2022, police stopped a truckload of Patriot Front members on their way to disrupt an LGBTQ program on health care. More than 30 members of Patriot Front were arrested and charged with conspiracy to riot.[16]

Patriot Front activities have been informational for the most part and this has caused some alt-right critics to dismiss them as inconsequential, if not downright wimpy. Patriot Front has received some embarrassing pushback from counter-demonstrators at their events and rallies—or by people who may actually share their political views but who do not want to be associated with Rousseau's group.[17]

In May of 2023, Patriot Front members showed up at the National Mall in Washington, D.C., for a "Reclaim America Rally." They held upside-down flags and offered the usual rhetoric about the decline of white men and the need to make America great again. There was no phalanx of dread Antifa fighters to challenge their message and to refute their mission of reclaiming America. Instead, a lone bicyclist named Joe Flood decided to ride down to observe the assembled demonstrators and check out the scene. Someone took a video as Flood transformed from a silent observer to an effective heckler of the alt-right group.

Washington Post journalist Theresa Vargas included Flood's biting comments and heckling for her column on the seeming defenseless and humiliated men of the Patriot Front: "You wear Walmart khakis," shouted Flood. "No one likes you. Your mom hates you. You were the losers of your high school class." Flood did not let up: "You're not even matching. You all have different types of pants on. Cargo pants are out. You look like General Custer's illegitimate son." The Flood video was posted on TikTok, and he began getting comments on social media from friends who recognized the bicyclist, as well as from unknown admirers: "Not all heroes wear capes," read one online comment about Flood's actions. "Some wear backpacks and ride red bicycles." Columnist Vargas observed: "On that day, Flood stood alone and countered hate. But the swell of support that has followed shows, that, in reality, he stands far from alone in believing that white nationalists should never go unchallenged."[18]

Alliance Defending Freedom

Alliance Defending Freedom(ADF) and Pacific Justice Institute are two organizations that are often on the same page on social issues as alt-right groups. The Pacific Justice Institute, founded in 1997 by attorney Brad Dacus, describes itself as a "legal organization specializing in the defense of religious freedom, parental rights, and other civil liberties." It specializes in fighting gay marriage and gay rights legislation. The ADF has been around for more than 30 years, but it found new energy with the ascendancy of the Trump administration. Among its founders were Bill Bright who discovered Campus Crusade for Christ; James Dobson of Focus on the Family; Christian radio personality Marlin Maddoux; and Alan Sears, former director of the Meese Commission under Reagan.

ADF supports traditionalist views on manhood with its opposition to same-sex marriage, legalized abortion, transgender rights, sex-change surgery, and restrictions on prayer at public meetings. U.S. Senator Hawley of Missouri has worked for ADF and drawn support from ADF as a paid speaker for its programs. The U.S. Senator's wife, attorney Erin Hawley, has worked on lawsuits to protect Christian speech to the detriment of gays and minorities. The Southern Poverty Law Center has labeled ADF as an extremist organization and a hate group against gay people, in part because ADF has praised countries like India and Russia for criminalizing homosexuality.[19] ADF is worth a close look, as compared to the Pacific Justice Institute, because of its national clout and the wider range of issues that it takes up in court battles.

Many of the alt-right groups mentioned in this chapter emerged during the Obama presidency, in part as a response to an administration perceived to be illegitimate, unmanly, globalist and contrary to American traditions. Many preexisting right-wing men's organizations also were energized by the first Black presidency for the same reasons. The considerable backlash by these groups against Obama, and their utter contempt for the prospect that a first woman presidency could follow Obama, helped catapult Republican Donald J. Trump to the highest office in the land in 2016.

Despite a win with the November 8, 2016, election of Trump, militant right-wing men's groups did not sit on their laurels. Rather than losing any momentum, they instead redirected their energy from candidate Trump to issues they championed. A lot of that energy outlay was corrosive, violent, and contrary to democratic norms. At many rallies and demonstrations, it was downright criminal. The irony here is that the disturbing spectacles were not necessary to achieve their aims. That's because their president, elected in 2016, was able to change the makeup of the U.S. Supreme Court by the end of his term. He put many of their goals on guns, abortion, immigration, gay rights, minority rights, and women's rights into effect or within reach through judicial actions.

The change in the makeup of the high court aligned well with the mission of many of the militant right-wing groups. It also meshed with some of the priorities of Alliance Defending Freedom. Trump's appointment of three justices to the court provided a 6-vote tilt to the right with a very conservative majority made up of five men and one woman—Amy Coney Barrett.

Barrett's bona fides with the right wing are well-established. She received overwhelming support from social conservatives with her nomination to the high court. Her work with the Blackstone Legal Fellowship from 2011 to 2016—a summer program for law school students that the Alliance Defending Freedom established to inspire a "distinctly Christian worldview in every area of law" was recognized.[20]

If anyone doubts the suggestion that the judicial stars have aligned for the far right men's groups, and for the Alliance Defending Freedom, consider the legal issues that the Trump court has its sights focused on now, or that the Supreme Court has already acted upon. In some cases, the court majority has actually acted with a big assist from the legal arguments and theories promoted by Alliance Defending Freedom. Consider these opinions:

Abortion—Right-wing men's groups and ADF oppose a woman's right to choose. ADF wrote the model for Mississippi's anti abortion law that was central to the 2022 Dobbs case, when the court nullified and discarded the 50-year Roe precedent establishing a right to abortion.

Contraception—Right-wing men's groups and ADF want to limit or eliminate morning-after pill contraception use. ADF has litigated for the right of employers to opt out of providing insurance coverage for contraception for female workers on religious grounds.

Home Schooling—Right-wing men's groups and ADF regularly blast public education as inept and ideological. They prefer home schooling. In 2017, ADF named Michael Farris as its CEO. He was a founder of the Home School Legal Defense Association. He got the nod for his dedication to protecting home learning from state and federal education regulations.

School Content—Alt-right men's groups and ADF often complain about teachers and school library content that they say normalize homosexuality. ADF supports so-called "parents' rights litigation," which allows for the removal of content that appears contrary to the traditional family structure and heteronormative relationships.

Bullying—Right-wing men's groups and ADF have opposed anti-bullying initiatives which are designed to protect LGBTQ students. ADF teamed up with Focus on the Family to oppose anti-bullying policies that may result in "public schools subjecting young students to books, lessons, and programs designed to advance the homosexual agenda and undermine traditional notions of sexuality and the family."[21]

Hate Crimes—Right-wing men's groups adamantly oppose hate crimes legislation and so-called Matthew Shepard laws that criminalize acts of violence—or attempts to commit violent acts—when motivated by actual or perceived gender, disability, sexual orientation, or the gender identity of victims. ADF attorney Erik Stanley told a 2014 conference in Nashville, Tennessee, that the Matthew Shepard murder was mythology. He said it was portrayed as an anti-gay "hate crime" to be used by pro–LGBTQ activists to advance homosexuality. However, claims that Shepard was likely murdered over drugs or for some other reason unrelated to his sexual orientation have been debunked.[22]

Marriage Equality—Right-wing men's groups and ADF have a history of opposing legalized gay marriage on the grounds that such laws normalize homosexual behavior. "By its very nature, homosexual acts are incapable of bearing fruit—indeed, strictly speaking, they are not sexual, as they are incapable of being generative or procreative," then-senior ADF Legal Counsel Piero Tozzi, told the World Congress of Families gathering in Madrid, Spain, 2012.[23]

The Alliance Defending Freedom has had a mixed record when it comes to judicial wins on all the issues near and dear to the hearts of alt-right men's groups. However, during the first term of the Biden administration, the U.S. Supreme Court—now often dubbed as the "Trump Court" by critics—made two dramatic decisions that show a rightward turn by the court. The first decision was the June 22, 2022, *Dobbs v. Jackson Women's Health Organization*, which effectively overturned *Roe v. Wade* on abortion rights protections. The second decision was the *303 Creative LLC v. Elenis* case of July 2023 which effectively voided consumer protections for gay people in certain circumstances.

The Supreme Court's decision in the Dobbs case threw abortion back to the states. The opinion authored by Justice Samuel Alito declared that the court returned authority to regulate abortion "to the people and their elected representatives." Thirteen states enacted near-total bans on abortion, and a dozen more approved new laws curtailing abortion access. In Wisconsin, abortion services were suspended due to uncertainty about the status of an abortion ban from 1849. Other states moved to strengthen reproductive rights, some with ballot measures to overcome resistance in state legislatures. Polls show the majority of Americans favor abortion access.

The first evidence of blowback to the ADF perspective on abortion, essentially validated by the high court, was an election shocker in red state Kansas in August 2022. By a significant majority, Kansans opposed a constitutional amendment—made possible by the Dobbs decision—that would have said there was no right to an abortion in Kansas. Kansas voters overwhelmingly rejected the abortion ban, and pro-choice groups like Kansas for Constitutional Freedom told the news media that the vote for safe, legal and accessible abortion was "huge and decisive."[24]

Voters in key states followed suit after the Kansas decision in the 2022 midterm elections. Voters affirmed pro-choice ballot measures in the wake of the high court's overturning of Roe v. Wade. Michigan voters enshrined abortion rights in the state constitution, a move to block a decades-old abortion ban from taking effect. California voters put abortion rights in their state constitution to ensure no future legislature or governor could interfere with abortion rights. Vermont voters approved an amendment to the state's constitution to protect individuals' rights to make their own reproductive decisions. Montana voters rejected an abortion measure that would allow criminal penalties on health care providers. Kentucky voters rejected a proposal that would have restricted abortion rights with a "trigger law" banning most abortions at all stages of pregnancy.

Meanwhile, Physicians for Human Rights, Pregnancy Justice, and several group supporting women's rights and reproductive freedom, issued a report, "Human Rights Crisis: Abortion in the United States." The report stated that not even a year after "this catastrophic legal decision, it is now apparent that the consequences are even worse than feared. Women and girls in need of reproductive healthcare are being met with systematic refusals, onerous financial burdens, stigma, fear of violence, and criminalization. Thousands are being forced to remain pregnant against their will."[25]

Civil libertarians agreed with the physicians and human rights groups. The ACLU emphasized that the court decision "allows extremists across the country to ban abortion and force women and others, who can

Alliance Defending Freedom played a major role in the Supreme Court decision to overturn abortion rights guaranteed for 50 years under *Roe v. Wade*. The court ruling prompted protests by women's groups. Physicians for Human Rights called it a "catastrophic decision" (courtesy Stacey Newman, Progress-Women.com)

become pregnant, into a second-class status by denying them control over their bodies and their futures…. The impacts of pushing abortion out of reach fall disproportionately on the same women and other people who have always faced systemic barriers to care—communities of color, people living on low-incomes, undocumented immigrants, young people, people with disabilities, and the LGBTQ community."[26]

With the *303 Creative LLC v. Elenis* decision, human rights groups and civil libertarians once again condemned the high court for undermining minority rights. Dobbs not only hurt women's reproductive rights but also sabotaged the legal underpinnings of same-sex marriage protections, according to the critics. They said the *303 Creative LLC v. Elenis* decision simply followed Dobbs in cutting back the constitutional guarantees on personal dignity and privacy.

In the *303 Creative* decision, the high court ruled in favor of a web designer, Lorie Smith, who did not want to assist same sex couples with websites because she said it impinged on her First Amendment rights. The website designer was represented by Alliance Defending Freedom. The *New Republic* magazine charged that any suggestion that website designer Smith had received an actual request from a gay male seeking a marriage website was misleading. The magazine said the man's request was a mirage. He was located and found to be a married with a family. His request was mythical, at best. Deciding cases in which identifiable people are harmed is a basic tenet of American law, according to legal scholars. It is part of the judicial restraint that reins in courts from making arbitrary decisions.

Gregory P. Magarian, the Thomas and Karole Green Professor of Law at Washington University in St. Louis observed, with regard to the *303 Creative* decision, "Clearly, the Supreme Court wanted to decide this case, wanted to hand down this ruling. And so they sort of stormed through the barriers that ordinarily kind of defined procedurally what they can do."[27]

Magarian also added this proviso: "There will certainly be instances of people coming out and saying, 'Hey, we provide an expressive service or an expressive good, we should be able to discriminate against African Americans, we should be able to discriminate against immigrants, we should be able to discriminate against women, we should be able to discriminate against Jews....'"[28]

Law professor Magarian was prophetic. *Time* magazine reported that days after the Trumpist Supreme Court embraced the ADF position for *303 Creative* on the right to discriminate against same-sex couples, a hairdresser in the small town of Traverse City, Michigan, publicly posted her intention to refuse service to clients who may have different pronouns than those that they were assigned a birth.

"If a human identifies as anything other than a man/woman, please seek services at a local pet groomer," the hair salon owner said in a Facebook post that was later deleted. "You are not welcome at this salon. Period."[29]

Threats against the LGBTQ community have multiplied with the rise of hostile, right-wing men's groups such as Proud Boys or the Fraternal Order of Alt-Knights. The Trump era also has ushered in right-wing state legislatures promoting bills to end gender-affirming care and protections for gay people. Katherine Frank, professor of law and director of the Center for Gender & Sexuality at Columbia University, said the high court's *303 Creative* decision provides a green light for bigotry and actions that were previously understood as discrimination: "People feel that they now are immune from any kind of consequences for engaging in that kind of violent bigoted speech."[30]

Proud Boys members have to feel some vindication now for their rancid history of shouting slurs against gay people, or for wielding their homophobic signs. Media-savvy characters like alt-right headbanger Gavin McInnes may feel more confident in taking swipes at "depraved homosexuals" on podcasts. McInnes might very well add that he now has the Trump wing of the U.S. Supreme Court in his anti-gay corner. As legal scholars note, a green light has been given for bigotry and actions that were previously understood as discrimination.

Alt-right men's groups of today can justifiably unfurl a "mission accomplished" flag on many of the issues that have inspired their street fights. Their brand of militancy and their successful messaging contrasts mightily with men's group activities of a previous century.

Section IV

Toward a New Definition of Manhood

13

Manhood: Old Icons Under Siege

Countries, religions, ethnicities, political parties, extremist groups, and even genders constitute human entities that seem to require inspiring icons. When those icons are questioned, or come under attack, there is predictable adverse reaction. Revered icons are not so easily jettisoned. The valued iconography of nations includes flags, sturdy monuments to founders, statesmen, and courageous warriors.

Iconography of religions includes statues, medals, and the symbols that are often found at the apex of places of worship. Iconography of ethnicities often involves symbolic representations that suddenly appear at holidays celebrating identity and culture. Most people in "melting pot" America can readily identify the ethnic icons for those who celebrate people of Irish, Italian, German, African, or Latin heritage.

The iconography of gender can be a little more complex. At its most basic, gender icons are the sex symbols involving circles with rudimentary stamens or pistils related to plant or flower reproduction. On a celestial level, masculinity is denoted by the symbol of planet Mars, whereas femininity is related to Venus. Hence, the literary allusion that women are from Venus, men are from Mars. This can be a reflection of the many miles apart the two sexes can be in their attitudes and their thinking. These two planets, as well as being symbols, also can refer to Greek and Roman deities related to gender.

In today's age of mass media, the heroes of popular music, and the charismatic actors and actresses of Hollywood movies, have provided us with gender icons. The cinema provides a constant supply of male and female icons. Indeed, the magazines of mass media even provide plebiscites for readers to vote on their favorite sex symbols. These sex symbols may offer the most cogent representations of gender icons at any given time. Among women, recognizable gender icons from the past include Marilyn Monroe, Jayne Mansfield, Brigitte Bardot, Marlene Dietrich, Kathleen Turner, and Raquel Welch. Among men, recognizable gender icons from the past include Douglas Fairbanks, Errol Flynn, Gary Cooper, Clark Gable, James Dean, and Marlon Brando.

Gender icons for the various men's movements covered in this study are a little more specialized and are not simply sex symbols that attract the notice of the opposite sex. These gender icons are not just about celebrityhood, but also represent certain manly values that average males should seek to acquire or exemplify. These traditional values or characteristics can involve strength, purpose, toughness, determination, loyalty, courage, independence, resilience, resoluteness, and responsibility. Examples of manhood for the conservative men's movements examined in this study include John Wayne, Charlton Heston, Clint Eastwood, Mel Gibson, Charles Bronson, Sylvester Stallone, and Tom Cruise.

John Wayne has been the idol and icon for conservative manhood for decades, and the proof of this is in the iconography available on the web. The "Code of The Duke Hand-Painted John Wayne Sculpture" has Wayne holding a rifle in front of a slate engraved with his manly provisos. Among his commandments: "Never stop fighting for that which you believe in. Talk low, talk slow and don't say too much. Always treasure the values of liberty and freedom." Other Wayne statues and posters for home shrines to The Duke include an armed shootist in *The Big Trail, Dakota, Texas Cyclone, The Big Stampede, Riders of Destiny, Westward Ho, King of the Pecos, Stagecoach, Dark Command, Tall in the Saddle, Fort Apache, Hondo, Rio Bravo, The Comancheros, How the West Was Won, Big Jake, True Grit, Chism,* and, of course, *The Shootist.*

No icon to manhood will ever match the number of manly cinema offerings of John Wayne and his era. The Duke is the king of manhood and actually became a spokesperson for the alt-right view of manliness. However, Wayne, with his 140 movies, does have a formidable challenger for the title as the king of manhood. After all, Wayne doesn't have the distinction of being Moses in the classic biblical story *The Ten Commandments* in 1956. He also was not a leader for the National Rifle Association or the most visible spokesperson for the organization's perspective on Second Amendment gun rights. One of Wayne's most famous quotes is: "If everything isn't black-and-white, I say why the hell not?" However, a quote of more longevity is that of the manly icon Charlton Heston: "From my cold, dead hands!"

Charlton Heston is immortalized in a 13-inch NRA bronze statue holding a rifle at his side. The statue of the famous actor, who said liberal gun regulators would have to pry his weapon from his "cold, dead hands" sells for $499.99. Heston achieved fame as a youthful, handsome Moses and as the patriarchal leader of the Hebrews in *The Ten Commandments.* Heston was a Hollywood liberal himself in the 1960s, but he did an about-face in the 1980s with his support of Ronald Reagan's bid for the presidency. In the years thereafter, Heston became an outspoken critic of academia, affirmative action, abortion, and gun control. He said he was proud to be a male culture warrior in service of defending evangelical Christian working stiffs. He slammed reporters and accused the news media of ridiculing the white marchers of the Promise Keepers, while at the same time celebrating Black men in the Million Man March on Washington.

Heston's credentials as an icon for white male movements are beyond dispute, and it's hard to beat a cinematic Moses unless, of course, you become a cinematic Jesus. Mel Gibson became the hero of white male Christian America when he produced, directed, and co-wrote *The Passion of the Christ* (2004), a controversial film about the trial, crucifixion and resurrection of the Christian savior that grossed hundreds of millions of dollars. Earlier Gibson had won awards and praise for his 1995 role as William Wallace in *Braveheart*. As Wallace, Gibson played a Scotsman fighting and dying for freedom against a cruel and effete British monarchy. In his role as Wallace and with *The Passion of the Christ*, Gibson won the loyalty of many in the evangelical men's movements. They later dismissed criticism of Gibson for his anti-Semitic language and for his legal difficulties for an assault-and-battery charge brought by an ex-girlfriend. These publicized offenses were dismissed by evangelicals as just indications of anti–Christian bias in the media and the judiciary.

Gibson has a propensity for extreme apocalyptic language, which has endeared him to the Rapture-oriented evangelicals. He has alienated others with his language. He became enraged at *New York Times* movie critic Frank Rich and was quoted as saying, "I want to kill him. I want his intestines on a stick…. I want to kill his dog."[1] In 2006, Gibson actually directed a film titled *Apocalypto*, which made the point that great civilizations such as that of the Mayans can decline and collapse. Gibson presented an ominous warning with a superimposed quote from historian Will Durant at the beginning of the film: "A great civilization is not conquered from without until it has destroyed itself from within."[2]

Clint Eastwood was offered an apocalyptic role in Francis Ford Coppola's epic about the Vietnam War titled *Apocalypse Now*. He also was offered the opportunity to replace Sean Connery and become a famous secret agent in the lucrative *007* movies. Both roles would have added more notches in Eastwood's reputation as a very masculine kind of guy. Eastwood turned both roles down, and some wonder if he resorted to his famous movie axiom: "A good man's got to know his limitations." In fact, Eastwood has had no limit for playing extremely masculine roles such as a tough cowhand in the TV series *Rawhide*; as a shootist in a classic series of Spaghetti Westerns such as *The Good, the Bad, and the Ugly*; and as a bad-ass detective ready "to blow your head clean off" in his *Dirty Harry* movies.

Audiences enjoyed Eastwood's Spaghetti Westerns because they were not as sappy and predictable as many of the John Wayne cowboy offerings. Also, Eastwood may have actually been more manly than Wayne with his unshaven face, his nub of a cigar, his squinty eyes, and his terse use of words. Eastwood became a hero for conservative men with his role as Inspector Callahan in the *Dirty Harry* movies. He detested political correctness and bristled in one movie in which he is paired with a woman officer. Inspector Callahan had no patience for crime laws written by liberals, nor for an inept political bureaucracy that tried to rein him in. He was never afraid to bend the rules to get the bad guy. The limitless manly Eastwood iconography for sale on the Internet is a testament to the man's unlimited manliness as a cowhand, a cowboy and a cop.

Charles Bronson, Sylvester Stallone, and Tom Cruise are significant, but lesser, lights in the shining cult of American manhood. These three do not enjoy the tremendous souvenir iconography of a John Wayne or a Clint Eastwood, though Stallone comes close. Still, they all are potent figures in the imagination of manhood in the United States. Charles Bronson won the allegiance of all men who fervently desire to take the law into their own hands to get revenge and to right wrongs. He is a hero for men convinced that the "law is an ass" and that the rigid application of the letter of the law is completely contrary to common sense.

Bronson had a respectable acting career in the 1960s, after acting classes at the Pasadena Playhouse in Hollywood and some minor TV roles in the 1950s. However, Bronson hit paydirt in 1974 with the film *Death Wish* about a respectable architect turned vigilante.[3] The architect takes up the gun after his wife is killed and his daughter is raped by a sexual predator. A violent role that Bronson played for much of the rest of his career, critics thought it was vicious and immoral, but men proved their love for it at the box office. Movie critics wanted to know about the real man behind the vengeful killer projecting violence on the screen. They were in for a shock on interviews to find that Bronson actually was a suspicious, bitter character who seemed violent in person.

Like Bronson, Sylvester Stallone has proved that good box office numbers can be testosterone-driven. Men have loved his pugilistic characters: a fighter named Rocky Balboa and a Vietnam War veteran with PTSD known simply as Rambo. Stallone as Rocky is an underdog boxer who must battle numerous opponents who bruise and abuse him. Critics have noted that Rocky is a masochist and that his movie audiences are sadistic. As Rocky, he is battered and bloodied in a series of movies in which he ultimately wins grueling championship fights.

Rocky's initiation into the fighting world has parallels to the bloody rituals that real men must undergo to achieve status in today's militant men's groups like the Proud Boys or the Fraternal Order of Alt-Knights. Rambo's personal history as a disillusioned Vietnam War soldier has parallels to the military backgrounds of men who join militias or groups like the Oath Keepers. Rambo is constantly enraged at the U.S. Government for callously ignoring his sacrifice and those of the men who fight its wars. In his many reincarnations in the *Rambo* series of movies, the Stallone character is terribly jacked around by his own government, but he does get his revenge. Rambo may be the ultimate icon for an angry slice of today's militant men's movements.

Inspector "Dirty Harry" Callahan played by Clint Eastwood was a renegade cop and a favorite male icon in movie theaters in the 1970s. However, the popularity of his patriarchal style of taking care of crime business diminished after years of mass shootings and police-brutality cases (Photofest).

Tom Cruise as the fighter pilot named Maverick cannot go unnoticed when discussing the iconography of masculinity. Movies like the 1986 *Top Gun* and the *2022 Top Gun: Maverick* were blockbusters full of fast-paced drama, electrifying aerial fight footage, and testosterone-filled patriotism. Men love that the fact that the Cruise character flaunts the rules, occasionally tweaks the noses of his superiors, but always beats the foreign bad guys and does it spectacularly. He also gets the women. There are two problems for Cruise as a manly icon: He has appeared as a metrosexual with "good hair" in many of his other movies. Also, his patriot bona fides are shed when he plays a Vietnam War protester in *Born on the Fourth of July*, and when he is an arrogant lawyer questioning what goes on in the U.S. military at Guantanamo in *A Few Good Men*.

In the era of the militant men of the Proud Boys, Oath Keepers and Patriot Front, the old cinematic male icons still have their ardent followers, but many of these icons have diminished in relevancy. Internet memes of militant right-wing men spilling the blood of Antifa and Black Lives Matter followers seem to have taken attention away from the cinematic idols. Donald Trump, a star of Reality TV and his own televised beauty pageants, may be the only male celebrity able to step in to fill the void left by fading icons and deceased stars like John Wayne or Charlton Heston. Like Wayne and Heston, the iconic Trump has had his own statues, posters, and iconography for placement in the shrines of suburban and rural man caves.

Trump won the 2016 presidency by echoing many of the same positions on affirmative action, civil rights guarantees, abortion, and gun control as espoused by Wayne and Heston. Also like Wayne and Heston, a stylish Trump considered himself to be a liberal in his younger years, before eventually adopting hardline conservative positions and traditionalist stances on gender issues. His political transformation, and his other "coming to god moments," sealed the deal with his far-right constituency. Trump has his own iconography as a male hero from the 2016 election in which he vanquished female candidate Hillary Clinton in an electoral college victory.

Trump also has new iconography as a male hero recovering from his failed election of 2020, when he lost the electoral college and the popular vote by a sum of more than 7 million. In some sense, the iconography from his defeat in what he insists was a "stolen election" brings to mind the grievances of Rambo against government betrayal and persecution. It also brings to mind the Bronson character in *Death Wish*, who can't rely on the legal establishment to defend the citizenry against some very bad people. Trump has clearly attempted to transfer all this grievance energy to those who see him as a double-crossed manly hero, and icon, who just may be America's last hope.

Trump is acutely aware of his stature as a male icon. He does nothing to dissuade this public perception among his loyal followers. In 2016 at a campaign stop at Dordt College in Sioux Center, Iowa, Trump declared: "I could stand in the middle of Fifth Avenue and shoot somebody, and I wouldn't lose any voters. OK?" … "It's, like, incredible."[4] Trump as an icon has been quite successful, irrepressible, and at times irresponsible.

His own belief in his iconic male status was evident in 2023 when he released his Trump Digital Trading Cards and sold them to collect literally millions of dollars from his devoted fans. Among the iconic images: Trump as a giant standing upon planet earth; Trump palming a basketball emblazoned with No. 45; Trump with a hard hat and boxing gloves; Trump tearing open his T-shirt to reveal a Superman vest; Trump in a cowboy hat with a raised, clenched fist; Trump in a hunting outfit with a shotgun over his shoulder; Trump holding a golf club while being showered with dollar bills—and the images don't stop there.

Iconoclasm: Bringing Down "The Duke"

Icons may appear impregnable, immortal, and immune to implosion, but the truth is that they are not made to last forever. Even Trump will not last forever. History shows us that, at some point, the iconoclasts begin chipping away. Sometimes it's not a matter of "chipping away" at all, but a wholesale destruction of an icon and an image—sometimes over the period of an evening. In the post–Gorbachev era after the fall of the Soviet Union, iconic statues to Vladimir Lenin and Joseph Stalin were brought down overnight in Moscow. Through the 1990s, the totalitarian icons laid face-down on the ground and languished in the parks of Russia's premier imperial city.

The demise of male political icons is a fairly common occurrence in history. When American troops entered Baghdad in 2003, statues of the Iraqi dictator Saddam Hussein were pulled down and never found upright again. Statues to Latin American dictators—and there have been many— suffered the same fate last century. During the French Revolution of the 1790s, the destruction of statues of kings was carried out by crowds of insurrectionists. Revolutions and changes of regime are often accompanied by the demolition of monuments of the previous order. Technically, the concept of "iconoclasm" has in the past been reserved for the smashing of religious icons.[5]

Religions have more permanence than nations and their political leaders, but even religious icons have met with desecration and exile. In ancient Egypt and Israel, the destruction of icons and idols seemed to happen periodically. For Jews and Christians, some of this can be attributed to the Second Commandment, brought to the fore by Moses, which banned sculptures of iniquity or "graven images." Hence, no idol, image, idea, or anything in the creation can ever attempt to capture divine essence. This is supposedly forbidden by divine providence. This dictum was reinforced in the 1500s with the rise of Protestantism. Religious Calvinists declared that all idols are cursed and deserve execration. Subsequently, icons of Christianity and statuary to the saints were destroyed in parts of Europe.

If historic political icons and revered religious icons of the world can be in jeopardy, should anyone be surprised that the American male icon of John Wayne was "shaking in his boots" on his pedestal in 2020? Orange County, California, was once a bastion of conservatism and its airport was renamed by its board of supervisors in 1979 to honor the late John Wayne. The John Wayne Associates commissioned a sculptor to create a bronze statue of "The Duke" to commemorate the airport's namesake. The nine-foot statue, created at the Hoka Hey Foundry in Dublin, Texas, sits in front of the airport and was dedicated in 1982 on a pedestal outside the Eddie Martin Terminal.[6]

Fast forward to four short decades later. The demographics of Orange County had changed substantially, going from white conservative to liberal and very diverse. Dissident voices began to be raised calling for the banishment of the film legend and icon of Caucasian manliness. A resolution by Orange County Democrats in early 2020 condemned the "white supremacist, anti–LGBT and anti–Indigenous views" of Wayne. The resolution asked for the removal of his iconic statue and a restoration of the original airline destination's name: Orange County Airport.

"Orange County is now a diverse region far different from the time when John Wayne was chosen as namesake for the airport," the resolution stated. It cited an annual survey that reported 79 percent of respondents saw the county's increasing ethnic diversity as "a source of great strength." Ada Briceño, chair of the Democratic Party of Orange County, stated: "An international airport that welcomes millions of people each year should not be named for someone whose beliefs oppose our nation's values of equal opportunity and justice for all."[7]

Donald Trump, always a champion of "The Duke," was outraged by the actions to remove Wayne in California and other icons of America's past, including Confederate generals at sites throughout America. He was not impressed by the efforts of those in Orange County "to remove white supremacist symbols and names" and other icons "widely recognized as racist symbols producing lasting physical and psychological stress and trauma particularly to Black communities, people of color and other oppressed groups."[8]

Trump responded to all of this in 2020 by declaring that on his watch the important monuments of America will never be desecrated; heroes will never be defaced; their legacies will never be diminished; and their achievements will never be forgotten. What's more, the ringleaders in any attacks on the eternal tributes to our forefathers and national luminaries can expect swift and severe punishment. Trump subsequently issued an executive order to make assaults on statuary punishable by ten years in prison. He vowed to make a new "National Garden of American Heroes." Among the 100 or more sculptures for the garden would be the likenesses of Davy Crockett, Billy Graham, Douglas MacArthur, Audie Murphy, George S. Patton, Jr., Ronald Reagan, Betsy Ross, and George Washington.[9]

"Sounds like the world's least dynamic amusement park, but perhaps they'll add some animatronics," quipped Crispin Sartwell, a philosophy professor at Dickinson College in Pennsylvania.[10] In a more serious vein, Sartwell asked whether Trump and his "Make America Great Again" acolytes understood anything about idolatry and iconoclasts. Great monuments and icons seem fated to become effigies, their destruction a premonition of the fall of a hero or leader and the transformation of the public order. Totalitarian regimes have come to learn that it's a lot easier to protect all the imagery and sculptures than it is to actually change people's minds about once-revered icons or the concrete conditions in which people live.

If John Wayne—the pre-eminent man among men—can be brought down, can Donald Trump be far behind? Trump's increasing number of detractors asked: How long can this man's diehard followers continue to ignore his sordid history, his trail of venality, his physical decline, his own mortality? When will the cult followers come to realize that all the shiny non-fungible tokens of Trump's greatness are just so much fool's gold—brittle, tarnished, broken, destined to be worthless?

The impermanence of icons, and their manipulation for nefarious purposes, can raise an age-old conundrum: Should humanity give it up when it comes to embracing icons? Did Yahweh have a point when he gave Moses a direction on the tablets that worshipping graven images is a cardinal sin? In the context of this study, can the icons for white, male hegemony withstand the hurricane-force winds of change and a new order? Will the iconic figures, who have clung tightly to the traditional definitions of manhood, find themselves relegated to the ash heaps of history? And what if all the sacred icons are not smashed to smithereens, just irretrievably altered? What about Barbie and Ken?

Kendom and a "Barbie Backlash"

The total meltdown of the right-wing yammering class—caused by a movie called, *Barbie*, in the summer of 2023—can go a long way in illustrating the depths of male anxiety over gender issues. Initially, the alt-right pundits were concerned about the new "twisted" messages being sent out by the doll, Barbie. She and her revered image were suddenly being hijacked by the women whom Rush Limbaugh once labeled as "feminazis." Male traditionalists were angry. Barbie, after all, was simply meant to be an alluring feminine symbol for conspicuous consumption and consumer capitalism. She was never designed to be a symbol of the choices that young girls should be able to make for their careers, for their lifestyles, or for their attitudes toward men. What in the hell was happening now?

Barbie was supposed to be a benign status symbol for little girls. The desire for status is part of what keeps the cash flowing, the credit cards processing, the e-commerce electronics buzzing. Some little girls get a Barbie, but then must beg their parents for something more than a cardboard box to keep all her accessories. Other little girls get a Barbie, and they also get a Barbie Stylized Dream House, and a Barbie Pink Luggage Collection, to store all those formal dresses and casual outfits. In either case, these girls' desires are good for the economy, and Barbie serves the needs of American commerce.

When Hollywood liberals got hold of Barbie, the game was turned upside down. The mission was compromised. Suddenly Barbie was troubled by existential questions related to human purpose and the meaning of life and death. Suddenly Barbie was transported from a paradise of beaches and great fun to a real world obsessed with who is in charge and who gets what. Suddenly, Barbie was no longer carefree and full of laughter. She was confused, and she was crying. No wonder the right-wing pundits were beside themselves, although they are always beside themselves.

The angst over Barbie's leftward turn had the male alt-right pundits setting fire to their hair—and to her hair. And, then there was the

Barbie and Ken dolls were once the prestige toys of little girls who loved to play with all their outfits and accessories. The 2023 movie *Barbie* transformed Barbie and Ken from consumer icons to curious characters exploring the meaning of life and of manhood (photograph by Courtney Martin).

Ken problem. The formerly happy Ken also was in depression in the Hollywood film. Ken's realization that he was a second-class citizen in his imaginary world—and that the patriarchy was losing ground fast in the real world of men—left Ken disoriented and in shock. His desperate plight also had the effect of upending the defenders of right-wing orthodoxy. They expressed their anger in the actual world—and in the virtual world of online media.

Ben Shapiro, editor of the right-wing *Daily Wire*, went on a 40-minute rant against the *Barbie* film and declared it the "most woke" and anti-male movie that he had ever seen.[11] Shapiro wore a black T-shirt with black pants, the precise outfit worn by Ryan Gosling as Ken in the film's musical performance, as he trashed the film in front of a *Barbie* movie poster. He dismissed the movie as a "flaming garbage heap of a film" and as feminist nonsense. He became increasingly enraged in his lengthy review of *Barbie* which began with him setting fire to the dolls in a trash can.

Fox News, still recovering from its $787 million libel suit settlement over fake news about Dominion Voting Systems in the 2020 election, wasted no time getting out its own version of the truth about *Barbie*. Fox News aired the boiler plate complaints against Hollywood employing actors and actresses of questionable gender, and also gave plenty of air time to Republican politicians who claimed the film was not only subversive sexually but also traitorous internationally. According to *Fox* reports, the *Barbie* film exhibited a global map that clearly played into the hands of Chinese communists who claimed vast sea rights off China's coasts.[12] Hollywood elitists were all part of a scheme to kowtow to the "Chi-coms" and to get Barbie's pink into Sino-pinko movie theaters.

Those charges were delineated and amplified by U.S. Senator Ted Cruz of Texas, who went after the film for its "pushing Chinese propaganda." A map of the disputed territory in the South China Sea was allegedly on display in one movie scene. An international political expert with Tufts University pronounced the suspect map in the film as mere nonsense with "squiggles and arrows and hashtags and dotted lines all over the damn place."[13] Nevertheless, Cruz persisted in hatching conspiracy theories about *Barbie* all over media spaces, including on the right-wing Internet platform, the *Daily Signal*.

David Joshua Rubin, a conservative political commentator and host of *The Rubin Report* and political talk time on the network *BlazeTV*, put his intellectual energy into the transexual conspiracy theories about left-wing Hollywood trying to confuse children about their sexuality. Like so many other outraged males, Rubin pointed a finger at the one actor in *Barbie* who was out as trans. Rubin decried his presence saying, "Why do they go out of their way to have a biological boy play a girl, who's supposed to be completely girl in *Barbie*, unless they are trying to confuse kids?"[14]

Right-wing commentator Charlie Kirk of *Turning Point USA* joined *The Daily Wire*'s Shapiro, as well as Fox host Rachel Campos-Duffy, in taking swipes at *Barbie* and Hari Nef, transgender model and actor. Kirk called the movie "trans propaganda that is in this hyper-feminine, ultra-pink propaganda thing, but it's really been taken over by the trans mafia." Kirk said the trailer for *Barbie* was "the most disgusting thing I've ever seen,"[15] and then proposed a boycott of the film. The boycott plan came on the heels of a boycott of the once-manly *Bud Light* beer, which fell out of flavor with real men after Anheuser-Busch marketers allowed a trans person to shill for its brew. A transgender woman promoted the beer brand during March Madness. The video triggered a backlash from right-wing conservatives, including singer Kid Rock, who resorted to firing his gun at Bud Light beer cans.

Not to be outdone by the right-wing bloggers and flamers on

Internet streaming, U.S. Rep. Matt Gaetz, Republican of Florida, went to the screening of *Barbie*, along with his wife, and then pronounced the movie to be trash. The couple lamented that the movie had nothing to say about faith and family. They also noted that the Ken character was not very masculine and "disappointingly low T."[16] Of course, dolls with smooth plastic crotches and no genitalia are predictably low on testosterone. The Gaetz comments brought the savage right-wing nuttery to new heights, with the tallish Barbie character and her sidekick Ken in the crosshairs.

Most liberal media outlets did not take the bait and declined to rumble over some of the outlandish commentary by conservative media. They did take a bit of time to engage in mockery. "Admit it, you hated the film because Barbie is taller than you," one liberal troller wrote taking aim at Ben Shapiro. "They finally make a movie for people who are 12 inches tall, with no genitals, and those people don't even like it," observed comedy writer Jesse McLaren about the feigned outrage.[17] Senior writer Amanda Marcotte wrote in *Salon* that the movie was a joyous occasion for quality mother-daughter time. She added that "Republicans, of course, can't let people have a good time without getting angry about it."[18]

Some feminist writers were concerned about a blasé response to all the right-wing *Sturm und Drang* over movie dolls. They noted that even though all the hyperbolic reactions by Gaetz, Cruz, and other right-wing men were absurd and not based in reality, they could still do real harm. They noted how trans people were being targeted and losing their rights to gender-affirming health care. They noted how ridiculous paranoia has become lethal policy in male-dominated legislatures obsessed with drag queens. They noted how a male-dominated U.S. Congress has blocked passage of the Equal Rights Amendment for women and the Violence Against Women Act. They noted how a male-dominated Supreme Court has destroyed reproductive care protections for women.

Nation magazine editor Katrina vanden Heuvel emphasized that Barbie is an obvious target for right-wing men because she represents female choice, female empowerment, and females' expanded career choices. However, if Astronaut Barbie wants to study aerospace engineering, Republican men have canceled her student assistance. If Teacher Barbie wants to educate kids, Republican men decide what she will teach in school and bust her union. If Paramedic Barbie wants to save lives, she can't afford the job because Republican men block childcare support. On issue after issue, according to vanden Heuvel, reactionary forces are now seeking to undermine Barbie's motto: "We girls can do anything."[19]

The film *Barbie* does make the case that "girls can do anything," especially given the achievement of writer-director Greta Gerwig, and the acting success of the tallish star Margot Robbie who plays Barbie. The boycott of the film proposed by such right-wing mouthpieces as Ben Shapiro and the Fox News team clearly fizzled. America proved its love for the new Barbie—and proved it quickly. The right-wing media most often measures the success of any enterprise in terms of dollars and cents. In the case of Barbie, she clearly won, and they dramatically lost. The box-office take for the film just 17 days after its release was a record $1 billion.[20]

Perhaps even more important, level-headed reviewers in the mainstream media declared that *Barbie* was neither anti-male nor anti-female, but a movie at the cultural crossroads of thinking about gender. And these critics found much to like in Ken's journey from a mere accessory to Barbie, to a dramatic manhood rebellion after he gets a taste of patriarchy in his visit to the real world. Then Ken finally comes to a new understanding that he and other Kens can find their own meaning and their own triumphs—even in a "Barbieland" where women have the right to succeed.

"By the end of the movie, when Barbieland is re-instated back to the way it was, Ken isn't any weaker or stronger than he was at the start of the movie," writes Evan Romano for *Men's Health*. "But one thing he is, is more aware of the world around him, how he fits into it, and how, in the future, he *can* fit into it. And that's something that doesn't hurt any man to think about."[21]

Can *Barbie*'s Ken become a new icon for manhood as males continue to ask what their role is in society? Can Ken provide insight on how men can navigate a world that is changing all around them? The reactionaries will, of course, shriek: "Oh, hell no!" They will cringe as they recall Ken donning his luxurious Sylvester Stallone–inspired white fur coat in a movie all about a girl, Barbie.

They also will point out that Ken is just a sexless doll and a movie character not suitable as an icon for real men. It must be pointed out, however, that characters like "The Duke," Dirty Hairy, Rambo, and Maverick are also all movie fantasies. The man palming a basketball emblazoned with No. 45, or tearing open his T-shirt to reveal a Superman vest, is something even less than a movie character. He's a poor candidate for a lasting icon. He's a Non Fungible Token, an NFT, a virtual collection of pixels on a screen display from cyberspace.

Manly Men in Search
of Manhood

When Herb Goldberg published, *The Hazards of Being Male: Surviving the Myth of Masculine Privilege* in the 1970s, he was tarred by critics as a deluded reactionary. He had the audacity to question whether men actually had male privilege in American society. Many of his male readers, however, agreed with him that it was not a privilege to fight the nation's wars, to be the family's breadwinner, to pay the alimony after divorce court, to die early and leave the family nest egg to survivors. They wanted a new definition of manhood. By the 1990s, men's rights groups were out in the streets, quoting Goldberg and protesting sexism at the cinema and at the county courthouse. Were they a bunch of radicals?

When a consortium of sports figures and ministers published *Seven Promises of a Promise Keeper* in the 1990s, their motives were suspect. They were inviting men to sports stadiums to hear religious sermons and homilies on how to be faithful husbands and better family providers. Promise Keepers leaders filled the stadiums with men who were often troubled and disgusted with their lives. They wanted a new definition of manhood. Men of the Promise Keepers discussed whether Christ was the battler of money changers in the temple or a just a gentle friend of vagabonds, the sick, and the poor. Were the Promise Keepers a bunch of wide-eyed Jesus Freaks?

When Minister Louis Farrakhan and his coterie asked a million Black men to come to Washington, D.C. in the 1990s for a day of atonement and a call to action, white folks were flustered. Were these rebellious Black Panthers in sheep's clothing? Would there be race riots and violence? The Black men came, and they sought a new definition of manhood. They peacefully assembled on the National Mall to hear about reconciliation and also to learn about the terrible holocaust of past enslavement and the need for societal reparations. Were they a bunch of mendacious extortionists?

When Robert Bly and his mythopoetic philosophers called on men to go to the woods and find their "inner warriors" and undergo purification, some opinion-makers in the media pronounced them as "loons." It all sounded like a poor excuse to get away from the drudgery of suburban life and nagging wives—and to do a little camping in a few smoke-filled wigwams. Regardless, the men came to the woods to enter a sweat lodge and to purge their physical and psychological impurities. They wanted a new definition of manhood. The opinion columnists mocked their flutes, their lutes, their drumming, and their ritual chanting. Were they a bunch of tree-hugging deadbeats?

Those who dismissed the men's movements at the end of our last century were free to ridicule them as radicals, freaks, frauds, and deadbeats. It should be remembered, however, that these men did not willfully kill, maim, or torture anyone. They did not engage in blood sport or participate in initiation rituals that harmed others. They did not storm the American Capitol while bringing down police officers with bear spray, flag poles, and deadly projectiles. These men were not out to "save" the republic from perfidy, or to intimidate those with different gender orientations, or to try to re-establish male hegemony over uppity women and incendiary "feminizers." These men were looking inward for the most part, trying to find a way to better themselves, to find a sense of balance in a world that was often shaking them to the core.

Contrast these men and their movements of the past to the most visible manifestations of men in today's militant groups. Today's manly men are of Proud Boys, Oath Keepers, Patriot Front, Crusaders, Fraternal Order of Alt-Knights, White Power, and various and sundry militias and alt-right splinter groups. These men are not inward-looking, and they are not interested in atonement, reconciliation, or redefining manhood. These men are cocksure of their identities and their mission. Their stated goal is to Make America Great Again in some fantasyland of male dominance, white supremacy, and evangelical orthodoxy in which a man is a man and a woman is woman—and never the twain shall meet.

The problem with the fantasyland of MAGA world is that the good ship Patriarchy has already sailed. America is now a diverse country with free-thinking women and plenty of men who are actually embracing the quest for a new definition of manhood. Any would-be sage—in an honest quest for a new definition of manhood—cannot simply ignore the ground work that was established by past men's movements, including some not covered in this text.

A sincere exploration of manhood in present times has to give due deference to what has come before The immediate questions that come to mind about the past manhood quests concern what the groups did right and what did they do wrong. Where did they flail and fail? Where did they succeed? And how did we all arrive at the disturbing point where we are today?

The most obvious failing of the groups of the past is their mistaken belief that they could arrive at a new definition of manhood without more than half of the population contributing to the effort, the segment consisting of females. Manhood has to be a joint project. The Black women who critiqued the Million Man March had it right when they went after the patriarchal nature of that event. The men argued back that they needed time with themselves, that men have a much harder time relating to each other and need coaching. Beyond that, the expressed purpose of the March was to sensitize men to their responsibilities to wives, family, and society as a whole.

A group of Black feminists formed an alliance called the African American Agenda 2000 to challenge the Million Man March. They called out the sexism implicit in an event that was largely all-male. Among the women critics were Angela Davis, Barbara Ransby, Evelynn Hammonds, and Kimberlé Crenshaw. According to these Black feminists, the march sent a message that men could do the hard work of improving themselves alone and that women should just stay at home where they belong.[1]

Robert Bly's mythopoetic men's movement came in for much the same criticism. Women were sidelined while men packed up and headed to the woods on their own to find themselves. Bly's movement may be the most interesting from an intellectual standpoint, and its adherents continue to explore in such areas as Jungian psychology, literature of other cultures, and Native American ritual. A valid criticism is that this movement is that it seems oriented for educated, upper-middle-class men and does not offer much for blue-collar males, a demographic hit hard by declines in social and economic status.

Men's rights and fathers' rights groups cannot be spared the criticism of seeming to be anti-women, either. Several men's rights groups started out as pro-feminist but became increasingly hostile to women as feminist movement leaders became more strident about women's rights. Ever on the lookout for "conflict journalism," major media outlets loved to report when the sexes were at each other's throats.

To their credit, fathers' rights groups sometimes enlisted women in their cause through their "second wives clubs." After difficult divorces and alimony fights, these men drafted their second wives into auxiliaries in their battle against what they perceived as an unfair judicial system and domestic laws at odds with their interests. Critics might dismiss these "second wives" as mere adjuncts, but the point is that the alienated dads still were talking to women. Contrast this with the involuntary celibate males of today, the "incel" men who have completely cut themselves off from women and who pose a danger to women and to themselves.

Men's rights and fathers' rights groups have taken aim at the media

Fathers' rights groups have attacked Hollywood for making movies with a bias against men. In *Kramer vs. Kramer* (1979), Dustin Hoffman and Justin Henry portrayed a father-son relationship threatened by divorce. Hoffman's character revealed a sensitive and caring father figure (Photofest).

and Hollywood in much the same manner as today's unhappy, militant men. They protested outside cinemas showing *First Wives Club* or *War of the Roses*, films deemed sexist against men.[2] Although this may have shown their sophistication regarding the power of popular culture in influencing the nation's attitudes, their protests did not acknowledge that Hollywood did a reasonable job of showing the other side in the struggles of men in the workplace, at home, and in the courtroom. Movie offerings of the time that were especially sympathetic to men were *Kramer vs. Kramer*, *Tootsie*, and *Mrs. Doubtfire*. These films showed sympathetic males often struggling in the workplace, at home, and in court. *Kramer vs. Kramer* in particular revealed how men, who want to be caring fathers, can be crushed in divorce courts.

Cinematic tastes for the Promise Keepers ran more to *Gladiator*, *We*

Were Men, and *Braveheart*, as opposed to *Tootsie* or *Mrs. Doubtfire*. Of all the men's groups of late last century, the Promise Keepers were probably the least wed to the idea of finding a new definition of manhood. What they wanted was a return to traditionalist attitudes about how men should behave. They seemed to be arguing for a pact with women. If you women return to the kitchen and your duties as childbearers and the nurturers of our children—then we men promise to get sober, stop carousing with other women, and buckle down in the workplace to assure steady support for the family enterprise.

Promise Keepers, a predominantly evangelical movement, was on the verge of having some serious discussions about Jesus Christ and his message for Christianity. As noted previously in this book, Promise Keepers sometimes divided over Jesus as an example of a servant leader or as the warrior in a corrupted temple of money changers. In her study, *Jesus and John Wayne: How White Evangelicals Corrupted a Faith and Fractured a Nation,* author Kristin Kobes Du Mez makes the case that the Promise Keepers chose the vision of the crusader and warrior. She posits that the argument among the men in this group was pretty much decided when the twin towers came down on September 11.[3]

With the death and chaos of September 11, Christian warriors were needed to fight the Islamic terrorists, the infidels, the appeasers, the sinners, and anyone who might take joy in weakening the vital character of American men. The Promise Keepers initially pledged to be nonpartisan, but after the cataclysm of passenger jets crashing into the towers and the Pentagon, it was time to circle the wagons. It was time to defend a traditional paradigm of Christian culture and masculinity. It was time to call out political liberals and all those who allied themselves with abortionists, gender benders, humanists, secularists, globalists, wild-eyed feminists and soft men.

Interestingly enough, the evangelical leaders who founded the Promise Keepers also came to found the Alliance Defense Fund. Its goal was to save the American culture under attack from the harmful forces of secularists and globalists. Since its founding, the Alliance Defense Fund has expanded its many operations in the United States and in 2012 became the Alliance Defending Freedom.[4] Although its mission is ostensibly to preserve the free speech rights of Christians, women and minority groups argue that its legal efforts are curtailing their freedoms and endangering constitutional rights. The Alliance Defending Freedom has advised courts and judges, written legislation, and engaged in litigation in the service of moral clarity and traditional manhood.

Of all the late twentieth-century men's groups examined in this study, the Promise Keepers provide the best segue into a new century of more militant men's movements. For one thing, the group has the continuing legacy of its American Defense Fund, which has become the activist Alliance Defending Freedom. For another, the new militancy of the Promise Keepers members after the attacks of September 11, 2001, so well-documented by Kristin Kobes Du Mez, seems to have continued unabated.

The militant men's groups of this century are on the same page as the post 9/11 Promise Keepers when it comes to opposing reproductive rights, gay rights, gun restrictions, or public school curricula and library content deemed as "woke." The rhetoric of the new militant men's groups, however, can be far more extreme and a provocation to violence. Alt-right men's groups' forays into criminal violence are now apparent and, in many cases, their leaders actually brag about their bloodletting and their physical attacks on others. The new militant men exhibit toxic masculinity at its worst and the most dramatic manifestations of it were evident at the 2021 Insurrection in Washington, D.C.

The violence of toxic masculinity, whether committed en masse or by so-called "lone wolves," has become a major problem on the American social and political landscape. Police departments, the military, schools, civic groups, churches and individual families are asking: How do we dismantle the radicalization pipeline that has produced so many militant masculinists? How do we stop the physical attacks on others? How do we get to a saner and healthier kind of manhood?

Obviously, the first step is to admit that toxic masculinity does actually exist. This first step is not so easy for everybody. Too many politicians and media entities on the right profit from denying that it exists. Male supremacist kingpins of the media have become expert at fueling alt-right males exaggerated sense of persecution and grievance. The resulting polarization and the extremist challenge America faces is daunting. Some authorities on radicalization and de-radicalization argue that the U.S. needs a Marshall Plan to address extremist propaganda and the violence engendered by a very real toxic masculinity.

Manly Quests and Toxicity

There's sad irony in the phenomena of a U.S. Senator positioning himself as an authoritative commentator on masculinity, yet casting himself as the foremost denier that toxic masculinity even exists. The children who have hidden under their desks while a male adolescent stalks school hallways with an automatic weapon know toxic masculinity exists. The battered and bruised women who call a help crisis line after an encounter with an abusive domestic partner know about toxic masculinity. The gay demonstrators at a Pride March, who endure insults and slurs and get punched in the face, know that toxic masculinity exists. And yet somehow, members of Congress, educated in elite U.S. schools, not only remain ignorant about toxic masculinity's existence but can actually personify it themselves.

In early 2023 Josh Hawley sent out a fundraising letter several months before his book on manly virtues was published: "The radical Left is poisoning our men," Hawley wrote. "They say that being strong and masculine is 'toxic masculinity.' They want to make our men's spirits diminutive, their courage nonexistent, and their protective instincts GONE altogether. The socialist Left is selling our men a lie, and it's up to US to stop it. Let me be clear: there is nothing 'TOXIC' about being a man!

"We don't need more feminine men: we need men to step up and be husbands, fathers, and leaders," Hawley continued. "I'm leading the fight to DEFEND masculinity and save the next generation of men from the radical Left! America's men need to rebel against the radical Left, Fellow American. Be confident. Start your own family. Have your own ideas and stand up for them. We need men to be brave leaders against the woke Democrats more than ever."[5]

Hawley' rhetoric is disturbing, dangerous—toxic. Who are all these radical, leftist, socialist, woke people out to destroy manhood? Hawley talks about all these poisonous forces, but there is something terribly poisonous in this militarist language of culture war, even if its purpose is just to solicit twenty bucks of campaign money. If all these horrible people exist—people who want to destroy men's courage, their spirits, their protective instincts—then maybe it is time to grab a handgun and join the Proud Boys. Hawley says these insidious foes are, indeed, everywhere and it's time to rebel and be brave. So, does this actually require more than just going out and getting a family started?

Hawley and other right-wing senators will cry "free speech" and defend their noxious words as purely "aspirational," rather than being an incitement to violence. Perhaps one over-charged, raucous plea for campaign money by a desperate politician can be overlooked. However, Hawley takes up page after page of his book, *Manhood: The Masculine Virtues America Needs*, hysterically ranting about the term *toxic masculinity* and how it is a twisted and evil radical liberal invention. Hawley says no menace to this nation is worse than the collapse of American manhood, and liberals welcome the demise of manly men: "In the power centers they control, places like the press, the academy and politics, they blame masculinity for America's woes. The tribunes of elite opinion long ago decided that male strength is dangerous—toxic, leading inevitably to oppression and hateful patriarchy."[6]

Authors of right-wing diatribes contend that subversives in the universities have confused and harmed American men. Hawley refers to the academic "Epicurean liberals" who have no moral compass. These Epicureans tell men they are "the biggest threat our society faces; that the male longing for adventure is dangerous, that a man's desire for accomplishment is oppressive: that masculinity is toxic, inherently ... no wonder young men feel bewildered."[7] And, it's not just the university professors who are shrinking masculine values and diminishing men. The brainwashing even is perpetuated by grade school teachers who have young boys in their sights to demoralize and squash them.

American schools have a mission that is "not so much to educate boys as to subdue them, to wring out of them any proclivity for aggressive play and adventure, to rid them of their boyishness." It starts early ... if boys don't comply, they are drugged…. For some clinicians, the very boyishness of boys is now something to be controlled and medicated away…. The left's ultimate aim is to separate men from manhood, to create "a new breed of men who view gender as a choice rather than anything rooted in reality— and masculinity as a construct individuals can pick up or discard at will. Leftists aim to create a generation of androgynous individuals…."[8]

The right-wing mantra on the coming extinction of men and manhood is quite simply ridiculous. The rhetoric is nonsensical, but dangerous at the same time. Nevertheless, think about it: If divine providence has made men to be kings and warriors, then why are these same men so susceptible and vulnerable to mere words of soft-headed and depraved academics? Why does Hawley suggest these godly warriors and kings are folding up their tents and curling into fetal positions—all because of college professors, feminist politicians, or liberal Hollywood actresses? It's illogical. It does not compute.

Logical or not, the right-wing agitprop about the man-haters continues. Hawley insists the anti-male lessons have been rehashed and recycled for decades by the media, Hollywood, and various politicians. The hateful pedagogy is now even found in elementary schools, where proposed curricula teach the youngest children that masculinity is shameful and oppressive: "It has become the conventional wisdom of our Epicurean age: manhood is toxic. ... And there you have it. To be a man is, of itself, to contribute to the supposed tyranny of the social order. It is to be trash. An entire generation of cultural Marxists and other liberals have drummed this theme into the head of anyone who will listen."[9]

Hawley has some explaining—and not mansplaining—to do. For example, he needs to be called out on who exactly describes our age as "Epicurean" besides Hawley himself? What does the economic theory of Marxism or socialism have to do with being anti-male? Maybe one explanation is that when all else fails, it's time to bring out the "communist" red herring of McCarthy Era vintage. Hawley needs to identify some of the schools where Marxist grade school teachers are telling little boys that they are shameful because they are male. Where are the lesson plans for saying "men are trash" in our public schools?

Hawley and most conservatives know full well that sociologists, feminist women, and even the American Psychological Association are not saying that men are trash, or inherently toxic, or that toxicity is ingrained in the DNA of the male gender. These professionals are simply saying that a dangerous number of men are exhibiting toxic behavior. There is a big difference. Behaviors can be changed for the better. Extremism can be moderated. Even disquieting culture war language can be exchanged for something better.

As previously noted, the first step to a saner masculinity, and a more positive vision of manhood, is to concede that toxic masculinity exists and to move away from all the culture war disinformation. This may require tuning out the noise and distraction of certain social media platforms. This may also require exiting from the harmful relationships that thrive on a commonality of hatred and bigotry. In the years since the Capitol Insurrection, desperate families have turned to counselors, psychologists, and a number of family organizations for help in "deprogramming" sons, brothers, fathers, uncles and grandfathers. Families have sought answers on how to pull loved ones back from the precipice of extremism, violence, racism, and contempt for women, feminist or otherwise. Resources for rehabilitation are available.

Partners for Peace is a volunteer counseling organization that has dealt with a growing number of young men attracted to the ideology of white supremacy. The group also has experienced an avalanche of helpline calls related to the January 6 attack and concerns over QAnon conspiracy talk among family members. Its executive director, Myrieme Churchill, explains that extremism and hate mix to make a drug of choice to numb the pain of underlying personal issues.[10] It's a dependency that must be addressed with a curative similar to what gets results with other addictions. The remedy includes compassion and a sympathetic ear because harsh rebukes and self-righteous reproaches are counterproductive.

Life After Hate is another program that has seen its caseload grow exponentially. Movements like QAnon, Proud Boys, and the men of the angry incel phenomenon have instigated far-right violence. It's extremism that results in injuries and death such as what occurred at the "Unite the Right" tragedy in Charlottesville in 2017. These events call out for interventions and for the compassionate rehabilitation of participants. The participants are just as often victims of extremism as their targets, according to Sammy Rangel, a founder of Life After Hate.[11] Rangel said militant men can, and do, leave the far-right and are capable of redemption, with informed and constructive personal counseling.

Two women who have chronicled the process of counseling and rehabilitation are Hannah Knowles of the *Washington Post* and Paulina Villegas, formerly of the *New York Times*. They have worked with Brian Hughes, founder of American University's Polarization and Extremism Research and Innovation Lab (PERIL), to understand the deradicalization process.[12] Hughes breaks down the circumstances of radicalization into three parts: there are the men who are "circling the drain" and taking in far-right ideas and conspiracies; the "hard core" who have marched in Charlottesville or who have stormed the Capitol; and then there are the troubled human beings in between.

The most opportune time to intervene is at the "circling the drain" phase when there may be an opportunity to teach basic media literacy and identify fake narratives. A more difficult challenge is reaching the "hard core" members of far-right militant male groups. A transformation at this point may require a "jolt" to the extremist's personal life, or the trauma of witnessing fellow conspirators' behavior, or the terrible violence that they may inflict on others. Hardened extremists are not so easily reached, but those who are merely following them can find their way back to sanity.

Many of the more passive participants in the Capitol Insurrection riot did get a "jolt" of reality and have reconsidered their associations with white nationalists and militant men's groups. A number of active participants expressed sincere remorse before judges and courts after being indicted for serious legal offenses. These conscience-stricken people sometimes recounted their psychological journey into anarchy and savage behavior. "They witness the full ugliness and how far people are willing to go," said Rangel of Life After Hate. "A lot of people then want to separate from that."[13]

After decoupling from the disinformation and the toxic leadership of extremist movements, those who have a corrective epiphany commonly desire to reach out and find a way back to reality. They seek a redemptive future. This can mean revitalizing past male and female relationships and also finding support from extended family members who are willing to take the initiative. Clinical psychologists advise that compassionate friends can be an antidote to the blind security of a cult. Sympathetic family members provide a much better forum to work through pain and disorders than the "gang atmosphere" provided by groups like Proud Boys or Patriot Front.

The process of de-escalating the toxic masculinity syndrome involves personal reflection, serious thought, and discussion for redefining individual manhood in a positive manner. Women should not only be welcome in this process but also be integral to it. Younger men may need new mentors and father figures whom they never actually enjoyed or benefited from while growing up. Some key items to work through together include retracing the path that took an individual to extremism in the first place; determining what psychological benefits accrued from joining an alt-right group; finding palliatives for misogynist or racist attitudes—this can actually include trips to Holocaust memorials or Black history museums; and evaluating the risk factors for recidivism or falling back into the trap of extremist behavior.

Finally, redefining manhood in a serious way requires jettisoning all of the old, tired stereotypes and icons. In his attempt to "recapture manhood," author Hawley devotes several of his book chapters to re-establishing past male roles as family patriarch, as "King," as "Warrior," as "Priest," and as "Builder." These kinds of prescriptions have been offered by similar alt-right guides, but there's a major impediment when the rest of the family does not cooperate in viewing the man of the house as a priest or warrior. And this rejection is precisely what drives some men into the willing arms of extremist groups. In any case, it's inconceivable that today's families desire a father who wants to play king, priest, or magician. Also, in a society where women now are welders, firefighters, home builders, and CEOs, they may not be so interested in having a know-it-all "Builder" around the house.

Society has changed. Women often have higher education attainment and economic status now than men. These women may be looking for a cooperative partner and companion, rather than an overbearing patriarch. Women are no longer sitting alone waiting for Camelot to materialize or Prince Charming to come rescue them from a dreary existence. Sleeping beauty has awakened without the help of a powerful male. Men who latch onto alt-right guides for reestablishing manhood may just want to consider a one-way ticket to an Isis stronghold in the Middle East or to the Taliban-ruled Afghanistan. Sadly, some young American men actually have made that ticket purchase, and their final destinations have proven far more disastrous than even a two-year prison sentence due to a hitch with the Proud Boys.

Redefining manhood requires new icons and new adjectives for masculinity, but the old identifiers and attributes for manhood do not all have to be consigned to history's dustbin. Manhood can still be served by courage, daring, enterprise, independence, spirit, and determination. However, masculine identity also can be served by such traits as empathy, tolerance, forbearance and collaboration. Men who sincerely desire to live more holistic and healthier lives will put new emphases on compassion over stoicism, sympathetic collaboration over aggressive independence, and reconciliation over belligerence. Clinical psychologists addressing toxic masculinity in therapy sessions offer the following advice for their clients:

- Do an inventory of past actions that would classify as toxic masculine behavior; resolve to end such conduct and to call it out when exhibited by other male acquaintances.
- Realize there is no single path or profession for masculinity. A florist or a nurse practitioner can be just as much of a man as a coal miner or an oil driller.
- Discourage admiration for toxic male icons of the past (or present) who appear in the worlds of sports, entertainment, politics, or cinema.
- Support male candidates who are non-toxic, whether at the level of Congress and the presidency, or in races for local school boards and city councils.
- Be vocal. Do not be afraid to denounce bullying, or shaming, or joking at others' expense; and do not be afraid to put down autocrats who fear that democratic norms threaten male privilege.
- Be a change agent. Encourage young men to be activists on climate change, or sensible gun laws, or campaigns against bullying—and provide helpful examples for youth by welcoming a more inclusive society.

New Icons for Manhood

George Washington is often cited as the "Father of the American experiment," a man whose courage in the Revolutionary War against the British secured independence for the United States. In November 2017, some thirty members of the Patriot Front demonstrated at the University of Texas at Austin. The alt-right males gathered around a statue of George Washington on the school campus with their torches and flares

George Washington was an effective military leader in the Revolutionary War against Britain. In civilian life, he was soft-spoken and polite. Scholars say Washington did not worry about his manliness wearing his powdered wigs, leggings, and stockings (Library of Congress)

ablaze. Their leader, Thomas Rousseau, raised his voice and delivered an alarming speech: "America, our nation, stands before an existential threat. The lives of your children, and your children's children, and your prosperity beyond that, dangle above a den of vipers. A corrupt, rootless, global, and tyrannical elite has usurped your democracy and turned it into a weapon, first to enslave and then to replace you."[14]

In gathering around a statue of America's first president, the manly guard of the Patriot Front apparently did not realize that George Washington was not a "real man" by their own standards. When Washington was young, he suffered from a viral infection that caused an inflammation in the lining of his lungs. His pleurisy as a child left him with a very high, weak, and breathy voice. His contemporaries described him as a soft man and very soft-spoken. Biographer Steve Yoch has explained that his high voice, and his notoriously bad teeth, gave him the habit of keeping his mouth shut. He was not gregarious or strident as might be expected of a manly patriot.[15]

Washington appeared as likeable rather than menacing, both as first president and in his later years. On the dollar bill found in most wallets, he appears rather droll and nonthreatening. He's in a powdered wig that makes him look rather womanish. He wears a smirk at best, and his lips seem pursed, with a mouth closed tightly. He wears a ruffly neckerchief in the image on the currency, and were a full frontal portrait available, Washington would be in leggings and stockings. Appearances be damned. The worst aspect of George Washington was that he fancied himself to be a philosopher—and a liberal one at that. He was a man of grace and quiet dignity who may very well have been an Epicurean liberal who enjoyed indulging in domestic pleasures.

Maurizio Valsana, author of *First Among Men: George Washington and the Myth of American Masculinity*, states in his biography: "Washington didn't fear that his being graceful and his being a true 'philosopher'—a term that would today translate as 'liberal' today—would trigger exclusion from male company. Washington didn't worry he would be called a 'faggot,' or a 'snowflake,' or a hypocrite in seeking to act in ways that did not trample on what he referred to as 'delicacy of my feelings.'"[16]

Recently the alt-right men who have learned of Washington's manly shortcomings and his imperfections have expressed a desire to cancel him out and to replace his image with that of Andrew Jackson or with Jackson's outspoken admirer, Donald Trump. Manly men of the right express aversion to males who sport longish locks like George Washington—or even Jesus Christ. It's tough to find manly images of Jesus with his occasional halo; his silky, lengthy hair; his wispy lips and mustache, his flowing gowns and robes. In recent decades, the men of the Promise Keepers have sought to portray him as an angry prophet chasing Pharisees or money-changers from the temple. However, the temple event was a rare moment of anger and aggression for an otherwise peace-seeking Jesus Christ.

In truth, George Washington and Jesus Christ are more likely figures for enlightened men of the liberal persuasion, men who seek to claim new—and some old—icons for a transformative definition of manhood. An outdated, angry patriarch of today cannot easily accommodate the most treasured quotes of such a gentleman as George Washington. He believed in the liberal arts and was also a patron of the arts. He declared that "heroes have made poets, and poets heroes." Washington also used that dread word *progressive*, which has been canceled as "woke" in the hateful lexicon of today's alt-right men. Washington once conceded a certain suspect obsession: "For I love to indulge the contemplation of human nature in a progressive state of improvement and melioration...."[17]

The words of Jesus Christ should be even more problematic for a rabble of alt-right male traditionalists. His Sermon on the Mount gets very little air play among the shock jocks of the right or on conservative talk radio. Among the eight Beatitudes, which comprise the wisdom of Jesus, and that appear in the Apostle Matthew's recounting are:

- Blessed are the poor in spirit, for theirs is the Kingdom of Heaven.
- Blessed are those who mourn, for they will be comforted.
- Blessed are the meek, for they will inherit the Earth.
- Blessed are the merciful, for they will be shown mercy.
- Blessed are the pure in heart, for they will see God.
- Blessed are the peacemakers, for they will be called the Sons of God.[18]

The Apostle Luke's recordings of the words of Jesus Christ can be even harder to swallow for conservative traditionalists. They not only contain the *Beatitudes* but also the listing of the *Woes*: "But woe to you who are rich, for you have already received your comfort. Woe to you who are well fed now, for you will go hungry. Woe to you who laugh now, for you will mourn and weep. Woe to you when everyone speaks well of you, for that is how their ancestors treated the false prophets."[19] The *Woes* are decidedly not a right-wing prosperity gospel. Jesus leaned to a Bernie Bros' perspective, not to the dictums of the Proud Boys. Enlightened males in the liberal column of the political equation are perfectly justified in claiming Jesus Christ, as well as George Washington, for their own as icons for an informed manhood.

Redefining manhood in a serious way does require thoughtful discussion as to what figures from religious heritage, past history, and contemporary culture belong in a pantheon of best examples of iconic men.

It's a discussion to decide which icons are best left to alt-right males, and which ones can rightfully be claimed by George Washington progressives looking for a new manhood paradigm. It's a discussion that should capture a new diversity in manhood with consideration of such iconic males as Sidney Poitier, Tom Hanks, Harry Belafonte, Barack Obama, Dwight Eisenhower, Mark Milley, Matt Damon, Chris Martin, Dave Meggyesy, Dave Kopay, and Jim Thorpe, to name just a few. It's also a discussion to compartmentalize icons, to identify personal successes and failings, and to draw comparisons between real live men and outright fantasies.

Those who value the frontier spirit are slowly beginning to realize that the celluloid cowboys of the John Wayne Era are simply not authentic. They don't hold a candle to an actual frontiersman like Daniel Boone. Rugged Daniel Boone could be an icon for a new definition of manhood. Yes, handsome John Wayne is the darling of the right, with his adoring ladies, and his ever-sharp six-shooter. However, Boone was the real man. Granted, pop culture and the mass media attempted to transform Boone into a benevolent slaveholder, a savage "Indian killer," a wrestler of bears, a tall fellow with a raccoon pelt on his head. The real story is quite different. Boone was condemned as an "Indian sympathizer" who was adopted by the Shawnee. He was a literate explorer who read from books around the campfire. He was not a big man, and he loathed those coonskin caps as coarse and scratchy.[20]

Many women prefer characters played by actor Alan Alda to those played by Clint Eastwood or Sylvester Stallone. Alda could be an icon for a new definition of manhood. Yes, Eastwood showed traditional manliness in threatening to blow a bad guy's "head clean off." Stallone showed manliness in *Rambo* by severing a head with a knife and running off with it. In marked contrast, Alan Alda as Dr. "Hawkeye" Pierce in *M*A*S*H* was in the business of repairing and attaching appendages. His prominence on TV and in film gave him a platform to speak out on political topics. He supported women's rights and the Equal Rights Amendment. A self-described feminist, he was appointed to the International Women's Year Commission. He worked on the critically-acclaimed children's album, *Free to Be You and Me*, which counseled girls and boys that it was okay to be friends.[21]

In 1972, veterans groups loathed Senator George H. McGovern and supported Richard M. Nixon for the U.S. presidency. McGovern was a critic of the Vietnam War and advocated American withdrawal from a bloody and futile effort. McGovern knew what he was talking about. McGovern could be an icon for a new definition of manhood. Yes, Nixon mined harbors, mercilessly bombed Hanoi, and received the American Legion's Distinguished Service Medal in 1969. However, McGovern had a far more distinguished record of military service, which he refused to brag about or exploit in the 1972 political campaign. McGovern volunteered for the U.S. Army Air Force in World War II. As a B-24 Liberator pilot, he flew 35 dangerous missions over German-occupied Europe. He saved his flight crew and barely escaped death on several occasions. McGovern was a distinguished U.S. Senator, but his insistence on humility kept most Americans in the dark about his military bravery.[22]

Monuments to early colonizers, slaveholder presidents, Confederate soldiers, vapid movie heroes, and general political nincompoops have understandably come under increasing attack. As the statues dedicated to Christopher Columbus, Robert E. Lee, and John Wayne start to come down, does it make sense to erect statues to new, more progressive male icons? Some historians answer in the negative. Heroes very often have feet of clay. Even the suggestion in this chapter that George Washington become an icon for a new manhood will inevitably draw fire. After all, Washington may have possessed desired qualities of compassion, comity, and quietude, but he was also an unrepentant slaveholder.

On 1960s television shows, Fess Parker played Daniel Boone. He was a big man in a coonskin cap who threw axes and killed varmints. Scholars say the real Daniel Boone (portrait from 1876) was a much smaller man who read books around the campfire and hated coonskin caps (Library of Congress).

The fact that very few human beings come away from the experience of life without failings and some very obvious flaws, should not preclude a search for some more satisfactory icons than those we may have in place now. The very realization of male frailty should be one of the animating forces behind a new perspective on manhood. All men are imperfect. Deal with it. Icons need not become idols.

Real men should be wise enough not to fall into an idolatry or worship of "heroes" that can drive the daffs to crashing through U.S. Capitol windows and defecating on the floors of the nation's house of democracy. Real men should be wise enough to avoid the raging iconoclasm that can devolve into tearing down everything and loosing mere anarchy upon our country and our world. A soft parade of soft men is what the times demand now. Moderation in all things. That is a virtue to be championed by all rational men of good will.

Postscript

To Be, or Not to Be—a "Girly Man"

Progress in the struggle to achieve a rational definition of manhood is generally measured in inches—not in feet. Every so often, however, there is one small step for man and a giant leap for mankind. Such a leap may have occurred in 2018 when the handsome body builder and alleged groper, Arnold Schwarzenegger, apologized for his years of using the homophobic insult "girly man." The ultimate "he man" of the late 20th century expressed his regret for using the hurtful term that some have likened to pejoratives like wimp, weakling, milksop, milquetoast, or crybaby. Of course, none of these epithets are as potent as the derogatory "girly man."

I know. I was a pre-school "girly man."

Schwarzenegger borrowed the insult from *Saturday Night Live.* It was from a sketch written for "Pumping Up with Hans and Franz," a routine about President George H. W. Bush and his political opponents in the late 1980s. Schwarzenegger repeated it in a 2004 speech at the Republican National Convention and as California's governor. He told *Men's Health* magazine some years later that he regretted using the girly-man term that was associated with misogyny and homophobia. Kenzie Bryant wrote in *Vanity Fair* that Schwarzenegger did not go far enough with his apparent apology. She said that in his expression of regret, the former governor of California tried to pass off the slur as part of partisan politics rather than as a damaging phrase in itself.[1]

In the long journey to male enlightenment, it seems even a half-hearted small step should be applauded, although I do tend to agree with Bryant's analysis. Schwarzenegger did not go far enough in his apology for normalizing the use of the term *girly man* in America. In truth, I have my own related complaint: Where was Arnold Schwarzenegger when I was in kindergarten and the neighborhood boys were calling me a sissy? They threw rocks at me and chased me home. I was denigrated as the sissy of the neighborhood because every afternoon I loved crossing the street from my house to play with my good friend, Margaret. My chief crime in childhood was probably that I liked playing with girls like Maggie.

At Maggie's, we would "play house" in her basement. Actually, she would play house setting up her little kitchen with a miniature stove, refrigerator, cupboard, table, and place settings. I would "play tornado" spinning around and knocking over all her kitchen appliances, chairs, tables, soup spoons and bowls. In retaliation for all my enjoyment of playing with Maggie, I was chased around the neighborhood by the Baird boys and the Czarnecki gang. At some point, my father had enough of my crying, my bruises, and my behaving like the "coward of the county"—or at least of the neighborhood. He told me to put up my dukes, stand my ground, and defend myself. Be a man—and start playing with some boys for heaven's sake.

So, the next time I was chased by David Baird, my father locked the screen door on me as I ran to seek refuge in my own home. I was forced to remain outside and defend myself. To my surprise, my display of pugilism was successful. The boys in the neighborhood were impressed. My father was pumped up with pride. I told a tearful Margaret goodbye for good and joined the Baird brothers every afternoon at their house to drink bottles of orange soda and to watch *The Three Stooges* on Channel 11. And what episodes of the Stooges did we boys most enjoy? Why, of course, the ones about their "Women Haters Club." And who could blame Moe, Larry, and Curly for being upset with women. These gals were always trying to trick them, always acting like they were in love—only because they wanted to take Moe's money.

I will not proceed with any more early biography—about how I started my own "Women Haters Club" in grade school, thanks to the Stooges. Or how by seventh grade, I had joined the Young Americans for Freedom and enlisted in the quest to elect Barry Goldwater to the presidency. Or how I also joined forces with Phyllis Schlafly in my home state of Illinois to oppose the subversive Equal Rights Amendment. For now, let's go back briefly to my struggle as the crybaby of the neighborhood—and my personal battle to end the label of "sissy" from becoming a permanent brand on my tender hide.

The point of this piece of postscript is to give an example of how boys learn, sometimes the hard way, about the need to be "manly." Lessons about gender differences and the way to behave appropriately, according to prevailing gender constructs, are forcibly taught quite early in life. It's harsh. Sometimes those instructions are taught by the bullies who shout insults like *sissy* or *pansy*. Sometimes those gender lessons are taught by a concerned father, who tries to do his best to protect a young son from humiliation. Later in life, those lessons may be taught to a young man by a brawny governor wielding terms like *girly man*. According to magazine writer Kenzie Bryant, the term *girly man* is just a hop, skip, and a jump to uglier slurs such as *fag* or *homo.*

Joining the Women's Pages

Less than two decades after being chased around my neighborhood and called a sissy, I ended up on the women's page desk at *The Columbia Missourian* at the University of Missouri School of Journalism. Apparently, I did not take those early lessons about minding my own gender to heart. Maybe the truth is that I just didn't care to show up at a school meeting to fight hard for a good story beat and editing desk position. So, I found myself stuck on general assignment and relegated to the women's pages at the school's Columbia daily newspaper. Every week, I was in charge of tracking down, and typing up, school lunch menus for the Columbia area's education districts: Monday—hot dog, macaroni and cheese, Rice Krispie treat. It was humiliating.

On the *Missourian* women's desk, I occasionally would land an actual feature story assignment. One was a feature profile on a pioneer woman priest, the Rev. Katrina Swanson, whose male elders in the Episcopal Church refused to acknowledge her ordination for the priesthood. I interviewed Swanson after she gave a speech to a group of young women at Stephens College in 1974. Later in the semester, I landed a front-page story on Corporal Klinger from the CBS-TV series *M*A*S*H.* I interviewed Jamie Farr in the backseat of his limousine ride from the airport in Jeff City for a celebrity appearance at Hickman High School in Columbia. Farr told me that he never tried on women's clothes for his TV job. He was a cross-dresser seeking a military discharge in the TV series. The show producers "have a mannequin for me who's a cross between Raquel Welch and Cybill Shepherd," Farr insisted.[2]

Stories on Corporal Klinger and the Rev. Swanson were worthy and publishable, but I was not going to get a passing grade for Reporting 105 at the graduate school of journalism without a legitimate story beat. My big break came when one of the regular student police/fire reporters told the newspaper editors she could not break a story because she could not break a date. The editors immediately fired her from police/fire and gave the beat to me. So what was my first assignment? I wrote a late-breaking story on Melinda Collins sporting the headline: "City's first woman firefighter says she's no blazing liberationist."[3] My new beat allowed me to write up the arrest blotter every day—much better than writing about Rice Krispie treats. I wrote regular police and crime stories, which allowed me to pass the reporting class and graduate.

My next stop in journalism—and next encounters with gender issues—came at the daily *Bloomington Pantagraph*. With my crime story news clips from *The Columbia Missourian* in hand, I was hired by the central Illinois newspaper for the evening police and fire beat. However, the editors told me there was another opening that they wanted me to consider. The new opening was an opportunity to be the first male reporter on the paper's women's page section, which was being renamed "Living Today." This was a revolutionary trend at newspapers all over the United States, one in which men were integrating the women's pages and the sections were being renamed "Scene," "Tempo," "Style," and "Family Living."

At the *Pantagraph*, I accepted the gracious offer to be a part of an American newsroom revolution. My reasons for accepting the challenge had less to do with an ambition to be on the cutting edge of journalism and much more to do with the hours. If I signed up with "Living Today," I would have a regular eight-hour shift during the day and could write features. Otherwise, I would be "Working Tonight," listening to the police scanner and chasing down crime stories at all hours of the night. I failed to realize that male *Pantagraphers* would harbor a lot of suspicions about a guy who would voluntarily enter the second-class purgatory of the women's pages—no matter what kind of fancy new name camouflaged the indignity of this section of the paper.

At the *Pantagraph*, I was not invited out to have "beers with the boys" for quite a long time. When I finally got an invite to the local bar, it was primarily because I was an object of curiosity. At an interrogation session over Budweiser drafts, a barrage of questions confronted me: "Was it true that I actually volunteered to write with the women?" "How could I look at myself in the mirror every morning as I prepared to write women's stuff?" "Weren't journalism schools ruining journalism with all this diversity in the newsroom crap?" "Why did I study for a master's degree in journalism? Who needs that?" After the beer session, the fellas in the newsroom removed me from pariah status and just put me on probation.

"You know, Corrigan, you are okay," said one sympathetic male colleague. "You seem to be a regular guy. When we heard some jerk was going to go to work on the women's pages, we figured he had to be some sort of fish." I began to feel like "some sort of fish." I got a hearty taste of the second-class treatment women have received in newsrooms since they were first allowed to enter the sacred domain as "sob sisters" for William Randolph Hearst and Joseph Pulitzer.

Our "Living Today" section of the paper was housed in a glass cage next door to the editor and managing editor. This proximity allowed the newspaper's patriarchs to conveniently "put a lid on the girls," if there was too much yakking and all their engagement announcements weren't getting typed fast enough. Unlike the real reporters in the newsroom, the girls were scrupulously timed for one-half hour for lunch. The assumption was that women would fritter the day away if left to their own devices. In contrast, the newsroom males could take as much time as they needed for lunch, after all, they were likely discussing late-breaking stories on the city or state desk.

I found myself caught in a bind one day, when I was out to lunch with the guys, and had to hurry back to the "Living Today" section in a timely fashion. "We're not through here yet," said the ringleader of the roundtable lunch discussion. "What's a matter, Corrigan? Got to get

Arnold Schwarzenegger was once the envy of the average male with his bulging biceps and super-human, tough-guy movies. The aging body builder apologized in 2018 for his many years of using the term "girly men" to describe mere mortal men (Photofest).

together some new recipes this afternoon?" Recipe jokes at my expense never grew stale, and the male newsroom crew gave me a nickname, "Donita." This made sense since the past women's page editor was named Lolita. The guys in the newsroom would frequently stick their heads in the glass cage where I sat with the female reporters and blurt out: "Hey, Donita, got any good recipes today?"

For the record, I did serious lifestyle stories every week, and only once published a recipe given to me by a visiting Nigerian delegation to Illinois State University. Needless to say, this strange sexual harassment that I encountered soon had me looking for another job. I took a much higher paying job to teach journalism at Lewis University in south Chicago, where I joined some new colleagues to start a weekly newspaper called *The Lockport Free Press*. One of the first letters to our newspaper enterprise came from one of the chauvinist males back at the *Bloomington*

Pantagraph. The letter to our weekly in the Lockport-Joliet area took aim at my photo and my credentials published in our first edition. It read:

> As a practicing journalist and a former president of the highly respected SDX chapter at Southern Illinois University, I must say I am appalled at the lack of veracity in the very first edition of your newspaper.
>
> The gall of one particular member of your editorial staff is enough to knock back the journalistic code several years.... Of what do I write?
>
> I quote from the summary of the qualifications of one Don Corrigan who serves as feature editor ... "he later spent a year as a member of the editorial staff at the Bloomington Pantagraph."
>
> I thought it was a simple coincidence and perhaps another Don Corrigan had once held a position of merit with our newspaper. But no, the mug shot (and I use that term literally) adorning your column erased all hopes of the paper's credibility.
>
> For the record, the closest Corrigan got to the editorial department was the day he was walking by the office and one of his engagement forms floated out of his fish-like hands and under the door. Our secretary kindly handed it back to him, through the mail slot, and he shuffled back to his desk in the women's department....
>
> Corrigan was a purveyor of panty hose, an editor of engagement announcements. Only, let's face it folks, Corrigan couldn't make it on his own. He didn't even know what a double-ring ceremony was. (He thought it was a Eubangie ritual, one ring for the finger, one for the nose.)
>
> Not only has he apparently falsified his records, Corrigan has evidently had his facial features reconstructed. He was never that cute when he was working here. Of course, he just didn't have the figure for gaucho pants.
>
> As a member of the working press, I would like to see competition among the media thrive and wish well to all sapling ventures. But you're doomed Free Press. Doomed by Corrigan.
>
> Sincerely,
>
> A Well-Wisher
>
> p.s. Donita, can I have your recipe for fried Dodo?[4]

Since my trials and tribulations in the late 1970s as the first male on the women's pages at the daily newspaper in Bloomington, many of the patriarchal ways in newsrooms are now a thing of the past. Women have achieved prestigious jobs as investigative reporters and as newsroom managers. In fact, females now comprise well over 50 percent of newsroom staffs. The chauvinists do have a new term for these predominantly female newsrooms. They are dismissed as "pink ghettos." Also, some news corporations have been accused of hiring more female journalists simply because they think they can pay them less.

Despite progress for women in the workplace, there is still a long way to go. And there are still plenty of men who want to turn back the clock. They are blue collar and white collar. They are walking the halls of Congress and sitting on the Supreme Court. They want to cancel out childcare programs, equal pay guarantees, sexual harassment prohibitions, and reproductive choice. Sometimes these men grow angry over these issues. Some are disposed to violence.

Another area of progress since the days of the "women's pages" 50 years ago is on the LGBTQ2+ front—on matters involving respect for gay men and women. After encountering homophobic slurs, being addressed as "Donita," and being dismissed as a "purveyor of pantyhose" at my first newspaper job, I must admit I was once pretty defensive about those slurs. I testified to my heterosexual credentials and made sure news staffers were aware that I had a girlfriend. This was not necessary. It smacks of cowardice. It's kind of like caving in to bigotry. There is no shame in being a gay human being.

Despite progress on gay rights, on protections against hate crimes, and the legalization of gay marriage in America, there are still many men who want to turn back the clock in this area of human relations. They are counting on a reconstituted U.S. Supreme Court to do their bidding. They drag out the specter of Sodom and Gomorrah to justify reactionary thinking and ugly talk. They contend that true manhood is inconceivable without the "correct" sexual orientation. Sometimes these men grow angry. Some are disposed to violence.

Manly Message: "Moderation in All Things"

After my time with the *Lockport Free Press* in south Chicago and the *Bloomington Pantagraph* in central Illinois, I moved to St. Louis to teach journalism at Webster University and to start several weekly newspapers in the Gateway City with graduating students. An editor job at the newspapers, and the professor job at the university, was the perfect combination. As an editor and co-publisher at *Webster-Kirkwood Times, Inc.,* I had the freedom to write stories on gender issues and area men who were active in the emerging men's groups in the 1980s and 1990s. This kind of journalism, and the necessary story research, was perfect for academic papers written for presentation at the Men's Studies Division of the American Culture Association, which later merged with the Popular Culture Association. This research proved to be germane for this work, *In Search of Manhood: American Men's Movements Past and Present* .

The academic papers I composed for the Popular Culture Association drew on interviews and stories with men of the Million Man March, Promise Keepers, Mythopoetic Men, and several different fathers' rights groups. In every case, I found these men to be sincere, contemplative, and committed to making their relationships with women and family better.

This is important to get on the record to dispel any suggestion of personal bias or hostility on my part to members of men's groups that arrived on the American scene during the period from the 1970s to 2000. I did not personally agree with all the tenets of these groups—and especially I did not agree with all the views of their leaders.

At the paper, I researched and interviewed members of militia groups, which may well have been forerunners of such organizations as Proud Boys or Oath Keepers of this century. While I disagree strongly with the philosophy and leadership of the militia movements, I never felt personally threatened by the members whom I interviewed. For the most part, I found that these men were looking for a sense of purpose and seemed genuine when they said they were training to help out in the event of weather disasters, local emergencies and civil unrest. However, like many Americans, I would prefer to rely on government for these kinds of services. Like many Americans, I also disagree with militia groups on their Second Amendment interpretations. I do not believe the Second Amendment sanctions unregulated militias or guarantees the right to open-carry and use powerful military-force weapons.

On April 21, 1995, I published interviews with members of 1st Missouri Volunteers. My story noted that militia members read from the U.S. Constitution, then took an oath to defend it. Following that, the citizen soldiers entered a field where they practiced combat exercises, bayonet training, and martial arts. According to their militia guidelines at that time, each member was to have at least 1,000 rounds of ammunition, an M-14 or M-1 Garand or a Russian SKS rifle. Personal sidearms could include a .45 ACP, 9 MM, or .38 Special. The militia leader said they were all about protecting America. It was silly, he implied, to liken them to the Ku Klux Klan or to some kind of extremists itching to get into an armed conflict with the U.S. government.[5]

One week after my visit with the militia, I was writing about the Oklahoma City bombing, a domestic terrorism incident that destroyed the Alfred P. Murrah Federal Building and killed 168 people. The perpetrators were Timothy McVeigh and Terry Nichols, both members of the Michigan militia. In the April 28, 1995, edition of my newspaper, I wrote about anger and backlash against the militia movement. Stephanie Seleman was regional director in St. Louis for the Anti-Defamation League at the time. She told me militias disseminate hate literature that can incite violence against Blacks, Jews, gays, feminists, liberals, and the government.

"The militias are a festering ground for paranoid extremism and when groups give out information that is essentially hate literature against the government, then they have to take some responsibility for what results.... There was not any urgency about the militia situation until last week's tragedy in Oklahoma City," said Seleman. "Now our eyes have been opened as a nation.… I'm encouraged both Republicans and Democrats are closing ranks on what needs to be done."6

Are our eyes open today? Have we forgotten all the babies killed in the smoldering ash heap of the Murrah Federal Building in Oklahoma City? Have our Republicans and Democrats closed ranks on what needs to be done in the face of increasing violence and domestic terrorism today? Are our leaders, male and female, taking the steps to turn down the volume on hateful and divisive speech—or are they simply adding to the irresponsible noise?

This book is meant to pose more questions than it answers. Some of the questions that I am left with are: How did we move from an era of Promise Keepers and a Million Man March to an era of Proud Boys, Oath Keepers and extremist militia groups? What is the best way to end the dangerous political polarization that we now have in America? In a country as blessed and prosperous as America, does extremist rhetoric simply create problems for us that don't really exist? Can the search for manhood be moderated to unite men and women and redirect a lot of wayward energy to simply make America a better place?

The "M" in manhood is the same "M" that begins the word *moderation*. Moderation can be a manly virtue. Now, more than ever, we need to moderate all the manly manifestos and deescalate the dangerous rhetoric of so many angry people. "Moderation in all things" originated with the great poet and Greek philosopher Hesiod of 700 BCE. I resolve to learn more about the Greek philosopher Epicurus, whom Missouri Senator Josh Hawley blames for the decline and crisis of American men in his *Manhood: The Masculine Virtues America Needs*. Perhaps Hawley will accept an invitation to learn more about Hesiod, originator of "moderation in all things."

Chapter Notes

Introduction

1. Alex McNeil, *Total Television: The Comprehensive Guide to Programming from 1948 to the Present* (New York: Penguin, 1996), p. 209.

2. Kenzie Bryant, "Arnold Schwarzenegger Regrets Using the Term 'Girlie Man,' but Not for the Obvious Reasons," *Vanity Fair,* October 10, 2018. https://www.vanityfair.com/style/2018/10/arnold-schwarzenegger-girlie-men-regret.

3. Editorial Board, "Words Matter. Especially in the MAGA Era. Reckless rhetoric shows that some politicians learned nothing in the MAGA era," *St. Louis Post-Dispatch*, September 9, 2023, p. A11.

Chapter 1

1. Calder M. Pickett, *Voices of the Past: Key Documents in the History of American Journalism* (New York: John Wiley & Sons, 1977), p. 373.

2. Frank Lyn, "Agnew Depicts McGovern as 'Fraud' on P.O.W. Issue," *The New York Times*, July 1, 1972. https://www.nytimes.com/1972/07/01/archives/agnew-depicts-mcgovern-as-fraud-on-pow-issue-agnew-attacks-mcgovern.html.

3. Thomas Alan Schwarz, "Nattering nabobs of news criticism: 50 years ago today, Spiro Agnew laid out a blueprint for attacking the press," *Nieman Lab Reports*, November 13, 2019. https://niemanlab.org/2019/11/nattering-nabobs-of-news-criticism-50-years-ago-today-spiro-agnew-laid-out-a-blueprint-for-attacking-the-press/.

4. Flavia Medrut, "50 Famous Quotes from John Wayne and His Movies," *Goalcast*, undated. https://www.goalcast.com/john-wayne-quotes-2/.

5. Rebecca Harington, "Roger Ailes produced one of the most infamous political ads of all time, and it helped George H.W. Bush win the presidency," *Business Insider*, May 18, 2017. https://www.businessinsider.com/roger-ailes-revolving-door-ad-bush-election-2017-5.

6. Roger Cohen, "Rumsfeld Is Correct—The Truth Will Get Out," *The New York Times*, June 7, 2006. https://archive.nytimes.com/www.nytimes.com/iht/2006/06/07/world/IHT-07globalist.html.

7. Jacob Weisberg, "W.'s Greatest Hits: The Top 25 Bushisms of All Time," *Slate,* January 12, 2009. https://slate.com/news-and-politics/2009/01/the-top-25-bushisms-of-all-time.html.

8. Political Staff, "White House Disputes Carter Analysis," *NBC News,* September 15, 2009. https://www.nbcnews.com/id/wbna32869276.

9. Christopher Orr, "Clint Eastwood: Political Wanderer," *The Atlantic*, August 30, 2012. https://www.theatlantic.com/entertainment/archive/2012/08/clint-eastwood-politicalwanderer/261808/.

10. Peter Howell, "Think before you shoot, Clint says of war interview," *Toronto Star*, January 16, 2015. https://www.thestar.com/entertainment/movies/think-before-you-shoot-clint-eastwood-says-of-war-interview/article_8d169699-b87d-502c-8672-d35e76f4c20f.html.

11. Tessa Berenson, "John Wayne's Daughter Endorses Donald Trump," *Time*, January 19, 2016. https://time.com/4185378/donald-trump-john-wayne-iowa/.

Chapter 2

1. Flavia Medrut, "50 Famous Quotes from John Wayne and His Movies," *Goalcast*, undated. https://www.goalcast.com/john-wayne-quotes-2/.

2. Flavia Medrut, "50 Famous Quotes from John Wayne and His Movies," *Goalcast*, undated. https://www.goalcast.com/john-wayne-quotes-2/.

3. Porter McKeever, *Adlai Stevenson: His Life and Legacy* (New York: William Morrow, 1989), pp. 45–60.

4. Jean H. Baker, *The Stevensons: A Biography of An American Family (New York: W.W. Norton, 1996), pp. 246, 257.

5. Jason Thompson, "Endorsement Watch: A Final Roundup of Editorial Support," *The Washington Post*, October 29, 2000. https://www.washingtonpost.com/wp-srv/politics/early/archive/early110200.htm#charlotte.

6. Allison Turner, "Flashback Friday—Today in 1973, the APA Removed Homosexuality from List of Mental Illnesses," *Human Rights Campaign Website*, December 15, 2017. https://www.hrc.org/news/flashbackfriday-today-in-1973-the-apa-removed-homosexuality-from-list-of-me.

7. Stephen Ambrose, *The Wild Blue: The Men and Boys Who Flew the B-24s Over Germany, 1944–45* (New York: Simon & Schuster, 2001), pp. 240–245.

8. Jonathan Karl, "Bravery, Activism in Kerry's War Record," *ABC News*, February 13, 2004. https://abcnews.go.com/WNT/story?id=131505&page=1.

9. Andrew Glass, "George W. Bush suspended from Texas Air National Guard," *Politico*, August 1, 1972. https://www.politico.com/story/2013/08/this-day-in-politics-aug-1-1972-095023.

10. Kate Zernike, "Veterans Rebut 'Swift Boat' Charges Against Kerry in Answer to Challenge," *The New York Times*, June 22, 2008. https://www.nytimes.com/2008/06/22 /us/politics/22kerry.html.

11. Janice Lane Polko, "Mr. Rogers' Legacy," *Franciscan Media*, July 2019. https://www.franciscanmedia.org/st-anthony-messenger/july-2019/mister-rogers-legacy/.

12. James Peron, "Why They Hated Mr. Rogers and His Neighborhood," *Medium*, February 26, 2021. https://medium.com/the-radical-center/why-they-hated-mr-rogers-and-his-neighborhood-514020 1ede30.

13. David Zurawik, "Checking back in with Mr. Rogers, a reminder how unneighborly America has become," *The Baltimore Sun*, January 31, 2019. https://www.baltimoresun.com/columnists/zurawik/bs-fe-zontv-mr-rogers-documentary-20190129-story.html.

14. Olivia Waxman, "Bill Clinton Said He 'Didn't Inhale' 25 Years Ago," *Time*, March 29, 2017. https://time.com/4711887/bill-clinton-didnt-inhale-marijuana-anniversary/.

15. Margy Rochlin, "New Again: Pee-Wee Herman," Interview, March 16, 2016. https://www.interviewmagazine.com/culture/new-again-pee-wee-herman.

16. Paul Grein, "In 1991, MTV Gave Pee-wee Herman a Perfect Comeback Moment at the Video Music Awards," *Billboard*, July 31, 2023. https://www.billboard.com/music/awards/pee-wee-herman-mtv-video-music-awards-1991-comeback-1235382327/.

Chapter 3

1. Shushannah Walsh, "RNC Completes 'Autopsy' on 2012 Loss, Calls for Inclusion Not Policy Change," *ABC News*, March 18, 2013. https://abcnews.go.com/Politics/OTUS/rnc-completes-autopsy-2012-loss-calls-inclusion-policy/story?id=18755809.

2. Shushannah Walsh, "RNC Completes 'Autopsy' on 2012 Loss, Calls for Inclusion Not Policy Change," *ABC News*, March 18, 2013, https://abcnews.go.com/Politics/OTUS/rnc-completes-autopsy-2012-loss-calls-inclusion-policy/story?id=18755809.

3. Matthew Continetti, "Barack Obama: First Woman President," *National Review*, March 8, 2014. https://www.nationalreview.com/2014/03/barack-obama-first-woman-president-matthew-continetti/.

4. John Hudson, "Kathleen Parker: Obama Is 'First Woman President,'" *The Atlantic,* June 30, 2010. https://www.theatlantic.com/politics/archive/2010/06/kathleen-parker-obama-is-first-woman-president/340606/.

5. Jerome Corsi, "Obama Hid Gay Life To Become President," *WND.com*, September 11, 2012. https://www.wnd.com/2012/09/claim-obama-hid-gay-life-to-become-president/.

6. Elias Isquith, "Alex Jones Calls Michelle Obama 'first Tranny,'" *Salon*, July 10, 2014. https://www.salon.com/2014/07/10/alex_jones_calls_michelle_obama_first_tranny/.

7. Amanda Robb, "Anatomy of a Fake News Scandal," *Rolling Stone*, November 16, 2017. https://www.rollingstone.com/feature/anatomy-of-a-fake-news-scandal-125877/.

8. Jason Silverstein, "U.S. reported more COVID-19 cases in November than most countries had all year," *CBS News*, November 30, 2020. https://www.cbsnews.com/news/covid-november-cases-united-states/.

9. Elizabeth Williamson, "Alex Jones and Donald Trump: A Fateful Alliance Draws Scrutiny," *The New York Times*, March 7, 2022. https://www.nytimes.com/2022/03/07/us/politics/alex-jones-jan-6-trump.html.

10. Brian Naylor, "Read Trump's Jan. 6 Speech, a Key Part of Impeachment Trial," *NPR*, February 10, 2021. https://www.npr.org/2021/02/10/966396848/read-trumps-jan-6-speech-a-key-part-of-impeachment-trial.

11. Sam Levine, "Donald Trump says he plans to pardon U.S. Capitol attack participants if elected," *The Guardian*, September 1, 2022. https://www.theguardian.com/us-news/2022/sep/01/donald-trump-pardons-january-6-us-capitol-attack.

12. Alisha Rahaman Sarkar, "Madison Cawthorn calls for mothers to raise 'monster' men in terrifying speech against 'demasculation,'" *The Independent*, October 19, 2021. https://the-independent.com/news/world/americas/us-politics/north-carolina-madison-cawthorn-masculinity-b1940849.html.

13. Kali Holloway, "J.D. Vance's Empathy for Kyle Rittenhouse Is Revolting," *Daily Beast*, May 2, 2022. https://www.thedailybeast.com/jd-vances-empathy-for-kyle-rittenhouse-is-revolting.

14. Bill Donahue, "How 2022 Became the Year of Over-the-Top Masculinity in Politics," *The Washington Post*, June 20, 2022. https://www.washingtonpost.com/magazine/2022/06/20/he-man-politics/.

15. Bill Donahue, "How 2022 Became the Year of Over-the-Top Masculinity in Politics," *The Washington Post*, June 20, 2022. https://www.washingtonpost.com/magazine/2022/06/20/he-man-politics/.

16. Bill Donahue, "How 2022 Became the Year of Over-the-Top Masculinity in Politics," *The Washington Post*, June 20, 2022. https://www.washingtonpost.com/magazine/2022/06/20/he-man-politics/.

Chapter 4

1. John W. Brown, *Missouri Legends* (St. Louis: Reedy Press, 2008), pp. 33, 68, 86.

2. John W. Brown, *Missouri Legends* (St. Louis: Reedy Press, 2008), pp. 14, 45, 59.

3. Don Corrigan, "McCaskill vs. Hawley in a Show-Me State Showdown for U.S. Senate," *Webster-Kirkwood Times*, September 28, 2018, p. 1.

4. Josh Hawley, *Manhood: The Masculine Virtues America Needs* (Washington, D.C.: Regnery, 2023), pp. 240–248.

5. Josh Hawley, *Manhood: The Masculine Virtues America Needs* (Washington, D.C.: Regnery, 2023), p. 28.

6. Josh Hawley, *Manhood: The Masculine Virtues America Needs* (Washington, D.C.: Regnery, 2023), p. 52.

7. Josh Hawley, *Manhood: The Masculine Virtues America Needs* (Washington, D.C.: Regnery, 2023), pp. 67–68.

8. Josh Hawley, *Manhood: The Masculine Virtues America Needs* (Washington, D.C.: Regnery Publishing, 2023), pp. 67–68.

9. Lauren del Valle, "Jury finds Donald Trump sexually abused E. Jean Carroll in civil case, awards her $5 million," *CNN.com*, May 10, 2023. https://www.cnn.com/2023/05/09/politics/e-jean-carroll-trump-lawsuit-battery-defamation-verdict/index.html.

10. George Will, "Trump, Hawley and Cruz will each wear the scarlet 'S' of a seditionist," *WashingtonPost.com*, January 6, 2021. https://www.washingtonpost.com/opinions/trump-hawley-and-cruz-will-each-wear-the-scarlet-s-of-a-seditionist/2021/01/06/65b0ad1a-506c-11eb-bda4-615aaefd0555_story.html.

11. Ruari Arrieta-Kenna and Emily Kadei, "The Education of Josh Hawley," *Politico.com*, January 19, 2021. https://

www.politico.com/news/magazine/2021/
01/19/josh-hawley-senator-stanford-histo
ry-capitol-insurrection-ambition-460481.
    12. Rudi Keller, "Danforth says regrets
over Hawley make him feel like 'Dr. Fran-
kenstein,'" *Missouri Independent*, February 3, 2021. https://missouriindependent.
com/2021/02/03/danforth-says-regrets-
over-hawley-make-him-feel-like-dr-
frankensein/.
    13. Katie Bernard, "A Photographer and
a Fist Pump," *Kansas City Star*, January 7,
2021. https://www.kansascity.com/news/
politics-government/article248354085.
html.
    14. Tony Messenger, "With perfect
staging, Hawley becomes 'The Face of
Sedition,'" *St. Louis Post-Dispatch*, January 9, 2021. https://www.stltoday.com/
news/local/metro/messenger-with-
perfect-staging-hawley-becomes-the-face-
of-sedition/article_4d76f299-911b-510a-
9155-4a2a4db37191.html.
    15. Josh Hawley, *Manhood: The Mascu-
line Virtues America Needs* (Washington,
D.C.: Regnery, 2023), pp. 103–107.
    16. Jon Schwarz, "Josh Hawley Won't
Let Go of His Manhood," *The Intercept*, May 14, 2023. https://theintercept.
com/2023/05/14/josh-hawley-book-
masculinity/.
    17. Susan Faludi, *Stiffed: The Betrayal
of the American Man* (New York: William
Morrow, 1999), pp. 3–223.
    18. Susan Bordo, *The Male Body: A New
Look at Men in Public and in Private* (New
York: Farrar, Straus and Giroux, 1999), pp.
107–168.
    19. Gayle Sheehy, *Understanding Men's
Passages: Discovering the New Map of
Men's Lives* (Chicago: Third World Press,
1996), pp. 177–191.
    20. Rob Okun, "Josh Hawley on Man-
hood: Wrong on Everything," *Daily
Hampshire Gazette*, May 22, 2023. https://
www.gazettenet.com/my-turn-Okun-
Josh-Hawley-s-New-Book-on-Manhood-
is-Wrong-on-Everything-51053408.
    21. Rob Okun, "Josh Hawley on Man-
hood: Wrong on Everything," *Daily
Hampshire Gazette*, May 22, 2023. https://
www.gazettenet.com/my-turn-Okun-
Josh-Hawley-s-New-Book-on-Manhood-
is-Wrong-on-Everything-51053408.
    21. Rob Okun, "Josh Hawley on Man-
hood: Wrong on Everything," *Daily

Hampshire Gazette, May 22, 2023. https://
www.gazettenet.com/my-turn-Okun-
Josh-Hawley-s-New-Book-on-Manhood-
is-Wrong-on-Everything-51053408.
    22. Kevin McDermott, "The Mission of
Manhood: Even judged by his own retro-
grade criteria, Josh Hawley fails the man
test," *St. Louis Post-Dispatch*, May 28, 2023,
p. A15.
    23. Rebecca Onion, "Man Overboard:
Josh Hawley's long-threatened tome
about American masculinity is here,"
Salon, May 18, 2023. https://slate.com/
culture/2023/05/josh-hawley-manhood-
book-republican-senator-wife.html.
    24. Don Corrigan, "Skeptics Lam-
poon Hawley: Missouri senator's manly
virtues book delights jesters & satirists,"
Gateway Journalism Review, June 8, 2023.
https://gatewayjr.org/skeptics-lampoon-
hawley-mo-senators-manly-virtues-book-
delights-jesters-satirists/.
    25. Lloyd Green, "Manhood review:
Josh Hawley, moralizer, neo–Confederate
and Tucker Carlson of the U.S. Senate,"
The Guardian, May 13, 2023. https://www.
theguardian.com /books/2023/may/13/
manhood-review-josh-hawley-book-
tucker-carlson.
    26. Lloyd Green, "Manhood review:
Josh Hawley, moralizer, neo–Confederate
and Tucker Carlson of the U.S. Senate,"
The Guardian, May 13, 2023. https://www.
theguardian.com/books/2023/may/13/
manhood-review-josh-hawley-book-
tucker-carlson.
    27. Jonathan Capehart, "Josh Hawley's
problem with masculinity," *The Washington Post*, August 3, 2022. https://www.
washingtonpost.com/opinions/2022
/08/03/josh-hawley-masculinity-prob-
lem/.

Chapter 5

    1. Michael A. Messner, *Politics of Mas-
culinities: Men in Movements* (Thousand
Oaks, CA: Sage, 1997), pp. 1–3.
    2. Jon Snodgrass, *For Men Against Sex-
ism* (Albion, CA: Times Change Press,
1977), pp. 177–179.
    3. Jack Litewka, "The Socialized Penis,"
For Men Against Sexism (Albion, CA:
Times Change Press, 1977), pp. 16–35.
    4. Michael Kimmel and Michael

Messmer, *Men's Lives* (New York: Macmillan, 1989), pp. 1–3.

5. John Stoltenberg, "Refusing To Be a Man," *For Men Against Sexism* (Albion, CA: Times Change Press, 1977), pp. 25–29.

6. Carl Wittman, "Refugees from America: A Gay Manifesto," *For Men Against Sexism* (Albion, CA: Times Change Press, 1977), pp. 330–345.

7. Carl Wittman, "Refugees from America: A Gay Manifesto," *For Men Against Sexism* (Albion, CA: Times Change Press, 1977), pp. 330–345.

8. Jon Naito, "Husky legend and gay icon David Kopay is at peace and at home," *University of Washington Magazine*, December 2008. https://magazine.washington.edu/feature/husky-legend-and-gay-icon-david-kopay-is-at-peace-and-at-home/.

9. L. Sahagun, "Christian Men's Movement Taps Into Identity Crisis," *LA Times*, July 6, 1995. https://www.latimes.com/people/louis-sahagun.

10. Chanté Griffin, "The dark side of Kwanzaa's founder can't extinguish the holiday's beacon," *LA Times*, December 23, 2018. https://www.latimes.com/opinion/op-ed/la-oe-griffin-kwanzaa-20181223-story.html.

11. Cornel West, "Historic Event," *Million Man March: A Commemorative Anthology* (Chicago: Third World Press, 1996).

12. Francis Baumli, *Men Freeing Men: Exploding the Myth of the Traditional Male* (Jersey City: New Atlantis Press, 1985), pp. 3–8.

13. James Doyle, "Manliness in the Twenty First Century with James Doyle," WebMD Live Events, October 2003. https://www.medicinenet.com/script/main/art.asp?articlekey=53987.

14. Mimi Avins, "Men's advocate in a woman's world," *LA Times,* January 26, 2000. https://www.latimes.com/archives/la-xpm-2000-jan-26-cl-57738-story.html.

15. Pamela Warrick, "A new role for men: victim: former feminist Warren Farrell says he's sick and tired of guys getting bashed," *LA Times*, August 9, 1993. https://www.latimes.com/archives/la-xpm-1993-08-09-vw-22148-story.html.

16. Lionel Tiger, *The Decline of Males* (New York: St. Martin's Press, 1999), pp. 244–249.

17. Robert Bly, *Iron John: A book About Men* (Boston: Addison-Wesley, 1990), pp. ix–xi.

18. Michael Schwalbe, *Unlocking the Iron Cage: The Men's Movement, Gender Politics and American Culture* (Oxford: Oxford University Press, 1996).

Chapter 6

1. Jerry Adler, "Drums, Sweat And Tears," *Newsweek*, June 23, 1991. https://www.*newsweek.com/drums-sweat-and-tears-204220.*

2. Jerry Adler, "Drums, Sweat And Tears," *Newsweek*, June 23, 1991. https://www.newsweek.com/drums-sweat-and-tears-204220.

3. Michael Kimmel, *The Politics of Manhood: Profeminist Men Respond to the Mythopoetic Men's Movement* (Philadelphia: Temple University Press, 1995), pp. 12–33.

4. Alia E. Dastagir, "Psychologists call 'traditional masculinity' harmful, face uproar from conservatives," *USA Today*, January 10, 2019. https://www.usatoday.com/story/news/investigations/2019/01/10/american-psychological-association-traditional-masculinity-harmful/2538520002/.

5. Mark Gunnery, "Unlearning Toxic Masculinity: Learning Consent," WAMU, *The Kojo Nnamdi Show*, October 10, 2018. https://thekojonnamdishow.org/2018/10/10/unlearning-toxic-masculinity-learning-consent/.

6. Terry E. Gilchrist, "What Is Toxic Masculinity?" *Advocate*, December 11, 2017. https://www.advocate.com/women/2017/12/11/what-toxic-masculinity.

7. Terry E. Gilchrist, "What Is Toxic Masculinity?" *Advocate*, December 11, 2017. https://www.advocate.com/women/2017/12/11/what-toxic-masculinity.

Chapter 7

1. Jesse L. Jackson, "Remarks Before One Million Men," *Million Man March: A Commemorative Anthology* (Chicago: Third World Press, 1996), p. 32.

2. Eric Stirgus, "Million Man March: A Day of Atonement," *The Atlanta*

Journal-Constitution (Black History Month Edition), February 23, 2017. https://www.ajc.com/lifestyles/million-man-march-day-atonement/ETMzJ6cxBNlssIiM042GHM/.

3. Eric Nelson, Jr., "We Must Go to This March in the Name of God," *Million Man March: A Commemorative Anthology* (Chicago: Third World Press, 1996), p. 48.

4. William Nelson, Jr., "Black Church Politics in the Million Man March," *Black Religious Leadership from the Slave Community to the Million Man March: Flames of Fire*, edited by Felton O. Best (Lewiston, NY: The Edwin Mellen Press, 1998), pp. 243–257.

5. Haki Madhubuti and Maulana Karenga, *Million Man March: A Commemorative Anthology* (Chicago: Third World Press, 1996), p. 143.

6. Haki Madhubuti and Maulana Karenga, *Million Man March: A Commemorative Anthology* (Chicago: Third World Press, 1996), pp. 142–143.

7. Marc Fischer and Eric Pianin, "The Riots and D.C.'s Underclass," *Washington Post*, April 4, 1988. https://www.washingtonpost.com/archive/politics/1988/04/04/the-riots-and-dcs-underclass/d802a15a-45d5-4046-a539-5ce644d15816/.

8. Gene Park, "The Million Man March as Told by the People Who Were There 20 Years Ago," *Washington Post*, October 16, 2015. https://www.washingtonpost.com/news/post-nation/wp/2015/10/06/were-you-at-the-million-man-march-tell-us-your-story/.

9. Gene Park, "The Million Man March as Told by the People Who Were There 20 Years Ago," *Washington Post*, October 16, 2015. https://www.washingtonpost.com/news/post-nation/wp/2015/10/06/were-you-at-the-million-man-march-tell-us-your-story/.

10. David Joyner, "Remembering a March That John Lewis Sat Out," *The Eagle-Tribune*, July 25, 2020. https://www.eagletribune.com/opinion/column-remembering-a-march-that-john-lewis-sat-out/article_0bcafa92-ae3f-5dc4-b0eb-18483b1c2 bcd.html.

11. George Curry, "The Message and the Messenger," *Million Man March: A Commemorative Anthology* (Chicago: Third World Press, 1996), p. 128.

12. Herb Boyd, "Claimed by Black People," *Million Man March: A Commemorative Anthology* (Chicago: Third World Press, 1996), p. 88.

13. Herb Boyd, "Claimed by Black People," *Million Man March: A Commemorative Anthology* (Chicago: Third World Press, 1996), pp. 88–92.

14. Herb Boyd, "Claimed by Black People," *Million Man March: A Commemorative Anthology* (Chicago: Third World Press, 1996), pp. 88–92.

15. Charshee McIntyre, "Why Focus on the Man," *Million Man March: A Commemorative Anthology* (Chicago: Third World Press, 1996), pp. 114–116.

16. NYT Staff, "Facing Complaints of Bias, Farrakhan Speaks to Women Only," *New York Times*, July 3, 1994. https://www.nytimes.com/1994/07/31/us/facing-complaints-of-bias-farrakhan-speaks-to-women-only.html.

17. Nolan McCaskill, "Louis Farrakhan Praises Donald Trump," *Politico*, May 2014. https://www.politico.com/blogs/2016-gop-primary-live-updates-and-results/2016/03/louis-farrakhan-donald-trump-220021.

18. Haki Madhubuti and Maulana Karenga, *Million Man March: A Commemorative Anthology* (Chicago: Third World Press, 1996).

19. Haki Madhubuti and Maulana Karenga, *Million Man March: A Commemorative Anthology* (Chicago: Third World Press, 1996).

20. William Nelson, Jr., "Black Church Politics in the Million Man March," *Black Religious Leadership from the Slave Community to the Million Man March: Flames of Fire*, edited by Felton O. Best (Lewiston, NY: The Edwin Mellen Press, 1998), pp. 243–257.

Chapter 8

1. Tim Pettus, "Men Who Keep Their Promises to Families," *St. Louis Post-Dispatch*, May 21, 1996. https://www.newspapers.com/article/20087444/promise_keepers_kansas_city/.

2. Tim Pettus, "Men Who Keep Their Promises to Families," *St. Louis Post-Dispatch*, May 21, 1996. https://www.newspapers.com/article/20087444/promise_keepers_kansas_city/.

3. Tim Pettus, "Men Who Keep Their Promises to Families," *St. Louis Post-Dispatch*, May 21, 1996. https://www.newspapers.com/article/20087444/promise_keepers_kansas_city/.

4. Ron Stodghill, "God of Our Fathers," *Time*, October 6, 1997. https://content.time.com/time/subscriber/article/0,33009,987116,00.html.

5. Editors, "Seven Promises of a Promise Keeper," *Roanoke Times*, June 25, 1996. https://scholar.lib.vt.edu/VA-news/ROA-Times/issues/1996/rt9606/960625/06250045.html.

6. Wayne Jackson, "What's Wrong with the Promise Keepers Movement?" *Christian-Courier.com*, October 1998. https://christiancourier.com/articles/sincere-but-wrong-dead-wrong.

7. Wayne Jackson, "What's Wrong with the Promise Keepers Movement," *Christian-Courier.com*, October 1998. https://christiancourier.com/articles/sincere-but-wrong-dead-wrong.

8. Kristin Kobes Du Mez, *Jesus and John Wayne* (New York: Norton, 2021), pp. 150–151.

9. Kristin Kobes Du Mez, *Jesus and John Wayne* (New York: Norton, 2021), pp. 152–155.

10. Kristin Kobes Du Mez, *Jesus and John Wayne* (New York: Norton, 2021), pp. 187–188.

Chapter 9

1. Don Corrigan, "Men Protest First Wives Club," *South County Times*, October 11, 1996, p. 1.

2. Don Corrigan, "Men Protest First Wives Club," *South County Times*, October 11, 1996, p. 1.

3. Don Corrigan, "Men Protest First Wives Club," *South County Times*, October 11, 1996, p. 1.

4. Don Corrigan, "Male Buffoons in Media: Misandry or Misogyny?" Popular Culture Association paper presentation, San Diego, California, March 2017.

5. Lindsay McIntosh, "There's Nobody Like Him...," *Sunday Times of London,* July 8, 2007. https://www.thetimes.co.uk/article/theres-nobody-like-him-except-you-me-everyone-6b05sctmwbh.

6. Seth Stevenson, "The Reign of the Doltish Dad," *Slate*, March 26, 2012. https://slate.com/culture/2012/03/huggies-diapers-first-its-ad-used-a-doltish-dad-then-came-the-outcry.html.

7. Elizabeth Gleick, "First Wives Club: Hell Hath No Fury," *Time*, October 7, 1996. https://content.time.com/time/specials/packages/artle/0,28804,1968770_1968790_1998719,00.html.

8. Herb Goldberg, *The Hazards of Being Male: Surviving the Myth of Masculine Privilege* (New York: Signet, 1976), pp. 177–182.

9. Herb Goldberg, *The Hazards of Being Male: Surviving the Myth of Masculine Privilege* (New York: Signet, 1976), p. 180.

10. Warren Farrell, *The Myth of Male Power* (New York: Simon & Schuster, 1993), pp. 356–357.

11. Christina Hoff Sommers, *The War Against Boys* (New York: Signet, 1976), pp. 63–64.

12. Don Corrigan, "The Flipside of Feminism," Webster-Kirkwood Times, August 5, 2011.

13. Warren Farrell, *The Myth of Male Power* (New York: Simon & Schuster, 1993), pp. 365–368.

14. Warren Farrell, *The Myth of Male Power* (New York: Simon & Schuster, 1993), pp. 365–368.

Chapter 10

1. Audrey McNamara, "Thousands gather in Washington, D.C., to show support for Trump," *CBS News*, December 13, 2020. https://www.cbsnews.com/news/trump-supporters-gather-washington-dc-million-maga-march/.

2. William M. Arkin, "'There Will Be Bloodshed': As night fell, the Million MAGA March Turned Violent," *Newsweek*, November 14, 2020. https://www.cbsnews.com/news/trump-supporters-gather-washington-dc-million-maga-march/

3. Courtney Subramanian and Jordan Culver, "Donald Trump sidesteps call to condemn white supremacists—and the Proud Boys were 'extremely excited' about it," *USA Today*, September 29, 2020. https://www.usatoday.com/story/news/politics/elections/2020/09/29/trump-debate-white-supremacists-stand-back-stand-by/3583339001/.

4. Kimberly M. Aquilina, "Gavin McInnes explains what a Proud Boy is and why porn and wanking are bad," *Metro Daily*, February 9, 2017. https://www.metro.us/gavin-mcinnes-explains-what-a-proud-boy-is-and-why-porn-and-wanking-are-bad/.

5. SPLC Staff Report, "Proud Boys," *SPLC Website Extremist Group Information* (updated regularly). https://www.splcenter.org/fighting-hate/extremist-files/group/proud-boys.

6. Andy Campbell, *We Are Proud Boys* (New York: Hachette, 2022), p. 14.

7. Andy Campbell, *We Are Proud Boys* (New York: Hachette, 2022), pp. 104–112.

8. Robert Evans, "Portland, Oregon, Is Ground Zero for Violent Culture War Clashes, and It's Spreading," *Rolling Stone*, September 14, 2021. https://www.rollingstone.com/culture/culture-features/proud-boys-oath-keepers-antifa-portland-violence-spreading-1224762/.

9. Andy Campbell, *We Are Proud Boys* (New York: Hachette, 2022), pp. 124–125.

10. SPLC Staff Report, "Proud Boys," *SPLC Website Extremist Group Information* (updated regularly). https://www.splcenter.org/fighting-hate/extremist-files/group/proud-boys.

11. Lauren White, "The Secret Service knew the Proud Boys posed a threat on Jan. 6. Why didn't they take it seriously?" *CREW*, June 29, 2022. https://www.citizensforethics.org/reports-investigations/crew-investigations/the-secret-service-knew-the-proud-boys-posed-a-threat-on-jan-6-why-didnt-they-take-it-seriously/.

12. NPR Staff, "Transcript of Trump's Speech at Rally Before Capitol Riot," *NPR*, February 10, 2021. https://www.npr.org/2021/02/10/966396848/read-trumps-jan-6-speech-a-key-part-of-impeachment-trial.

13. NPR Staff, "Here's every word of the first Jan. 6 committee hearing on its investigation," *NPR*, June 10, 2022. https://www.npr.org/2022/06/10/1104156949/jan-6-committee-hearing-transcript.

14. NPR Staff, "Here's every word of the first Jan. 6 committee hearing on its investigation," *NPR*, June 10, 2022. https://www.npr.org/2022/06/10/1104156949/jan-6-committee-hearing-transcript.

15. NPR Staff, "Here's every word of the first Jan. 6 committee hearing on its investigation," *NPR*, June 10, 2022. https://www.npr.org/2022/06/10/1104156949/jan-6-committee-hearing-transcript.

16. WBUR Newsroom, "Go Home—Trump Tells Supporters Who Mobbed Capitol to Leave, Again Falsely Claiming Election Victory," *WBUR*, January 6, 2021. https://www.wbur.org/news/2021/01/06/go-home-trump-supporters-us-capitol-transcript.

17. NPR Staff, "Here's every word of the first Jan. 6 committee hearing on its investigation," *NPR*, June 10, 2022, https://www.npr.org/2022/06/10/1104156949/jan-6-committee-hearing-transcript.

18. Andy Campbell, *We Are Proud Boys* (New York: Hachette, 2022), p. 267.

19. Andy Campbell, *We Are Proud Boys* (New York: Hachette, 2022), pp. 268–270.

20. Andy Campbell, *We Are Proud Boys* (New York: Hachette, 2022), pp. 261–262.

Chapter 11

1. Amanda Sakuma and Bradley J. Rayford, "Emergency Declared in Ferguson After Shooting," *MSNBC*, August 11, 2015. https://www.msnbc.com/politicsnation/revs-early-reads-aug-11th-2015-msna658736.

2. Amanda Sakuma and Bradley J. Rayford, "Emergency Declared in Ferguson After Shooting," *MSNBC*, August 11, 2015. https://www.msnbc.com/politicsnation/revs-early-reads-aug-11th-2015-msna658736.

3. Scott Malone, "Heavily armed 'Oath Keepers' inject disquieting element in Ferguson," *Reuters*, August 11, 2015. https://www.reuters.com/article/us-usa-ferguson-oath-keepers/heavily-armed-oath-keepers-inject-disquieting-element-in-ferguson.

4. Eric Ortiz and Ron Allen, "Why Are 'Oath Keepers' Allowed to Be Armed in Middle of Ferguson," *NBC News*, August 11, 2015. https://www.nbcnews.com/storyline/ichael-brown-shooting/why-are-oath-keepers-allowed-be-armed-ferguson-n408156.

5. SPLC Staff Report, "Oath Keepers," *SPLC Website Extremist Group Information* (updated regularly). https://www.

splcenter.org/fighting-hate/extremist-files/group/oath-keepers.

6. Stewart Rhodes, "My Personal Pledge of Resistance Against Any Attempt to Disarm Us by Means of an Assault Weapons Ban," *Oath Keepers Website*, December 19, 2012, https://usaoathkeepers.com/.

7. Stewart Rhodes, "Oath Keepers Call to Action: Border Operation," *Oath Keepers*, December 4, 2018. https://usaoathkeepers.com/.

8. Alex Jones Interviews Stewart Rhodes, "I don't trust the Pentagon," *InfoWars*, October 27, 2020. https://www.google.com/search?q=InfoWars+official+website&sca esv=561395159& source=hp&ei=35bvZJinDbSfptQPtu62yAw&iflsig=AD69kcEAAAAZO.

9. Stewart Rhodes, "Open Letter to President Trump: You Must Use Insurrection Act to 'Stop the Steal,'" *Oath Keepers*, December 14, 2020. https://usaoathkeepers.com/.

10. Alex Jones Interviews Stewart Rhodes, "Label It Pretend Legislation," *InfoWars,* January 20, 2021. https://www.google.com/search?q=InfoWars+official+website&sca esv=561395159& source=hp&ei=35bvZJinDbSfptQPtu62yAw&iflsig=AD69kcEAAAAZO.

11. Sam Jackson, *Oath Keepers: Patriotism and the Edge of Violence in a Right-Wing Antigovernment Group* (New York: Columbia University Press, 2020), pp. 142–148.

12. SPLC Staff Report, "Oath Keepers," *SPLC Website Extremist Group Information* (updated regularly). https://www.splcenter.org/fighting-hate/extremist-files/group/oath-keepers.

13. Sam Jackson, *Oath Keepers: Patriotism and the Edge of Violence in a Right-Wing Antigovernment Group* (New York: Columbia University Press, 2020), pp. 49–50.

14. Ryan J. Reilly, "Oath Keepers Founder Says 'Undercover' Poll Watching Effort Won't Intimidate Voters," *Huffpost*, October 27, 2016. https://www.huffpost.com/entry/oath-keepers-poll-watching_n_58122566e4b0990edc2f8178.

15. *William Arkin,* "'There Will Be Bloodshed': As Night Fell, the Million MAGA March Turned Violent," *Newsweek*, November 14, 2021. https://www.newsweek.com/there-will-bloodshed-night-fell-million-maga-march-turned-violent-1648658.

16. *William Arkin,* "'There Will Be Bloodshed': As Night Fell, the Million MAGA March Turned Violent," *Newsweek*, November 14, 2021. https://www.newsweek.com/there-will-bloodshed-night-fell-million-maga-march-turned-violent-1648658.

17. Sergio Olmos, "Guns, ammo ... even a boat: how Oath Keepers plotted an armed coup," *The Guardian*, January 14, 2022. https://www.theguardian.com/us-news/2022/jan/14/oath-keepers-leader-charges-armed-plot-us-capitol-attack.

18. Kierra Frazier, "Jan. 6 sentences are piling up. Here's a look at some of the longest handed down," *Politico*, May 30, 2023. https://www.politico.com/news/2023/05/30/january-6-arrest-sentencing-00099158.

19. Lindsay Whitehurst, "Witness: Oath Keepers head tried to reach Trump after Jan. 6," *Associated Press*, November 2, 2022. https://apnews.com/article/capitol-siege-texas-donald-trump-veterans-conspiracy-d159e7b101fd7fc63f7821a0bc7daa9d.

20. Michael Kunzelman, Lindsay Whitehurst, and Alanna Durkin Richer, "Two More Oath Keepers Sentenced to Prison for January 6," *Associated Press*, May 26, 2023. https://www.voanews.com/a/oath-keeper-gets-8%C2%BD-years-in-prison-in-latest-january-6-sentencing-/7111003.html.

21. Sam Jackson, *Oath Keepers: Patriotism and the Edge of Violence in a Right-Wing Antigovernment Group* (New York: Columbia University Press, 2020), p. 122.

Chapter 12

1. CNN Newsroom, "Report: Clinton Says Trump Campaign Built on Prejudice and Paranoia," *CNN.com*, August 25, 2016. http://www.cnn.com/TRANSCRIPTS/1608/25/ cnr.08.html.

2. Katie Reilly, "Read Hillary Clinton's 'Basket of Deplorables' Remarks About Donald Trump Supporters," *Time*, September 10, 2016. https://time.com/4486502/hillary-clinton-basket-of-deplorables-transcript/.

3. SPLC Staff Report, "Three Percenters," *SPLC Website Extremist Group Information* (updated regularly). https://www.splcenter.org/fighting-hate/extremist-files/group/three-percenters.

4. BBC Staff, "19-year sentence for second ringleader in Michigan governor kidnap plot," *BBC News,* December 28, 2022. https://www.bbc.com/news/world-us-canada-64112234.

5. *Peter* Barker, "Life sentence sought for mastermind behind governor's kidnapping plot," *Michigan News-Local Today,* December 6, 2022. https://localtoday.news/mi/life-sentence-sought-for-mastermind-behind-governors-kidnapping-plot-68274.html.

6. Jessica Garrison and Ken Bensinger, "The FBI Allegedly Used at Least 12 Informants in the Michigan Kidnapping Case," *BuzzFeed News,* July 12, 2021. *https://www.buzzfeednews.com*/article/jessicagarrison/fbi-informants-in-michigan-kidnap-plot.

7. Celia Llopis-Jepsen, "Garden City bomb plot reflects larger trend among anti-government circles," *The Topeka Capital-Journal*, October 18, 2016. https://www.cjonline.com/story/news/politics/state/2016/10/19/garden-city-plot-reflects-larger-trend-among-anti-government-circles/16570585007/.

8. SPLC Staff Report, "Three Percenters," *SPLC Website Extremist Group Information* (updated regularly). https://www.splcenter.org/fighting-hate/extremist-files/group/three-percenters.

9. Kirk Siegler, "Ammon Bundy ordered to pay $50 million. But will the hospital ever see the money?" *NPR*, July 25, 2023. https://www.npr.org/2023/07/25/1189953918/ammon-bundy-ordered-to-pay-50-million-but-will-the-hospital-ever-see-the-money.

10. David Debolt, "Far-Right Protester Kyle 'Based-Stickman' Chapman in Trouble Again," *East Bay Times*, July 10, 2018. https://www.eastbaytimes.com/2018/07/10/far-right-protester-kyle-based-stickman-chapman-in-trouble-again/.

11. Kevin Braouezec, "Identifying Common Patterns of Discourse and Strategy among the New Extremist Movements in Europe: The Case of the English Defence League and the Bloc Identitaire," *Journal of Intercultural Studies*, 2016, pp. 637–648.

12. Morgan Hines, "Avowed neo–Nazi James Fields sentenced to life in prison for Charlottesville hate crimes," *USA TODAY*, July 1, 2019. https://www.usatoday.com/story /news/2019/06/28/james-fields-jr-charlottesville-sentencing-heather-heyer-unite-the-right/1587233001/.

13. Elle Reeve, "How White 'replacement theory' evolved from elderly racists to teens online to the alleged inspiration for another racist mass homicide," *CNN*, May 21, 2022. https://www.cnn.com/2022/05/20/us/replacement-theory-white-supremacist-buffalo-shooter/index.html.

14. Elle Reeve, "How White 'replacement theory' evolved from elderly racists to teens online to the alleged inspiration for another racist mass homicide," *CNN*, May 21, 2022. https://www.cnn.com/2022/05/20/us/replacement-theory-white-supremacist-buffalo-shooter/index.html.

15. Elle Reeve, "How White 'replacement theory' evolved from elderly racists to teens online to the alleged inspiration for another racist mass homicide," *CNN*, May 21, 2022. https://www.cnn.com/2022/05/20/us/replacement-theory-white-supremacist-buffalo-shooter/index.html.

16. SPLC Staff Report, "Three Percenters," *SPLC Website Extremist Group Information* (updated regularly). https://www.splcenter.org/fighting-hate/extremist-files/group/three-percenters.

17. Andy Campbell, *We Are Proud Boys* (New York: Hachette, 2022), pp. 269–270.

18. Theresa Vargas, "Meet the Red Bike Guy who in a viral video heckled white nationalists," *Washington Post*, May 17, 2023. https://www.washingtonpost.com/dc-md-va/2023/05/17/cyclist-heckles-white-nationalists/.

19. SPLC Staff Report, "Alliance Defending Freedom," *SPLC Website Extremist Group Information* (updated regularly). https://www.splcenter.org/fighting-hate/extremist-files/group/alliance-defending-freedom.

20. Sofia Resnick and Sharona Coutts, "Not the 'Illuminati': How Fundamentalist Christians Are Infiltrating State and Federal Government," *Rewire News Group*, May 13, 2014. https://rewirenewsgroup.com/2014/05/13/illuminati-fundamentalist-christians-infiltrating-state-federal-government/.

21. Brian Tashman, "Alliance Defending

Freedom and Focus on the Family Unveil New Anti-Anti-Bullying Strategies," *Right Wing Watch*, September 5, 2012. https://www.rightwingwatch.org / post/alliance-defending-freedom-and-focus-on-the-family-unveil-new-anti-anti-bullying-strategies/.

22. Christine Maxouris and Brandon Griggs, "Two decades after Matthew Shepard's death, 20 states still don't consider attacks on LGBTQ people as hate crimes," *CNN*, October 12, 2018. https://www.cnn.com/2018/10/12/health/matthew-shepard-hate-crimes-lgbtq-trnd/index.html.

23. SPLC Staff Report, "Alliance Defending Freedom," *SPLC Website Extremist Group Information* (updated regularly). https://www.splcenter.org/fighting-hate/extremist-files/group/alliance-defending-freedom.

24. Dylan Lysen, Laura Ziegler, and Blaise Mesa, "Voters in Kansas decide to keep abortion legal in the state, rejecting an amendment," *NPR*, August 3, 2022. https://www.npr.org/sections/2022-live-primary-election-race-results/2022/08/02/1115317596/kansas-voters-abortion-legal-reject-constitutional-amendment.

25. PHR Briefing, "Human Rights Crisis: Abortion in the United States After Dobbs," *Physicians for Human Rights*, April 18, 2023. https://phr.org/our-work/resources/letter-to-un-special-procedures/.

26. ACLU Briefing Report, "ACLU Responds to Supreme Court Ruling on Dobbs," *ACLU*, June 27, 2022. https://www.aclu.org/cases/dobbs-v-jackson-womens-health-organization.

27. William II. Freivogel, "Chief Justice Roberts falling short on recapturing Supreme Court legitimacy," *Gateway Journalism Review*, July 27, 2023. https://gatewayjr.org/chief-justice-roberts-falling-short-on-recapturing-supreme-court-legitimacy/.

28. William H. Freivogel, "Chief Justice Roberts falling short on recapturing Supreme Court legitimacy," *Gateway Journalism Review*, July 27, 2023. https://gatewayjr.org/chief-justice-roberts-falling-short-on-recapturing-supreme-court-legitimacy/.

29. Solcyre Burga, "The Implications of Supreme Court's 303 Creative Decision Are Already Being Felt," *Time*, July 16, 2023. https://prod.web.time.com/6295024/303-creative-supreme-court-future-implications/.

30. Solcyre Burga, "The Implications of Supreme Court's 303 Creative Decision Are Already Being Felt," *Time*, July 16, 2023. https://prod.web.time.com/6295024/303-creative-supreme-court-future-implications/.

Chapter 13

1. Staff editors, "Frank Rich: Mel Gibson Threatened to Kill Me and My Dog—And I Don't Even Have a Dog," *Huffpost*, May 28, 2008. https://www.huffpost.com/entry/frank-rich-mel-gibson-thr_n_8136.

2. 19 Newsclips, "Mel Gibson Criticizes Iraq War During Movie Screening," *19 News Cleveland*, September 25, 2020. https://www.cleveland19.com/story/5455551/mel-gibson-criticizes-iraq-war-during-movie-screening/.

3. Obituaries, "Charles Bronson," *Daily Telegraph*, September 2, 2003. https://www.telegraph.co.uk/news/obituaries/1440296/Charles-Bronson.html.

4. Colin Dwyer, "Donald Trump: 'I Could ... Shoot Somebody, and I Wouldn't Lose Any Voters,'" *NPR*, January 23, 2016. https://www.npr.org/sections/thetwo-way/2016/01/23/464129029/donald-trump-i-could-shoot-somebody-and-i-wouldnt-lose-any-voters.

5. Crispin Sartwell, "American Idolatry Meets Woke Iconoclasm," *Reason Magazine*, October 2020. https://reason.com/2020/09/01/american-idolatry-meets-woke-iconoclasm/.

6. Terminal Info, "The John Wayne Statue," *John Wayne Airport Website*, May 2008. https://web.archive.org/web/20080512023812/http://www.ocair.com/terminal/jwstatue.html.

7. Janelle Griffith, "Leaders Want John Wayne name, statue gone from Orange County Airport," *NBC News*, June 29, 2020. https://www.nbcnews.com/news/us-news/leaders-want-john-wayne-name-statue-gone-orange-county-airport-n1232480.

8. Janelle Griffith, "Leaders Want John Wayne name, statue gone from

Orange County Airport," *NBC News*, June 29, 2020. https://www.nbcnews.com/news/us-news/leaders-want-john-wayne-name-statue-gone-orange-county-airport-n1232480.

9. Crispin Sartwell, "American Idolatry Meets Woke Iconoclasm," *Reason Magazine*, October 2020. https://reason.com/2020/09/01/american-idolatry-meets-woke-iconoclasm/.

10. Crispin Sartwell, "American Idolatry Meets Woke Iconoclasm," *Reason Magazine*, October 2020. https://reason.com/2020/09/01/american-idolatry-meets-woke-iconoclasm/.

11. Amanda Marcotte, "The 'Barbie' backlash isn't just cynical: The GOP is abusing its own supporters," *Salon*, July 25, 2023. https://www.salon.com/2023/07/25/the-barbie-backlash-isnt-just-cynical/.

12. Amanda Marcotte, "The 'Barbie' backlash isn't just cynical: The GOP is abusing its own supporters," *Salon*, July 25, 2023. https://www.salon.com/2023/07/25/the-barbie-backlash-isnt-just-cynical/.

13. E.J. Dickson, "The Right-Wing Backlash Against 'Barbie' Is Hilariously Flopping," *Rolling Stone*, July 19, 2023. https://www.rollingstone.com/culture/culture-news/barbie-movie-right-wing-backlash-ted-cruz-ginger-gaetz-1234791386/.

14. Amanda Marcotte, "The 'Barbie' backlash isn't just cynical: The GOP is abusing its own supporters," *Salon*, July 25, 2023. https://www.salon.com/2023/07/25/the-barbie-backlash-isnt-just-cynical/.

15. E.J. Dickson, "The Right-Wing Backlash Against 'Barbie' Is Hilariously Flopping," *Rolling Stone*, July 19, 2023. https://www.rollingstone.com/culture/culture-news/barbie-movie-right-wing-backlash-ted-cruz-ginger-gaetz-1234791386/.

16. Amanda Marcotte, "The 'Barbie' backlash isn't just cynical: The GOP is abusing its own supporters," *Salon*, July 25, 2023. https://www.salon.com/2023/07/25/the-barbie-backlash-isnt-just-cynical/.

17. Matt Pridge, "Ben Shapiro Got Dragged for Being So Triggered by 'Barbie' That He Recorded a 43-Minute Video Raging Against It," *UPROXX*, July 22, 2023. https://uproxx.com/viral/ben-shapiro-dragged-hating-barbie/.

18. Amanda Marcotte, "The 'Barbie' backlash isn't just cynical: The GOP is abusing its own supporters," *Salon*, July 25, 2023. https://www.salon.com/2023/07/25/the-barbie-backlash-isnt-just-cynical/.

19. Katrina vanden Heuvel, "Why does the Barbie movie have Republicans in such a tizzy?" *The Guardian*, July 20, 2023. https://www.theguardian.com/commentisfree/2023/jul/20/barbie-movie-republicans-reaction.

20. Eva Rothenberg, "Barbie makes history with $1 billion at the box office," *CNN Business*, August 6, 2023. https://www.cnn.com/2023/08/06/business/barbie-box-office-history/index.html.

21. Evan Romano, "*Barbie* Has a Lot to Say About Men; But It's Not Anti-Male," *Men's Health*, July 25, 2023. https://www.menshealth.com/entertainment/a44631534/barbie-anti-male/.

Chapter 14

1. E. Frances White, *Dark Continent of Our Bodies: Black Feminism and the Politics of Respectability* (Philadelphia: Temple University Press, 2001), pp. 25–47.

2. Don Corrigan, "Men Protest First Wives Club," *South County Times*, October 11, 1996.

3. Kristin Kobes Du Mez, *Jesus and John Wayne* (New York: Norton, 2021), pp. 179–180.

4. SPLC Staff Report, "Alliance Defending Freedom," *SPLC Website Extremist Group Information* (updated regularly). https://www.splcenter.org/fighting-hate/extremist-files/group/alliance-defending-freedom.

5. Josh Hawley, "Defend Masculinity," *Josh Hawley Victory Committee*, Campaign Appeal for January 2023.

6. Josh Hawley, *Manhood: The Masculine Virtues America Needs* (Washington, D.C.: Regnery, 2023), p. 7.

7. Josh Hawley, *Manhood: The Masculine Virtues America Needs* (Washington, D.C.: Regnery, 2023), p. 67.

8. Josh Hawley, *Manhood: The Masculine Virtues America Needs* (Washington, D.C.: Regnery, 2023), p. 111.

9. Josh Hawley, *Manhood: The Masculine Virtues America Needs* (Washington, D.C.: Regnery, 2023), p. 51.

10. Paulina Villegas and Hannah Knowles, "After Capitol riot, desperate families turn to groups that 'deprogram' extremists," *Washington Post*, February 21, 2021. https://www.washingtonpost.com/nation/2021/02/05/desperate-families-are-seeking-groups-that-deprogram-extremists/.

11. Paulina Villegas and Hannah Knowles, "After Capitol riot, desperate families turn to groups that 'deprogram' extremists," *Washington Post*, February 21, 2021. https://www.washingtonpost.com/nation/2021/02/05/desperate-families-are-seeking-groups-that-deprogram-extremists/.

12. Paulina Villegas and Hannah Knowles, "After Capitol riot, desperate families turn to groups that 'deprogram' extremists," *Washington Post*, February 21, 2021. https://www.washingtonpost.com/nation/2021/02/05/desperate-families-are-seeking-groups-that-deprogram-extremists/.

13. Paulina Villegas and Hannah Knowles, "After Capitol riot, desperate families turn to groups that 'deprogram' extremists," *Washington Post*, February 21, 2021, https://www.washingtonpost.com/nation/2021/02/05/desperate-families-are-seeking-groups-that-deprogram-extremists/.

14. SPLC Staff Report, "Patriot Front," *SPLC Website Extremist Group Information* (updated regularly). https://www.splcenter.org/fighting-hate/extremist-files/group/patriot-front?gclid=EAIaIQobChMImPCl362HgQMV6CqzAB0PgQ5YEAAYASAAEgJAjPD_BwE.

15. BPT News Service, "Did George Washington Sound Like a Wimp?" *Las Vegas Review-Journal*, September 10, 2015. https://www.reviewjournal.com/sponsor-old/did-george-washington-sound-like-a-wimp/.

16. Maurizio Valsania, *First Among Men* (Baltimore: Johns Hopkins University Press, 2022), pp. 168–169.

17. Maurizio Valsania, *First Among Men* (Baltimore: Johns Hopkins University Press, 2022), pp. 168–169.

18. Ján Majerník, Joseph Ponessa, and Laurie Watson Manhardt, *The Synoptics: Matthew, Mark, Luke* (Steubenville, OH: Emmaus Road,2005), pp. 63–68.

19. Ján Majerník, Joseph Ponessa, and Laurie Watson Manhardt. *The Synoptics: Matthew, Mark, Luke* (Steubenville, OH: Emmaus Road, 2005), pp. 63–68.

20. David Edward Aune, *The Westminster Dictionary of New Testament and Early Christian Literature and Rhetoric* (Louisville: Westminster John Knox Press, 2003),*pp. 70–78*.

21. Robert Morgan, *Boone: A Biography* (Chapel Hill: Algonquin Books, 2007), p. xi.

22. NPR Staff, "40 Years On, 'Free to Be' Still Resonates," *NPR Weekend Edition*, December 7, 2012. https://www.npr.org/2012/12/09/166735512/40-years-on-free-to-be-message-still-resonates.

Postscript

1. Kenzie Bryant, "Arnold Schwarzenegger Regrets Using the Term 'Girlie Man,' but Not for the Obvious Reasons," *Vanity Fair*, October 10, 2018. https://www.vanityfair.com/style/2018/10/arnold-schwarzenegger-girlie-men-regret.

2. Don Corrigan, "'Klinger' wore pants in Columbia," *Columbia Missourian*, April 17, 1975, p. 1.

3. Don Corrigan, "City's first woman firefighter says she's no blazing liberationist," *Columbia Missourian*, March 4, 1975, p. 1.

4. Don Corrigan, "Joining the Women's Pages," *The Women's Voice*, April 22, 1993, p. 1.

5. Don Corrigan, "Hate Mongers or Freedom Fighters?" *Webster-Kirkwood Times*, April 21, 1995, p. 1.

6. Don Corrigan, "Militias Under Fire Following Oklahoma City Bombing," *Webster-Kirkwood Times*, April 28, 1995, p. 1.

Bibliography

Adams, Jane. *Women on Top: Success Patterns and Personal Growth*. New York: Hawthorn Books, 1980.

Ambrose, Stephen. *The Wild Blue: The Men and Boys Who Flew the B-24s Over Germany, 1944–45*. New York: Simon & Schuster, 2001.

Arkin, William. "'There Will Be Bloodshed': As Night Fell, the Million MAGA March Turned Violent." *Newsweek*, November 14, 2021. https://www.newsweek.com/there-will-bloodshed-night-fell-million-maga-march-turned-violent-1648658.

Baker, Jean H. *The Stevensons: A Biography of An American Family*. New York: W. W. Norton, 1996.

Baumli, Francis. *Men Freeing Men: Exploding the Myth of the Traditional Male*. Jersey City: New Atlantis Press, 1985.

Beneke, Timothy. *Men on Rape*. New York: St. Martin's Press, 1982.

Betcher, William. *In a Time of Fallen Heroes*. New York: Atheneum, 1982.

Bird, Caroline. *The Two-Paycheck Marriage: Making It Work*. New York: Rawson, Wade, 1979.

Bly, Robert. *Iron John: A Book About Men*. Boston: Addison-Wesley, 1990.

Bordo, Susan. *The Male Body: A New Look at Men in Public and in Private*. New York: Farrar, Straus and Giroux, 1999.

Brown, John W. *Missouri Legends*. St. Louis: Reedy Press, 2008.

Burga, Solcyre. "The Implications of Supreme Court's 303 Creative Decision Are Already Being Felt." *Time*, July 16, 2023. https://prod.web.time.com/6295024/303-creative-supreme-court-future-implications/.

Campbell, Andy B. *We Are Proud Boys: How a Right-Wing Street Gang Ushered in a New Era of American Extremism*. New York: Hachette, 2022.

Continetti, Matthew. "Barack Obama: First Woman President." *National Review*, March 8, 2014. https://www.nationalreview.com/2014/03/barack-obama-first-woman-president-matthew-continetti/.

Corsi, Jerome. "Obama Hid Gay Life to Become President." *WND.com*, September 11, 2012. https://www.wnd.com/2012/09/claim-obama-hid-gay-life-to-become-president/.

Curry, George. "The Message and the Messenger." *Million Man March: A Commemorative Anthology*. Chicago: Third World Press, 1996.

Debolt, David. "Far-Right Protester Kyle 'Based-Stickman' Chapman in Trouble Again." *East Bay Times*, July 10, 2018. https://www.eastbaytimes.com/2018/07/10/far-right-protester-kyle-based-stickman-chapman-in-trouble-again/.

Dickson, E.J. "The Right-Wing Backlash Against 'Barbie' Is Hilariously Flopping." *Rolling Stone*, July 19, 2023. https://www.rollingstone.com/culture/culture-news/barbie-movie-right-wing-backlash-ted-cruz-ginger-gaetz-1234791386/.

Donahue, Bill. "How 2022 Became the Year of Over-the-Top Masculinity in Politics." *The Washington Post*, June 20, 2022. https://www.washingtonpost.com/magazine/2022/06/20/he-man-politics/.

Doyle, James. "Manliness in the Twenty-First Century with James Doyle." *WebMD Live*

Events, October 2003. https://www.medicinenet.com/script/main/art.asp?article key=53987.

Du Mez, Kristin Kobes. *Jesus and John Wayne*. New York: Norton, 2021.

Faludi, Susan. *Stiffed: The Betrayal of the American Man*. New York: William Morrow, 1999.

Farley, Lin. *Sexual Shakedown: The Sexual Harassment of Women on the Job*. New York: Warner Books, 1978.

Farrell, Warren. *The Myth of Male Power*. New York: Simon & Schuster, 1993.

Fausto-Sterling, Anne. *Myths of Gender*. New York: Basic Books, 1992.

Freivogel, William H. "Chief Justice Roberts falling short on recapturing Supreme Court legitimacy." *Gateway Journalism Review*, July 27, 2023. https://gatewayjr.org/chief-justice-roberts-falling-short-on-recapturing-supreme-court-legitimacy/.

Gerzon, Mark. *A Choice of Heroes*. New York: Houghton Mifflin, 1982.

Gilchrist, Terry E. "What Is Toxic Masculinity?" *Advocate*, December 11, 2017. https://www.advocate.com/women/2017/12/11/what-toxic-masculinity.

Gilmore, David. *Manhood in the Making: Cultural Concepts of Masculinity*. New Haven: Yale University Press, 1990.

Goldberg, Herb. *The Hazards of Being Male: Surviving the Myth of Masculine Privilege*. New York: Signet, 1976.

Hawley, Josh. *Manhood: The Masculine Virtues America Needs*. Washington, D.C.: Regnery, 2023.

Held, Virginia. *Feminist Morality*. Chicago: University of Chicago Press, 1993.

Henley, Nancy. *Body Politics*. Englewood Cliffs, New Jersey: Prentice Hall, 1977.

Howe, Louis Knapp. *Pink Collar Workers*. New York: Avon, 1978.

Hudson, John. "Kathleen Parker: Obama Is 'First Woman President.'" *The Atlantic*, June 30, 2010. https://www.theatlantic.com/politics/archive/2010/06/kathleen-parker-obama-is-first-woman-president/340606/.

Jackson, Jesse L. "Remarks Before One Million Men." *Million Man March: A Commemorative Anthology*. Chicago: Third World Press, 1996.

Jackson, Wayne. "What's Wrong with the Promise Keepers Movement?" *Christian-Courier.com*, October 1998. https://christiancourier.com/articles/sincere-but-wrong-dead-wrong.

Kanter, Rosabeth Moss. *Men and Women of the Corporation*. New York: Basic Books, 1977.

Keen, Sam. *Fire in the Belly*. New York: Bantam, 1991.

Kimmel, Michael. *Men's Lives*. New York: Macmillan, 1989.

Malone, Scott. "Heavily armed 'Oath Keepers' inject disquieting element in Ferguson." *Reuters*, August 11, 2015. https://www.reuters.com/article/us-usa-ferguson-oath-keepers/heavily-armed-oath-keepers-inject-disquieting-element-in-ferguson.

Marcotte, Amanda. "The 'Barbie' backlash isn't just cynical: The GOP is abusing its own supporters." *Salon*, July 25, 2023. https://www.salon.com/2023/07/25/the-barbie-backlash-isnt-just-cynical/.

McKeever, Porter. *Adlai Stevenson: His Life and Legacy*. New York: William Morrow and Company, 1989.

Messenger, Tony. "With perfect staging, Hawley becomes 'The Face of Sedition.'" *St. Louis Post Dispatch*, January 9, 2021. https://www.stltoday.com/news/local/metro/messenger-with-perfect-staging-hawley-becomes-the-face-of-sedition/article_4d76f299-911b-510a-9155-4a2a4db37191.html.

Messner, Michael A. *Politics of Masculinities: Men In Movements*. Thousand Oaks, CA: Sage, 1997.

Mill, John Stuart. *On Liberty*. 1859. Indianapolis: Hackett, 1978.

Montagu, Ashley. *The Natural Superiority of Women*. New York: Collier, 1974.

Morgan, Robert. *Boone: A Biography*. Chapel Hill: Algonquin Books, 1977.

Morrow, Lance. "Men: Are They Really That Bad?" *Time*, February 14, 1992.

Okin, Susan Moller. *Justice, Gender, and the Family*. New York: Basic Books, 1992.

Okun, Rob. "Josh Hawley on Manhood: Wrong on Everything." *Daily Hampshire Gazette*, May 22, 2023. https://www.gazettenet.com/my-turn-Okun-Josh-Hawley-s-New-Book-on-Manhood-is-Wrong-on-Everything-51053408.

Olmos, Sergio. "Guns, ammo … even a boat: how Oath Keepers plotted an armed coup." *The Guardian*, January 14, 2022. https://www.theguardian.com/us-news/2022/jan/14/oath-keepers-leader-charges-armed-plot-us-capitol-attack.

Peron, James. "Why They Hated Mr. Rogers and His Neighborhood." *Medium*, February 26, 2021. https://medium.com/the-radical-center/why-they-hated-mr-rogers-and-his-neighborhood-514020lede30.

Pettus, Tim. "Men Who Keep Their Promises to Families." *St. Louis Post-Dispatch*, May 21, 1996. https://www.newspapers.com/article/20087444/promise_keepers_kansas_city/.

Pickett, Calder M. *Voices of the Past: Key Documents in the History of American Journalism*. New York: John Wiley & Sons, 1977.

Pleck, Joseph H. *The Myth of Masculinity*. Cambridge: MIT Press, 1981.

Reilly, Katy. "Read Hillary Clinton's 'Basket of Deplorables' Remarks About Donald Trump Supporters." *Time*, September 10, 2016. https://time.com/4486502/hillary-clinton-basket-of-deplorables-transcript/.

Romano, Evan. "*Barbie* Has a Lot to Say About Men; But It's Not Anti-Male." *Men's Health*, July 25, 2023. https://www.menshealth.com/entertainment/a44631534/barbie-anti-male/.

Rothenberg, Eva. "Barbie makes history with $1 billion at the box office." *CNN Business*, August 6, 2023. https://www.cnn.com/2023/08/06/business/barbie-box-office-history/index.html.

Sartwell, Crispin. "American Idolatry Meets Woke Iconoclasm." *Reason Magazine*, October 2020. https://reason.com/2020/09/01/american-idolatry-meets-woke-iconoclasm/.

Scully, Diana. *Understanding Sexual Violence*. Boston: Unwin Hyman, 1990.

Sheehy, Gail. *Passages: Predictable Crises of Adult Life*. New York: Bantam, 1977.

_____. *Understanding Men's Passages: Discovering the New Map of Men's Lives,* Chicago: Third World Press, 1996.

Smith, Ralph E. *The Subtle Revolution: Women at Work*. Washington, D.C.: The Urban Institute, 1979.

Snodgrass, Jon. *For Men Against Sexism*. Albion, CA: Times Change Press, 1977.

Soble, Alan. *Pornography*. New Haven: Yale University Press, 1986.

Sommers, Christina Hoff. *The War Against Boys*. New York: Signet, 1976.

Stoltenberg, John. *Refusing to Be a Man*. New York: Meridian Books, 1990.

Tiger, Lionel. *The Decline of Males*. New York: St. Martin's Press, 1999.

_____. *Men in Groups*. New York: Marion Boyars, 1984.

Toffler, Alvin. *The Third Wave*. New York: William Morrow, 1980.

Valsania, Maurizio. *First Among Men*. Baltimore: Johns Hopkins University Press, 2022.

White, Frances E. *Dark Continent of Our Bodies: Black Feminism and the Politics of Respectability*. Philadelphia: Temple University Press, 2001.

Young, Iris. *Throwing Like a Girl and Other Essays in Feminist Philosophy and Social Theory*. Bloomington: Indiana University Press, 1990.

Index

www.ingramcontent.com/pod-product-compliance
Lightning Source LLC
Chambersburg PA
CBHW031128270326
41929CB00011B/1539